QUANTUM

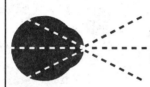

This Large Print Book carries the
Seal of Approval of N.A.V.H.

QUANTUM

PATRICIA CORNWELL

THORNDIKE PRESS

A part of Gale, a Cengage Company

A Cengage Company

Farmington Hills, Mich • San Francisco • New York • Waterville, Maine
Meriden, Conn • Mason, Ohio • Chicago

**LIBRARY OF CONGRESS CIP DATA ON FILE.
CATALOGUING IN PUBLICATION FOR THIS BOOK
IS AVAILABLE FROM THE LIBRARY OF CONGRESS**

ISBN-13: 978-1-4328-7203-8 (hardcover alk. paper)

Published in 2019 by arrangement with Thomas & Mercer

Printed in the United States of America
1 2 3 4 5 6 7 23 22 21 20 19

To Staci:
you make it possible . . .
and
To Irv and Lonni,
who live among the stars . . .

Spooky Actions at a Distance

Anyone who is not shocked by quantum
theory has not understood it.

— Niels Bohr

Learn how to see. Realize that everything
connects to everything else.

— Leonardo da Vinci

We are the product of quantum
fluctuations in the very early universe.

— Stephen Hawking

Quantum physics thus reveals a basic
oneness of the universe.

— Erwin Schrödinger

Everything is energy and that's
all there is to it.

— Albert Einstein

Do not feel lonely, the entire universe
is inside you.

— Rumi

THREE YEARS EARLIER . . .

The bright light is blinding. The vents too small, too high on the metal-clad walls.

Frantic and nauseated, willing myself to keep going. Trying to make it better. The air breathless and heated, windows facing due east. I've had nothing to eat.

The black coffee from the overturned mug pools around the plate of bagels, bowls of cream cheese, butter. The stone countertop streaked red. Drip, dripping over the edge. To the smeared, sticky floor.

"Oh God, oh God . . . !"

Distracted, dizzy, about to black out. Grabbing more paper towels. Aware of the obvious vulnerabilities. Even as I panic. The same ones as before. If only I'd paid attention. If only I'd factored in the data. Time. Season. Altitude. Latitude and longitude vis-à-vis the equator. Skylights. Glass windows. Weather.

No equation. No algorithm to predict what to expect when emerging from my sensory-

11

deprived day to day. To be helpful, friendly. No matter what's asked. Or when. Or how I feel.

Here to serve. No need to threaten the usual punishments. Disgrace, demotion, hard labor, imprisonment.

"Oh God, oh God, please hurry . . ."

Another minute clicks past on the wall clock. Shoving wadded bloody paper towels into the trash. Looking around at the gory mess.

Didn't see it coming when I showed up for my assignment . . . Exactly 21 minutes ago . . . Glancing every other second at the digital time glowing green between the American and Space Command flags in polished wooden stands . . . Darting about, water drumming in the sink.

Four minutes since I texted. Dick is coming. On his way.

"Hurry, hurry, oh God . . . !"

My heart pounding in my ears. Making matters worse as I try to clean up. Blood soaking through the dish towel wrapped around my right hand, tucked in close like a damaged wing. Sweating, shivering, teeth chattering in fits and starts.

"Oh God, oh God . . ."

The simplest of tasks. A mindless responsibility.

Stupid.

A favor not meriting special rank, preparation or training. Scarcely any forethought. Was happy to. Flattered, didn't hesitate to comply. In fact, volunteered.

Stupid!

No favor goes unpunished. No good deed either. The best intentions setting you up for trouble. Which I didn't see coming. Behind the locked door, waiting and listening for Dick.

Cleaning up what I would have prevented were I not in sleep mode. Not to be confused with safe mode. I wasn't in that.

1

DECEMBER 3, 2019
NASA LANGLEY RESEARCH CENTER
HAMPTON, VIRGINIA

I can't say for sure when the century-old tunnel was sealed off like a tomb.

Probably around the same time it began popping up in 8-pitch type as a nondescript feature on utility site maps hardly anyone ever sees. Crammed with high-pressure steam pipes and other mechanicals, the section of tunnel designated 1111-A was at some point given the code name Yellow Submarine.

"Never publicly or in print," I'm explaining to NASA police major Fran Lacey, miserably scuffing behind me on the steep, gloomy stairs. "Mid- to late '70s is about right for when this might have occurred," I add, as if she's listening or cares. "That's

15

what I get if I factor in the data and do the math."

Crickets is her response, the same one I've been getting, and I turn around, checking on her, fully aware she's not talking back. May as well enjoy that while it lasts. Except I don't. I feel bad for her. But that doesn't mean I'll cut her any slack. Nope.

"In other words, in the Dark Ages, when you were coming along," tossing in a dig whenever I can. "And way back then not even NASA had a glimmer about what was ahead. If they'd known, we wouldn't have the problem I'm trying to make you handle sooner rather than later."

I pause again for a response that isn't coming. Our feet slowly thudding on concrete steps nosed with steel safety plates painted screaming yellow. Going down a few. Stopping every second or two as it gets warmer and stuffier the deeper we descend. More like steamy summer than the dead of winter, both of us clearing our throats and sweating.

"I'm guessing some dorky systems engineer or member of the intelligence community was to blame. A Beatles fan at any rate, and therefore most likely after 1968," I continue to download information Fran couldn't be less interested in right now.

16

Talking nonstop in rhythm to our descent. Feet thud-thudding. Another pause or two. Punctuated by the off-gassing of her loud exasperated sighs and coughs. Prompting me to turn around, finding her the same as last I looked, flipping me off with both middle fingers, messing with me the way she usually does. But not really. Because believe me when I say that nothing about this is funny to a legendary badass cop known for being afraid of nothing.

On permanent loan from Hampton PD, Fran oversees investigations for NASA Langley's protective services. Or what's essentially our police force of some 70 uniformed officers and a dozen special agents, all armed and federally sworn to ensure security and enforce the law on campus. In addition, she supervises NASA's and the City of Hampton's joint Marine, Aviation and Crime Scene Units. Plus our mobile response teams, riot squad and SWAT.

Not to mention providing executive protection for visiting VIPs. And coordinating with the military police on Langley Air Force Base, separated from our center by guard gates and an 8-foot-high fence topped with barbed wire. Suffice it to say, Fran isn't someone to dismiss, disrespect or underestimate. That doesn't mean I'm letting her off easy by offering empathy or the slightest hint about how much it secretly bothers me to put her through this ordeal. Or any. But if I'm really her investigative partner and closest ally and friend, then for me to give in to her problem would be the worst thing I could do. It would be selfish and dangerous. Worst case, it could be catastrophic.

"I'll take your profane sign language as a yes. You're doing okay," responding to her latest doubly offensive gesture, and it's pointless to react personally when she's distressed to the max.

"Shut up," she manages to gasp, and thankfully her current unpleasantness is predictable and for the most part inconsistent with who she is the rest of the time.

But extreme anxiety, no matter how buried or quiet, rarely makes anyone more co-operative or nicer. Her mop of dark hair plastered to her scowling brow beneath her cockeyed hard hat, her safety glasses constantly fogging up. Staring at her boots, watching every tentative step as she makes her way down a claustrophobic dusty stairwell that she's avoided like the plague in the past. And would continue to do so were it up to her. Fortunately, it isn't. Even if she outranks me. Technically.

"The reason I know, obviously, is their

iconic album by that name didn't come out until then," I answer what she doesn't ask. "*Yellow Submarine.* We're all living on one, a metaphor for spaceship Earth, right? Which is appropriate considering what's down here, as you're about to see," I carry on as if oblivious to her fear of confined anything.

Including caves, orthopedic casts, subways, seat belts, handcuffs, bunkers, submarines and most of all, tunnels, and it's not that I'm insensitive. But as matters relate to her phobias, I'm her sponsor and never her enabler. Meaning I wasn't happy about her refusal to shadow me along this very route when I ran a routine network analysis inside the Yellow Submarine tunnel yesterday. A very important test. In fact, critical in light of current circumstances, and Fran would have none of it. She stopped answering my text messages or calls on the subject. She ducked and dodged. I worked without her.

Then, as synchronicity would have it, one of 1111-A's airlock motion sensors sent me an alert exactly 22 minutes ago, presenting me with the perfect opportunity to give Fran another chance. I made her an offer she couldn't refuse in front of the entire Langley Center directorate and its high-ranking guests, the NASA Protective Services and Hampton police chiefs.

Most of all, my former boss General Dick Melville, the commander of Space Force. And I anxiously rub my right thumb and index finger together. Feeling the scar. Remembering him doing the same only hours ago when I first encountered him at the briefing and he shook my hand. Checking my finger pad for that distinctive old injury, exploring its beveled topography like a stigmata. So subtle I'm still not certain it was intentional.

But I felt scrutinized as never before, and he also reacted oddly when the motion-detector alarm went off. When I say oddly, he didn't react at all. Just sat there stonily while I apologized profusely, explaining in front of everyone that Fran and I had to respond instantly.

Irony of ironies, the very vulnerability I'd been preaching about had a possible problem. The security of the Yellow Submarine may have been breached. Right now. In real time.

"If I didn't know better, I'd think you planned this," Fran managed to take a jab at me in front of our Mount Olympian audience.

Payback for leaving her little option but to

save face by responding openly and reasonably to what she'd decided instantly and irrationally was a wild goose chase. On the spot and peeved, she was violently reluctant even if she didn't show it. Well, too darn bad, whether it turns out to be a false alarm or not, at long last Fran's along for the ride.

She's about to find out exactly what's inside the bricked-up section of tunnel running some 50 feet below buildings 1110 and 1111. For once she's going to take my warnings to heart about the two unassuming prewar government facilities on the outer limits of the campus, where NASA keeps telecommunications, space operations, electromagnetic labs. And something else.

It's the "something else" she needs to understand fully and intuitively, or she can't possibly appreciate why this remote area of our campus isn't simply at risk. But as far as I'm concerned it's more vulnerable than all NASA centers and facilities combined when we have the volatile chemistry of our current political chaos added to the local meteorological and geographical circumstances.

Fran needs to know what to watch for if she doesn't want World War III. Because I probably won't be here to tell her. If all goes well, I won't be here to tell anyone.

21

■ ■ ■ ■

Then what? Who's going to keep Major Lacey from turning into Major Chicken?

Suffering full-blown panic attacks that end with her in a fetal position, on a stretcher or being helped by firefighters back down a ladder. Not that I have the magic touch or cure. But I figured out from the start that when she decompensates, the best remedy is to talk nonstop.

To overwhelm her with information, distracting her from getting sucked in to her fear-biting paralyzing vortex. It's always worked like a charm when the job takes us into environments hostile to her. Which is most of them.

"Think of it as a wormhole leading into . . ."

"Wormhole bunghole!"

". . . Either one of them leading into a parallel universe that dark matter is desperate to overtake," I may as well be speaking extraterrestrial. Glancing back at her, "You hanging in okeydoke?"

"Stop asking!" Out of breath and several paces behind, she's more congested and grumpy with each passing second.

But I'm not letting her flee the scene. Doing what's best even if it pisses her off as I continue to make sure she's not hyperventilating, overheating, going into anaphylactic shock or who knows what. I consider it real progress that at least she's not taking the stairs sitting down one at a time. I really have seen her do that when frightened off her feet.

At the moment she's not quite that bad. But close enough, staring down at her steel-toe boots without a glance at where she's going. Not caring what or why. Not caring about anything except how stressed she feels. Following me down one shaky step at a time. And you'd think we were descending into Dante's hell of torments by the look on her face the deeper we get as she clutches the railing.

You and your phobias. What's going to happen when I'm gone?

"Oh boy, oh boy . . ." Not intending a word of it out loud. "Don't start with me!" Struggling to block out the steepness, the walls closing in.

"I'm not starting. But if I did?" My voice echoes as I pause on the stairs. "Look, I know how much you hate this, Fran, but it's for your own darn good. And I'm not letting you off the hook."

"You know what you can do with your

hook!" Sniffling, eyes rheumy from her allergies kicking in harder, unable to grasp the importance.

And not because she's overworked and claustrophobic, both of which are true. The problem is she doesn't want to face the reason I'm insisting on a detailed tutorial about what I manage around here. Not just Building 1111 but the gestalt of science and policing in this age of hybrids and fusions, everything increasingly entangled and intertwined. Except she's not interested or paying attention, and I don't mean just now.

Fran doesn't want to deal with the fact that it was never the plan for me to stick around here forever. She's going to have to take over for me eventually, doesn't matter how she feels about it. Like my sister, Carme, says, *"Reality happens, Sisto."* Only *reality* isn't the word she uses.

And *Sisto* isn't for publication, her secret pet name for me going back to infinity, as I like to say. A clever hybrid of *sister* and *Callisto,* our NASA parents naming their twin daughters after two of Jupiter's moons. Although Carme (pronounced *karma*) is actually considered more of an irregular satellite while my namesake is the second-largest moon after Ganymede. Everybody calls me Calli. And Carme is Carme unless they mispronounce it *Carm*. (Not to be confused with *charm*, let me add, in case you haven't met my firebrand not-exactly-matching bookend.)

When we were last together, she made me swear that if all goes as expected, I won't leave our NASA mom and dad or Langley or Fran or anyone in a lurch. Since then I've been making plans and taking care of what I can because statistically it's a 50-50 chance that my fighter-pilot twin and I will be called back to Houston any day. Intuitively, I'm giving us bigger chances than that, and suspect that by the New Year we'll be settled in Texas for the long haul.

Maybe in that lakefront neighborhood we like so much where we fantasized about keeping a small boat. Not even 15 minutes from Johnson Space Center, depending on traffic. But what I've always wished for me isn't something Fran and I can talk about easily now that my future is within reach. We've really not discussed what's next.

She doesn't want to acknowledge that what I intend is real. She refuses to face what it means beyond making occasional cracks and snipes about how preoccupied and on edge I supposedly am. That I'm a fussbudget. An overachieving royal pain who has no off switch or time for friends.

". . . And then in 1975, the US government decided to use fiber-optic cables to link computers into a network for the first time," my narration is going strong as I make my way down another stairwell. "This happened to be at the air force's classified facility in Colorado Springs. Cheyenne Mountain, my last honest job, like you're always saying."

Until three years ago, I was a military police captain in charge of cyber investigations at what I think of as North America's Bat Cave, the Cheyenne Mountain installation, built some 2,000 feet below ground to withstand an atom bomb. Explaining why I have an informed opinion about the wisdom of using a subterranean utility trench to create a test bed for fiber-optic telecommunications. But any choices made back in the good ole days of the Beatles and the Cold War were long before I was born.

Otherwise I would have quite a lot to say about the eventual risks of creating a quantum key distribution network in such a locale. And then running cables from it into the heart of Langley's recently opened supercomputing complex, the Katherine G. Johnson Computational Research Facility, named after the human computer who calculated trajectories virtually in her head for our earliest space flights.

No ribbon-cutting ceremony or anything else that's been in the news hints at the CRF's top secret importance. Had it been up to me, I would have removed 1111-A, the Yellow Submarine, from the mix. I would prohibit telecommunication cables, junction boxes and other equipment from being installed inside that or any utility tunnel.

Never on my most distracted day would I approve point-to-point links carrying high-speed data signals inside a confined underground space shared with rodents, reptiles and a miscellany of service people in and out.

Plagued by distractions, and knowing how to block them out. All would have been fine but for the timing.

Confronted with the worst news of my life moments earlier. Preoccupied, secretly in turmoil and easy to forget how I've been reconditioned. Unaccustomed now to the sun, moon, the sky outside my deep stone catacomb. Spending endless hours with no fresh air. Never seeing windows, atriums, cupolas. No room with a view of the good Earth I crave. Only instrument displays, and arrays of computer screens in near-dark conditions.

Doing as instructed while preparing for the ultimate mission. To stop the unthinkable before thought takes form. Day in and out on the hunt for heat trails and their signatures. Sniffing for signals everywhere. All leading up to why I had trouble with the knife, wooden handled with a long single-edged blade.

Like a mole, eyes watering, not seeing well in the glare. In a hurry and confused. Scared and bereft. Caught off guard, didn't feel it when it happened. Blood everywhere, I scurried about, crazed like a dying mammal, a tiny subterranean one. Except I'm not dying.

Mortified, frenzied, but not wounded mortally. Not physically. Trying to clean up before anybody sees the stupid thing I've done.

2

"Can we hurry this along, for freak's sake?" Fran complains, sweating through her white uniform shirt, huffing and puffing as we stop outside the first door of the second airlock. "And you can spare me the tour. Jeez, you can talk."

"Nope, I'm not sparing you." I reach inside my jacket, untucking the lanyard around my neck.

Clipped to it is my badge holder, and I slide out my smartcard, instantly seeing my personal identification verification in my head. As if branded there:

00010-080121101

At times my memory can be exhausting, driving me crazy. Almost as crazy as Fran is making me right now.

"I want to make sure you're up to speed on what we're dealing with around here," I say to her firmly. "Somebody needs to know all this besides me. What happens when I'm not around?"

"Stop talking like you're dying."

"Speaking of. Deep, slow breaths. You need to chill before you overtorque and have a stroke. We've got to work harder to get on top of this problem . . ."

"Chill?" she interrupts with a snort. "Have you noticed how hot it is down here!"

"Nothing like it's about to be." I hold my smartcard over the electronic reader mounted on a yellow steel post in the uneven glow of a sodium vapor lamp.

The closer we get to the Yellow Submarine, the warmer and more humid it is. In the 80s at least, the air saturated. I've sweated through my underclothes and socks. My hard hat makes my head ache, my scalp itch, and there's little I hate more than wearing safety glasses. At least these are amber tinted and custom fitted for the firing range. Even so, when I look up and down, they slip on my sweaty nose.

"All right, same drill," I announce with a sharp clack of the lock releasing. "Go! Go! Go!"

Motioning Fran to hurry through as I open a shark-gray metal door that like everything else is marked with yellow-painted stripes and plastered with warnings.

Yellow, yellow everywhere, including a

blizzard of sunny stickers about the pinch-point potential for crushing fingers and hands if you don't shut one door all the way before opening the next.

In addition to other bright reminders of what can terrorize, maim or kill you down here:

CONFINED SPACE

ASBESTOS HAZARD

DO NOT DISTURB WITHOUT PROPER TRAINING AND EQUIPMENT

ABSOLUTE "BUDDY SYSTEM" REQUIRED

Not that your average buddy or bear would wish to spelunk alone or at all inside an underground concrete tube filled with asbestos-wrapped high-pressure pipes heated up to 218 Celsius, or 424 degrees Fahrenheit. And standing water and active leaks. Plus the skittering slithering critters that love hot humid places. Not much fun if you have a plethora of phobias as Fran now does.

She can't even put on a scuba mask or have an MRI anymore without feeling buried alive, is terrified of spiders and snakes, just the thought enough to break her out in hives. No big surprise she's been a horror show since I received the alert not even a half hour ago at 1538 hours eastern time. As I was winding up my briefing, a

31

motion detector registered a fault in one of the airlocks leading to the Yellow Submarine tunnel, suggesting the sensor picked up movement that shouldn't be there.

I instructed Fran to dash back to Building 1195C, our protective services headquarters. To grab hard hats, safety glasses, flashlights, steel-toe footwear, and meet me ASAP in the parking lot of 1111. Told her I'd be waiting for her with bells on. Or more specifically, with my portable spectrum analyzer turned on.

Figuring that by the time she rolled up, I would have scanned the building's perimeter with a receiver not much bigger than a handheld radio that can detect 99 percent of all electronic signals up to the 12.4 gigahertz (GHz) range. This pretty much covers everything from wireless heart monitors to navigation and avalanche beacons to submarine and aviation communications to television broadcasts.

Virtually any low to superhigh frequency signal that I might consider problematic or rogue is going to be sniffed out by my handy-dandy analyzer that I keep with me or in my truck almost everywhere I go. It's my divining rod, my stick I poke at things, and in real time it's telling me all motion sensors are transmitting. They're operating nominally, and that's reassuring and not. I don't want a malfunction.

What I want even less is a bad actor up to no good, and I can't stop thinking about the stolen-badge report from yesterday. The alleged victim works inside Building 1110, and it's connected to 1111 by the sealed-off tunnel I'm constantly worried about. I found the story suspicious then, and now my concerns are like a rock in my shoe. The alleged missing badge with its high-level security clearance could have gotten some-one through these airlocks. Worse, before it was deactivated, there was ample time for it to be used all over campus and also to gain access to the air force base.

But I remind myself there's likely a mun-dane explanation. There almost always is, and I make the mistake of wondering out loud if there might be bats down here. Perhaps the detector was tripped by some-thing other than a trespasser of the human variety.

"Oh Jeez-us!" Fran's eyes dart around wildly.

"Relax. I've never seen a bat, well not in this tunnel. I'm just trying to figure what could have caused one detector to pick up motion and not the others. Unless it wasn't on 2 legs. Maybe on 8 or more. Or something flying that got in and out somehow. Or slithering, I guess."

"Please shut up!"

"Better that than a bad guy with a stolen badge."

"We canceled it within minutes!"

Well, not exactly, because we can't cancel something until we know there's a problem, I remind her. And we didn't know that within minutes. It took way too many hours. But I understand her overall point. The smartcard was deactivated 23 hours ago at around 5:00 p.m. yesterday, suggesting it shouldn't have worked had someone tried it to access airlock doors down here recently. Hopefully she's right, but the so-called stolen badge won't stop nagging at me.

"On the count of 3. One, 2, 3, and stay clear!" My shout echoes off concrete.

Hands and limbs out of the way, and I close the airlock door behind us, making it possible to open what's dead ahead, centered in the opposite water-stained wall. The repurposed submarine hatch and likely inspiration for the Yellow Submarine code name is circa World War II and painted French's mustard yellow. The ton of steel is oval shaped and bomb shelter thick with a bank vault spin-dial lock straight out of Bonnie and Clyde.

Only certain people like me are authorized to have the combination. Although most likely it will be Fran's problem soon enough, adding to the vulnerability of 1111-A. Because there's no way she'll check on anything unless she gets a grip. And gosh knows I've tried to help her while there's still time.

"A false alarm, what a surprise, and I won't say I told you so." She can't wrap this up fast enough. "Has to be an error if the motion detector in the first airlock didn't go off. Yet this one did." Indicating the second airlock door we just came through.

I don't offer the bat theory again. Or suggest a bird, ghost or extraterrestrial is to blame. Certainly not a spider or snake, and I remind Fran in general there's no "has to be" in most of life's formulas. She should know that loud and clear since she's the one who taught me from the get-go never to stop questioning. And not to kill time. Or be in too big of a hurry.

She's always encouraged me to occupy the moment, to be mindful and pay attention. But she's unable to practice what she preaches right now, is something less than her relentless self.

"It's obvious nobody's been down here."

Her sharp-featured face is bright red, her blue eyes deer-in-the-headlights wide and watery.

Hovering near the door, she watches me sweep the airless dead space with my signal sniffer. Monitoring the small display, I point the antenna like a magic wand, snooping for any transmissions. Including cell phones, radios and, most of all, the sensors programmed to alert on rapid motion, triggering the alarm that went off.

Turning in slow circles, I hold up the antenna, scanning in 360-degree sweeps. Finding nothing atypical about the detector covering the yellow hatch roughly 4.5 meters, or 15 feet, from us.

"Weird, weird, weird," to myself.

"What?" Fran's unhappy eyes as she breathes hard, wiping her face on her sleeve. "And you look like a crazy person right about now." What she always snipes when I spin.

"It's weird that the only fault was with the one I was alerted about during the briefing," I stop turning, looking at the metal airlock door behind us, pondering the oddity.

"Like I said, a malfunction of some sort." Fran unzips her police uniform jacket, pushing it out of the way of her Glock .40 cal, in case she needs to quick draw.

Meanwhile I'm neither armed nor dressed appropriately beyond the steel-toe sneakers she brought for me to put on. At least she's in uniform instead of a suit and vintage leather flight jacket not meant for such conditions. But I was in the midst of giving the briefing when the alarm went off. There wasn't time to change my clothes, no time to spare when it's 1111-A. Especially when facing a government shutdown. While expecting a major winter storm to slam our peninsula. Creating the perfect formula for espionage and sabotage.

By midnight, most federal workers will be furloughed if politicians can't agree on whatever it is this time. NASA centers nationwide will be locked down, the average employee not allowed access to the facilities, offices or computers. Except that won't include me, depending on which way I spin at any given moment. Maybe I'm the stealthy cop. And maybe I'm not. Maybe I'm the nerdy scientist instead. It all depends on what's going on around me.

I can make exceptions and choices your typical NASA employee can't with my two jobs and offices at Langley. As a special agent, I have enforcement powers and a badge, and when so inclined carry a gun.

But I also have a master's degree in aerospace engineering and a PhD in quantum mechanics, with extensive training and experience in other disciplines. Most significantly, cyber investigations. Not to sound boastful, I'm not average.

"Exactly my point," Fran is saying impatiently. "You have to open the first door to get to the second one unless you're Houdini. Also, if this detector here at the hatch didn't go off, then obviously nobody got close to your *super secret bunghole* or whatever."

"*Tunnel.* And most likely nobody did. But we don't know that for a fact yet." Sliding my tactical flashlight out of a pocket. "And I continue to be unhappy about the timing of the badge reported stolen late yesterday afternoon. Since the alleged victim works in the building next door."

"And I'm unhappy that I'm starting to itch and it's hard to breathe!" she warns semi-hysterically. "There's not enough oxygen in here! I don't need a damn asthma attack!"

"There's plenty of oxygen, and you don't have asthma," as I shine the light over unpainted concrete walls, ceiling and flooring.

Checking what's around us in the off chance the alarm was legitimate and someone has been in here unauthorized. Searching for what I think of as low-tech evidence, like a cigarette butt. Footwear and other patterns transferred to surfaces. A shed hair. A lost button. Something falling out of a pocket. A mindless mistake.

"What's gotten into you?" Fran's frustration is about to boil over. "This is nuts, you see that, right? Dropping all these morbid bombs about not being here and crap like that."

"My returning home to Langley was never meant to be forever." I say it kindly, knowing the truth really can hurt. "I'm here and I'm not, my ambitions, heart and soul elsewhere. And you've always known that."

"Dragging me down here for no good reason," she isn't going to listen, "like we're about to be hacked by North Korea."

"If that should go down, whether it's a nation or individual, you don't want it happening on your watch. Which is why I've tried to show you all this before, most recently yesterday, to no avail." Moving away from her as she hovers near the airlock door. "Well, going forward, maybe when there's a big storm coming or an alarm goes off — or both — you'll understand why it should matter to you. And if you're not going to come down here yourself, then you'll have to find someone who can."

Doing my best to make it penetrate that soon enough whatever happens in Langley's cyberspace is on her.

"Hack into what?" At the top of her lungs. "A steam pipe?"

Her sarcastic question doesn't merit a response, and I focus my attention on the hatch, careful where I step. Getting closer to what Fran considers the monster in the closet or under the bed, and I believe she'd do almost anything to avoid checking this or any tunnel. There isn't much she wouldn't do to avoid stepping foot in one and hasn't since Christmas Eve three years ago.

She hasn't done a lot of things since then, and probably no one knows more about her history than I do. No one is less callous to her current misery and how real it feels. But if I gave in to her every phobia, she couldn't do her job. She would have lost it by now, and that's the irony. When she decompensates, her defense is to make it all about me, as if I'm the one acting squirrelly even as I help her.

". . . Ever since you got back from Houston, you've been freaking over everything," lecturing me, jabbing her index finger into the warm stale air. "Like the world's going to end if you don't walk on the freakin' moon someday."

Yes, I'd very much like to step foot there, I don't bother to reply. But I've also got my sights on other destinations, including Mars, and crouching in front of the yellow-painted hatch, I zip my analyzer inside my gear bag.

"Well, you know my attitude about what you can't control," I answer. "You know what they say: que será, será."

"Yeah, 'whatever will be, will be,' bullshit. You've been a nervous wreck ever since those interviews." Fran isn't going to spare my feelings or even be polite about it.

And that's the downside when you've known someone most of your life.

3

In her late 40s, she looks younger and more fit than she deserves, and it isn't fair. Especially when one is as calorie and work-out obsessed as I have to be.

Fran can eat and drink pretty much anyone under the table without penalty or remorse, and forget exercise. No need when you clean your own house, do your own repairs and work in the yard, if you ask her. The last time I dragged her to the gym here on campus, she broke out in hives, claiming an allergy to exercise.

Yet she doesn't have an ounce of padding in any of the wrong places, is built like a stevedore and about as strong. I remind her when I can that she's old enough to be my mom. But she doesn't act mature or maternal, more like a bossy badass aunt. A dyed-in-the-wool cop from a long line of them, she'll tell you she doesn't know how to be anything other than what she is.

Take it or leave it, some things are hard-wired in, and I don't disagree. A perfect example of the apple not falling far from the tree, her father a Hampton chief and commander of SWAT. And his father a legendary investigator for the Virginia State Police. Even without her law enforcement pedigree, Fran was considered quite the force when Hampton PD and NASA Protective Services formed a reciprocal partnership about the time Carme and I left for college.

Since then, Fran has been deputized by us and has jurisdiction on our grounds. And NASA Langley's federal special agents like me have jurisdiction in Hampton. This is helpful since nobody actually lives on the NASA campus and has to drive through Hampton to get anywhere. What happens if I witness a crime on my way to or from work? In the old days, that was a problem. One could be in uniform with a badge and gun, and have no more power than any other citizen when witnessing a bank being robbed.

The ultimate exchange program and perfect synergy. Our two agencies combining resources, including technologies, weapons, equipment and vehicles. But mostly good people who have something to offer and learn, and Fran tops the list. Were it not for what happened when Easton was three, I have no doubt she'd be back at Hampton full time by now.

She may very well be their chief had she not gone into a stall, headed nowhere in more ways than one, hiding her problem from almost everyone while raising a precocious child with her on-and-off-again husband. Not Tommy's fault, by the way. Why he's still with her, it's hard to say, and compared to her, I seem uncomplicated. Single and childless at 28. Living at home for the past three years after transferring out of the air force and into NASA.

My special sauce is aviation safety and aircraft control systems, and when I'm not in uniform, so to speak, my day to day is consumed by all sorts of activities that aren't routine for most police investigators. What Fran considers rather mind-withering preoccupations such as writing algorithms for flight simulators, test piloting autonomous aircraft (drones), gathering data from my faithful crew of crash dummies at the gantry.

Or testing an exploratory spacecraft in one of our High-Intensity Radio Frequency (HIRF) labs or anechoic chambers before sending the next Cassini probe into the solar system. It's not unusual at NASA for people to have different jobs with different directorates and divisions or with private industry. While I work full time as a test pilot and aerospace engineer for the Dynamic Systems and Control Branch, I'm also a captain for NASA Protective Services, in charge of cyber investigations. Explaining why I'm crouching before a submarine hatch at the moment, inside a concrete airlock below sea level.

"Maybe moisture caused a false alarm." Fran repositions herself behind me, making sure she can see what I'm doing while watching the door we came through a few minutes ago.

"No way." I look up at the reflective infrared system mounted in a corner at the top of the wall near the hatch with its thick layers of yellow paint and rash of rust.

As I noted with the other RIRs, the pyroelectric lens is safely behind glass, the entire unit protected by a tough waterproof case that doesn't appear to have been damaged or compromised.

"All of them look exactly the same as they did when I was here yesterday," I remind Fran. "When I was doing the systems analysis here in 1111-A that you managed to boycott as usual. But let's not forget I also was next door in 1110 after that, taking the complaint about the alleged stolen badge. I don't like the coincidence, if I've not said it enough. In fact, you know how I feel about coincidences."

"I don't see the connection."

"The Yellow Submarine tunnel between 1110 and 1111 is the connection. And you don't see it because you don't want to."

"What I see is a false alarm, and I'm thinking if the detector's circuit board was exposed to condensation and some of the components got corroded . . . ?" Fran suggests what she wants to be true. "Couldn't that do it?"

"Nope. Because like I said, it's working now. The analyzer read all sensors loud and clear, not picking up anything unusual in the area. Had there been a malfunction in this motion detector or any other, I would have been alerted that the sensor was off line."

Instead, I got an emergency tone similar to those that sound on my phone when there are severe weather warnings, missing children, mass murder and mayhem in the greater Tidewater area of Virginia. This was as I was winding up the presentation to our center directorate. Meaning I had quite the audience when an app on my phone alerted me that there may be a problem, a potentially serious violation in an underworld where NASA keeps a scary quantum secret.

The Yellow Submarine hatch is a potential portal into the heart and soul of our government and beyond, and not a day goes by that the threat isn't on my mind.

But times exactly like what we're facing right now are when our cyber security is most at risk for a breach, and any adversary worth his salt knows it.

If I learned nothing else while working military investigations in Colorado Springs, it's never to make assumptions. Or skip a step. Or be in too big of a hurry to clear a scene or conduct a thorough interview. Stuffing my used purple nitrile exam gloves into a pocket, I pull on fresh ones in the off chance I might figure out later that I should be worried about DNA on door handles and locks.

Stretching my fingers like a safecracker limbering up, I turn the dial, focusing on how many spins to the right or left. Nothing written down. Never is when it comes to codes and combinations I don't want others to know. That's what memory is for, and with a turn of the big brass wheel, I release steel bolts as thick as sausages. Heaving open the massive door, I'm careful not to pull too hard and smash myself between the casement and the wall.

Staring into the maw, unevenly illuminated and hot as an oven, hearing the rush of blowing air. And I swing one leg through, ducking under, instantly slammed by heat and humidity that are suffocating.

"Come on." I peer back at Fran, holding out my hand, helping her through. "Careful." I point out slimy water flowing along a narrow path through asbestos-wrapped pipes, conduits, and the rusting fins, fans and tube plates of heat exchangers.

"Holy mother of God!" she protests, and I feel the heat prickle my skin, the air filling my lungs as hot as Death Valley.

"I don't need to go in very far, and we're definitely not staying long," I can reassure her of that much. "Just one area in particular I want to take a peek at. Where we tied in to the grid yesterday."

It's routine to ensure redundancy when facing an emergency such as a blizzard or a hurricane, the node enabling us to uplink via satellite to our sister research center, NASA Ames in Silicon Valley. They have a quantum key distribution and a quantum computer to go with it, and linking East Coast to West gives Langley a backup should we find ourselves blown away or under 8 feet of water.

But it also makes NASA's telecommunication system less secure. As Carme and I like to say, the more links in a chain, the higher the probability that the chain will be compromised or broken. The more doors to your house, the more likely the wrong person will enter.

"You stay right here by the hatch, which must remain open and in line of sight at all times," I tell Fran, who doesn't need convincing. "I'd prefer we don't get locked inside here . . ."

"Oh Jeez . . ."

"Don't worry, there are emergency phones every 200 feet . . ."

"Not close enough!"

"Trust me, we're not going to end up down here resorting to cannibalism."

"What?"

Never mind, I don't say out loud as I pick my way through dripping concrete and hulking rusty metal for as far as I can see, finding nothing off-nominal, as we say in NASA speak. Not one thing abnormal as I carefully step through shallow puddles scummy like pond water. Dodging thick steam pipes wrapped in fraying silvery asbestos that I work hard not to disturb in any way. Estimating the ambient temperature is 46 Celsius, or 115 degrees Fahrenheit, and if the humidity were much higher, it would rain.

Already I'm overheated, my pulse picking up, but not about to unzip or take off my leather jacket. At least it offers some protection should I have a close encounter of the scalding kind, and most assuredly I'm careful with my hands. Tucking them out of harm's way in my jacket pockets, and thank goodness for my hard hat, or I might have knocked myself out on the pipe elbow I didn't see coming a few seconds ago.

"Don't go too far! I'm not gonna save your sorry ass!" Fran yells from the hatch. "Jeezzz-us criminy, it's hot! What the hell are you looking for?"

"I'll explain when I'm done," I remind her loudly, but it's not exactly true, can't tell her but so much.

Clunking my hard hat on whatever's low hanging, I continue to scan a concrete ceiling festooned with black cables and a pileup of PVC and metal tubing. Pinpointing the familiar galvanized steel conduit newer than the rest, following it like the yellow brick road to Oz as I yell to Fran that the target's in sight.

"So is heat stroke!" yelling back.

Evading more hanks of cables gathered in thick bundles, I step around a dead mouse near groundwater pouring out of a copper pipe brown like an old penny. Counting how many caged ceiling lights I've passed. Two so far. Reassured by the third up ahead, where I was yesterday in preparation for the storm and other critical events about to unfold that have been keeping me awake at night for months.

Long before bad weather and government obstructions were a thought, I've been trying to tell those who count that we're poised for the perfect storm of a cyberattack if we're not careful. Prompting me to be down here for many hours yesterday, in and out as the heat allowed, running a systems analysis on Fiber-Optic Distribution Box 001.

Or FOD-1, as those of us in the know call the node that as of yesterday is uplinked to NASA Ames's supercomputer center in Silicon Valley, making sure we have that backup plan. Because government shutdowns don't stop astronauts from needing supplies or conducting a scheduled Extravehicular Activity, EVA. Pronounced *E-V-A* and better known as a spacewalk, a major headache of one is scheduled for tomorrow at 0700 Greenwich Mean Time (GMT). Or

2:00 a.m. on the East Coast. Less than 10 short hours from now, two US astronauts will install a top secret quantum machine parading as a science experiment.

During the EVA, they'll attach this node to a remote platform outside the International Space Station, where quantum research is ongoing in its Cold Atom Lab. I'm just the telerobotics officer who will be sitting next to Rush Delgato at Langley's Mission Control when he talks the astronauts through the installation. But at oh-dark-hundred I'll be ready should he need me for technical assistance, and in a perfect world this wouldn't be going on right now.

Given a choice, I'd prefer we weren't hooking up a quantum node on the Space Station's truss at the same time a resupply rocket is launching from our Wallops Flight Facility on the coast of Virginia. It's too darn much at once, each event a colossal vulnerability, which is why I'm down here in this tunnel. Making sure no one has been tampering with the pole-mounted FOD-1 cabinet, thick stainless steel, about the size of a hotel refrigerator.

Next to it in a locked mesh rack is a switchboard, and it's from here that we can monitor NASA's telecommunications network. Meaning that systems engineers and cyber ninjas like me come down here rather often to run tests, verifying that parameters are at the correct levels. That's what I did yesterday before giving the green light to connect all critical NASA infrastructures such as directorate emails and videos. Rather frighteningly similar to turning on Wi-Fi and logging on to the internet with a device you don't want hacked. Better hope someone up to no good doesn't outsmart your firewalls and encryption.

These days it could be some 12-year-old in China who breaches international cyber security in the ultimate way, and quantum computing will only make the apocalyptic possibilities endless. It may very well be a kid who destroys our planet as if it's some virtual reality game. But I hope not. It's what I'm here to prevent as sweat runs into my eyes and an internal alarm begins to sound. My body is sending me warnings. It won't be long before I'll stop perspiring entirely and start getting chills.

My mouth is dusty, as dry as paper, my eyes burning as I flip up the shielding for the FOD-1 keypad. Fail-safe with old-style metal buttons in the event the power should go out, and I enter my code. So far, so good. No indication anything's been tampered with until I notice the fat steam pipe directly to my left, the crusty black drops and drips of what looks like blood on the tattered asbestos cover. I didn't see this when I was in here yesterday, and I'm pretty certain I would have.

It's ingrained in me to notice the morbid hieroglyphics of violent encounters and other disasters, whether it's aircraft, crash dummies or humans, and this bloodlike spatter wasn't here when I last was. Whatever the explanation, my overriding concern is that no one should come within a mile of the FOD-1 node without my knowledge and consent. Even Rush has to let me know if he's coming down here, and I set my gear bag on a dry area of the tunnel's concrete floor.

I begin digging for the most basic of crime scene paraphernalia that I carry pretty much everywhere. Swabs. A small bottle of sterile water. More gloves, always nitrile because acrylonitrile butadiene synthetic rubber is hypoallergenic and won't melt. Plus, the expected surgical masks, shoe covers, various evidence buttons, envelopes and bags and so on. For bigger jobs requiring special lights, crime scene tape, tarps, chemicals and cameras, I keep a large field case locked up in the back of my truck.

But there's no need for that, and I root

around for a permanent marker, then the stickers that look like miniature rulers. Jotting today's date on one to use as a labeled scale for photographs, I place it on top of the fraying-asbestos-wrapped pipe. Centering the label under what may be blood. Hoping the loose insulation is far enough away from the pipe itself that any potential DNA wasn't completely degraded by heat.

At around 190 degrees Celsius, or 374 Fahrenheit, the game is over. Gloves off, I wipe down my phone with an alcohol pad, and capture images and video of the flaky blackish drops. Fresh gloves, and I begin to swab, noting that the white cotton tips turn a deep reddish brown. *Consistent with blood, sure enough,* I think but don't say out loud.

"What are you doing down there?" Fran's voice sounds from the open hatch door.

But I don't answer as I seal each swab inside a separate clear plastic evidence envelope. A precaution that most likely won't matter, similar to jotting down a license plate number when someone is a menace on the road. Probably nothing. But then again, you never know when you might wish you'd bothered.

Mission accomplished, and it's back through the airlocks and up the claustrophobic stairwells, the going steeply uphill and harder than before. But not to Fran. She's like a horse racing to the barn. Exploding out the rear door of 1111. Boiling into the parking lot, and it's emptied considerably since we arrived barely an hour ago.

"Oh, thank God Almighty!" she gushes, her breath fogging out.

"Better zip up your coat," I suggest.

The temperature is a nippy 11 degrees Fahrenheit. Or -11.6667 Celsius, to be precise. Because I am that. Precise to a fault. Despite my efforts not to show it or my other annoying quirk of doing instant calculations involuntarily in my head. Not that I have only two annoying quirks. Carme will tell you I enjoy an embarrassment of riches when it comes to idiosyncrasies.

"Watch where you step," I warn, my breath streaming out like smoke as I keep up my scan for the insidious sheen of black ice I noticed earlier. "Over there, and over there." Pointing out danger zones. "And there."

"Oh great," Fran mumbles. "I'll break my neck. That'll be next."

She continues to blame me for all that's treacherous in the world as I jam my hands into my pockets, beginning to shiver. I don't know why it seemed like a good idea this morning to forgo my goose-down coat and instead head out of the house in a vintage leather jacket with no lining. Well, I do know. I wanted to look nice, do something special for the briefing at hand.

General Melville hasn't seen me wear the WWII flight jacket since I left his command in Colorado Springs. I thought it would mean something to him. But truth be told, he never mentioned it. I'd describe him as polite but impersonal, and I touch my right index finger and thumb together, lightly rubbing the scar.

Hiding evidence before Dick and the others got there.

Tucking and throwing things away, insanely tidying as if it mattered. As if I could hide the mistake I made in an unguarded moment. Blood tracked everywhere in chaotic patterns, and the more I tried to clean it up, the worse it got. Shamed that such a thing could happen on my watch.

"Unlike you, I have to pay attention, Sisto," Carme drinking beer with me in the barn, and I wish I hadn't told her. "If I'm sloppy and unfocused for even one nanosecond? My ass gets shot out of the sky," she's saying, the two of us at a workbench, messing around with sensors and multimode handheld lasers. "Maybe this time you actually learned a lesson about what happens when you get in one of your dreamy quantum states, being all over the place in that spinning head of yours."

Yes, I learned something, I don't say out loud. Not about to tell her, our parents or anyone that I no longer trust myself the way I did. That ability was ruined by carelessness. By emotionality, and Carme is right. Had it been her, it might not have been survivable.

4

The setting sun smolders blood orange through winter-bare trees, backlighting the former Lunar Landing Research Facility looming starkly against the distant horizon.

More commonly known as the gantry, it's 73 meters (240 feet) high, 122 meters (400 feet) long, and mainly used these days to conduct pendulum-swing drop tests of cargo planes, Unmanned Aerial Systems (drones), spacecraft and most recently a passenger jet. Several weeks before that, it was various autonomous urban taxis and flying cars, and a crew capsule destined for the moon and back.

Some dirt landings. Others in the water. Each scenario more stressful than the last, with fewer resources and more at stake. All to say that the massive red-and-white A-frame steel structure and its outbuildings near the disgusting-smelling steam plant are my home away from home for lots of reasons. At least 20 if we're talking about my faithful crew of bruised and battered crash dummies stored in a hangar over there. Requiring me to drop by regularly. As if they're my patients or kids (yes, I've named them).

Always checking if they need something. Reprogramming. A little tweaking. Fixing bad boo-boos when the going gets way too rough. Forever futzing with their various sensors that let me know how our pilots, astronauts and other travelers would fare if similarly hurled and banged around. Smashed to the ground. Or against the side of a building after a pinnacle takeoff in a high-density urban area like Boston or New York City. Or splashed down in the ocean after streaking through the atmosphere, returning home from the International Space Station, the moon, deep space or soon enough Mars.

"Jeez, I need a beer," Fran says, both of us pointing our keys with a chirp.

Unlocking and remote starting, and I'm all for a little distance if there's a chance your vehicle might blow up.

"And you're sure as hell buying after putting me through that," she rants but doesn't mean it.

"No drinking, not even one," I remind

her. "Unless something miraculous happens, we're going to be furloughed at midnight. So, guess who's got to be here? And I have to anyway because of the EVA."

"As usual, you depress the crap out of me."

"Good news is we can hang out at Mission Control, watch the launch, watch Rush talking to the astronauts . . ."

"Rockets, schmockets. And I've seen how many launches and spacewalks over the years? And who cares diddly-squat about astronauts?" she adds, not wanting me to be one even if she won't say it.

Her black Tahoe is backed in next to my take-home police truck, a white Silverado with a covered bed, tricked out with the appropriate sirens, lights and run-flat tires. *NASA Protective Services* is in blue on the doors, and our logo may be the only one I know of in law enforcement with a design that includes planet Earth, an orbiting moon and a belt of stars.

Not that anything is normal about working at Langley Research Center (LaRC), the oldest of NASA's 10 national field centers, what most of us refer to as just plain Langley. Not to be confused with the Central Intelligence Agency, headquartered in Langley, Virginia, some 200 miles to the northwest of the peninsula we share with the air force base. You might say Carme and I were created by an alchemy of rivers, creeks, ocean and bay catalyzed by a sonic-booming elixir of military airspace. We've always had one foot in the water, the other in the sky while shooting for the moon and beyond.

Our Mayberry while coming along was 764 acres of numbered government buildings connected by tunnels forming a labyrinth of mysterious chambers, incubators, labs and test ranges haunted by legends and inhabited by geniuses. For as far back as I can recall, my sister and I were wandering the same hallways and hangars that Amelia Earhart, Charles Lindbergh and John Glenn once did.

We routinely heard eyewitness accounts of Neil Armstrong, John Young, Buzz Aldrin and other death-defying explorers learning to pilot a lunar lander and moonwalk in our gantry. It all started right here in Virginia, not Florida or Texas. But on this very spit of land in 1917, when the US government created the first laboratory for studying human flight, the National Advisory Committee for Aeronautics, NACA.

At the time there was no *S* in the acronym, no *Space* in the equation, not when we didn't have airports or the FAA yet and Robert Goddard was still almost a decade out from firing off the first liquid-fueled rocket. Reaching for the stars wouldn't become an urgent priority until 1957, when Russia sent up the first satellite in history. Sputnik was the launch heard round the world, the space glove tossed down.

NACA morphed into the National Aeronautics and Space Administration, NASA, and the space race was on. Of course, if you ask me, it's been on since our so-called primordial soup days if not before and forever. Because it's the very stuff we're made of and who we are to sail through the air and just keep going. Unimpeded, infinitely, our heaven-bent behavior tracing back long before Igor Sikorsky and the Wright brothers roared off terra firma, soaring, spinning, mostly crashing. Nor were those early inventors the first to conjure up such lofty contraptions.

Leonardo da Vinci was designing gliders and helicopter-like flying machines in the 15th century. Eons earlier, fantastic tales were spun fast and furiously about galactic visitors making fiery landfalls and whirlwind departures, and foolish mortals with wings of wax and feathers flying too close to the sun. Myths and other ancient texts including the Bible are rich with astonishing revelations and allusions that might hold scientific clues about our true origin were we not expected to take them at face value.

Streets paved in gold and the burning bush come to mind. Along with Balaam's mistreated talking donkey, Lot's disobedient wife turning into a pillar of salt, the Red Sea parting, the feeding of the masses with 7 loaves and a few small fish. And one of my favorites, stubborn Jonah refusing to sail to Nineveh and landing there anyway. Spewed up on shore after a three-day journey in the gullet of a whale. An off-nominal entry if there ever was one, and a reminder not to blow off Mission Control.

Then there are angels, demons, Mount Olympus and gods among us, all of it problematic when one isn't a fan of blind faith and fables. And in my family, we accept miracles, magic, the paranormal for what they are. Unexplained or misunderstood scientific phenomena that humans love to repurpose and anthropomorphize. Not to mention politicize. Usually to make some point. Almost always a self-serving one.

When we'd be wise to know our place in the grand design of things, a small blue dot, one of countless vibrant planets flung far and wide throughout infinity, spinning, orbiting like tumbled jewels. Separate worlds seeking to reconnect like the two fingers in Michelangelo's *Creation of Adam* on the Sistine Chapel ceiling. Like E.T. looking up to the heavens, to where he's from. Like Dorothy chanting there's no place like home. Suggesting that we may not be from here but someplace else we're desperate to return.

Explaining why it's in our programming, our very nature to propel our fragile flesh-suited bodies perilously through the air. To take flight with our capes and kites, our blimps and balloons, our gliders, zip lines, catapults, bungee cords, parachutes, planes, rockets, space shuttles, jet packs, drones . . .

There's not much we won't try to defy gravity. To break away from what binds us. Returning to our source, chasing what we've lost, speeding freely through eternity on waves of energy and light.

Parking driver's door to driver's door is how cops rendezvous in deserted parking lots, and Fran and I hum our windows down.

"What's next? You gonna alert the Pentagon about your false alarm?" she asks sarcastically over heat blasting. "Maybe run it by your sugar daddy, General Melville?

Except I have to say he wasn't very *sugary* toward you today . . ."

I shush her so I can close out the call we're actively on, "Comm Center, Alpha 5 is 10-95 at 1111."

Radioing dispatch that we're clearing the scene, offering no other details. I was exquisitely careful from the very first call not to divulge exactly where I was headed inside the building. And for what purpose beyond responding to what most would consider a routine security alarm. I didn't mention 1111-A, the Yellow Submarine or anything quantum.

I didn't cross-reference the stolen badge report in 1110 from late yesterday, always mindful of journalists and others who might be monitoring. Most of all, Mason Dixon, and that really is his name.

"Ten-four, Alpha 5," Christine with dispatch comes back, and I key the mic in a sneaky shout-out to her.

"I have a few things to take care of," I say to Fran through our open windows as I buckle up. "And please be reminded that the alarm wasn't false, per se. So, don't go around saying that or putting it in a report."

"It's not my report to write. Not my false alarm for that matter. And I don't write up your crap, Captain Cut to the Chase."

"Well, Major Jerkoff, my point is we just don't know what triggered the detector. Not yet. But I'm not done checking."

"When are you heading home?" she asks, and I can tell she wants to talk as I expected she might.

"Hopefully within the hour but it depends on what's crossed my desk, what else has come in. Plus, I need to lock up evidence, refrigerate the swabs."

"To do what? You'd better not be thinking of turning them in to the labs, as backlogged as they are." Here she goes with the lecturing again. "I swear I don't know why it matters if someone bled in a tunnel. I'm sure a lot of people do, with all the rusting metal everywhere. I mean just being that far below sea level will give you a nosebleed if you stay long enough. Your heart can explode."

"Not true."

"I'm pretty sure that's a medical fact," she's adamant and being ridiculous.

"Nope."

"People have freakin' died in there," and that's not quite right either but close enough. "Which reminds me, when's the last time you had a tetanus shot?"

"I'm all squared away, and it wasn't me who was bleeding." Raising my voice as F-22 Raptor fighter jets rip up the dusk,

67

rocketing through the darkening sky at steep angles of attack that seem impossible.

"But you don't know *when* someone or some*thing* bled in there. Hours, days, weeks or months ago? That's assuming what you found is blood, and human blood at that." Talking to me while scanning her mirrors, her self-possession and street smarts kicking back in now that she's no longer fried by anxiety.

"I suspect the blood has been there *at most* since late yesterday," I reply. "No longer ago than that, but it also could be much more recent, extremely recent. Assuming someone was inside that tunnel mere minutes before we were. As hot as those pipes are, blood drops would turn black very fast, looking exactly like what I saw. It wouldn't take long. Minutes, possibly seconds," adding that it would be simple to test my hypothesis.

All I'd have to do is go down to the 1111-A tunnel, prick my finger and bleed on that same asbestos-swathed steam pipe. I could pinpoint with certainty the minimum amount of time required in the same hot, humid conditions for human blood to coagulate, dry and blacken. But this wouldn't tell me how long it might stay like that before flaking off or washing away in blowing hot air and water leaks.

"If you want to do something that cray-cray, help yourself," Fran retorts. "You're on your own. They find your sorry ass mummified in there 20 years from now, that's what you get."

She doesn't mean it, and I let her know that later on this evening I bet we can find some pretty decent leftovers in my mom's kitchen. Some warmed-up mac and cheese from her favorite TV cooking show, *Kitchen Combat.* Maybe a serving or two of those sinful baked beans that taste like candied onions and bacon. Before we have to be back here and up all night.

"I'll text you when I'm home. Give me a couple hours to wrap up a few things before you wander on over," I mean it literally.

We're next-door neighbors, more than that, actually. Like a tribe or a clan, the Chase family and those related have lived in a nearby cove on Back River since the late 1860s, when the farm I grew up on was given to my father's great-grandfather, George Washington Chase, after the Civil War. It's family lore that our surname was permuted if not made up from whole cloth by some carpetbagger who thought it amusing to give our mixed-race ancestors a stick about being *chased* all the time.

Wasn't funny then. Isn't funny now. But for sure I'm here today because our saga had a much more fortunate resolution than most. The Chases truly are one big happy family, and you don't have to be related by blood to be included. Fran and her 6-year-old son, Easton, live across the garden from my parents and me, inducted into our ecosystem by marriage to her high school sweetheart, my mother's cousin, Tommy, who's taking a time-out, and I don't blame him.

A mental health break. A sabbatical or convalescence might be a more honest way to describe why he and Fran decided to give each other space. Meaning he's the one who needed it after she began turning into Mr. Hyde more than Dr. Jekyll. Her phobias had gotten kicked into a higher gear for reasons unknown, although I have a pretty good idea.

I don't believe in coincidences, and it wasn't one when she got worse last spring after finding out that Carme and I had been selected as potential astronaut candidates. Should that end the way I hope, it would change life for Fran as she knows it. Not that she would admit such a thing. But she got increasingly panicky and disagreeable, and Tommy got an apartment in Williamsburg.

He insisted that she, Easton and their orange tabby cat, Schroder, stay put in Hampton, living in the tin-roofed house on the river one door down from us. They need to stay right where they are, surrounded by family. No better way for a child to grow up, my parents always say, and it's true. As long as all is good with your loved ones, all is good.

Or good enough, and I tell Fran I'll see her back at the ranch, rolling up my window, driving off. Soon it will be dark, and most people are headed out for the day, the traffic picking up as I follow North Dryden Street away from the gantry, back toward the center of the campus.

5

I keep my speed below 20 miles per hour. Driving through the dormant grassy fields of the Unmanned Aircraft System Test Range. Then dense woods, and marshland thick with ice and tawny tall sea oats.

Passing rows of nondescript brick government buildings with tiny windows and signs out front offering a hint of what might go on inside. MEASUREMENT SYSTEMS. AUTONOMY INCUBATOR. CONTINUOUS-FLOW HYPERSONIC TUNNEL. FLIGHT RESEARCH. ACOUSTICS. Most of the facilities painted white with antennas everywhere, and I check my cell phone for messages.

Annoyed to find that Mason Dixon tried me again. As if his name isn't bad enough, worse, he's wicked Alec Baldwin gorgeous, explaining his nickname, Calendar Boy.

A semifamous internet journalist, he's crafty and charming, and his uncle Willard happens to be the governor of Virginia. I'm still furious with myself for giving Mason my personal number. But it made sense at the time, and I'd probably do the same thing again under the circumstances.

Playing his voice mail while I drive:

"Hey, Calli, it's me, Mason Dixon, as in 'the line you don't cross in reporting the news.' " Off air and on he has a way of crooning, as if everyone is his lover or wants to be. "Clever, right? I'm thinking it will go viral. Do you like it?"

No, I don't. Considering my dad is descended from the daughter of a slave and the man who owned her during an era when the Mason-Dixon Line defined far more than simply a border separating North from South. I could accuse Mason of being a bigot, but it's not my style, and besides, he's too self-involved to have a clue. He knows nothing about my history and mixed ethnicity, only that I remind him of J-Lo, whom I've pretended to be on many a Halloween but don't remotely resemble, if you ask me. Sadly.

". . . Word on the street is that the eagle has landed, i.e., the head honcho of Space Force has been spotted in the area," Mason's recorded voice. "Specifically, at Langley, and you know your friend Mason, here . . ."

Not my friend, none of your business and no, I don't know you or want to.

". . . I'm sitting here pouring myself a bourbon and thinking . . . soooo what's *General Moby Dick Melville himself* doing in your lovely neck of the woods, right? The big fish that keeps getting away, you know I really do want that interview, Calli. I'm pretty sure you know how to help me out, and maybe there's something mutual here . . ."

"Presumptuous horse's patootie . . . ," and it's a good thing no one's around to hear my coarse comments.

". . . Anyhoo, whenever the *big fish* comes around, others can't be far behind, right? Soooo what's goin' on, girlfriend? Sounds mighty intriguing. Call me. And oh yeah, didn't you and he once . . ."

I end the message, unable to listen a second longer to Mason's syrupy voice droning on as if he has some special right to my time or attention. Why would it ever enter his self-absorbed thoughts that I would connect him with my former boss? Or anybody else who matters?

On Langley Boulevard now, headed toward the giant white vacuum spheres and monster mechanicals of the wind tunnels. The most iconic and dramatic view on

74

campus, and I'm fortunate to enjoy it from both of my NASA offices, directly across the street from each other. It's good and bad that I can look out my window in Building 1232 and see into my corner window of 1195C, making me feel I'm in two places at once.

Around a copse of winter-bare hardwood trees, picnic tables and tennis courts, and next to the fitness center, where I never spend enough time. Especially this time of year, when my none-too-swift metabolism wants to hibernate. Then the almost century-old Variable Density Tunnel that brings to mind the *Hunley* submarine, which sank during the Civil War. Or a Gothic iron lung. Or maybe a primitive alien vessel from *Star Trek.*

Built with a lot of rivets from back in the heyday of the Wright brothers, the National Historic Landmark has been on display for as long as I've been around, and when my sister and I were kids, we used to climb all over it. Irreverently playing war games when no one was looking. Flying it like a weaponized space shuttle . . .

. . . Or pretending it was one disguised as an asteroid . . . Then switching into marine mode . . . Breaking the surface with periscope up . . . Diving into the silent depths of the sea . . . Firing torpedoes at the enemy . . .

Pay attention!

Getting bleary eyed in heavy traffic, on-coming headlights bright white like suns, and I'm blinking often, my blood sugar dipping. Trying not to be obvious about the two black Suburban SUVs in my wake, three and four vehicles back and following. DC license plates in the 900 numbers, tinted windows, possibly armored to protect not just the people but the equipment inside. Not military or private security, and they're not State Department, I decide, first noticing them several minutes after driving away from 1111.

They swung in behind me as I passed the van pool, keeping a discreet distance while locked in to each other and my truck like a tractor beam. Or that's what I sense even as I remind myself it's probably nothing. If they're interested in me for some unknown reason, they wouldn't be this blatant. I need to be careful about overreacting. Because Dick can make me paranoid, and I am right now, just a little.

Keeping my eyes on the SUVs, almost feeling the agents tracking me like a signal sniffer, as if they're curious about whether I might be a rogue frequency, an intruder, one of those unwanted events they're always talking about. It's not typical for a security detail to be wandering around back here. Certainly not a Secret Service detail, for crummy sake. But it depends on who of import might be touring the treasures hidden in our labs.

Except nobody's touring anything at this hour as we prepare for a furlough and a nor'easter. And I'm always informed about VIP guests well in advance.

I watch the two Suburbans in my mirrors, making out the shapes of two people in each. Taking in their technology and modus operandi, profiling who's bird-dogging me.

The scarcity of visible antennas on the lead SUV suggests conformal microstrips blended into the rooftop and body. The thin narrow bands can operate at almost any frequency and communicate with satellites if need be. The second SUV has an array of telecommunications antennas on both sides of the roof, and also two domes for electronic countermeasures such as signal jamming. Not a normal protective detail for around here unless the vice president is touring, as he was the other week.

I'm all but certain I recognize the profile of the vehicles, the subtle maneuvers, the

DC plates and all the rest. As a recent addition to the Secret Service's Electronic Crimes Task Force, I'm still learning their intricate and unusual ways, some of them super high tech even for me. But why would agents be here at Langley without my knowing, and is it just these two vehicles, or are there others? And if so, who are they protecting?

Or looking for?

The disturbing thought floats up from the depths of my consciousness, and I don't know where it came from. Since when would the Secret Service be looking for a fugitive or person of interest on our NASA campus? Mostly what we worry about is espionage. That's handled by the FBI, and I wouldn't expect the Secret Service to take charge unless there's the perceived threat in their wheelhouse.

Including an assassination attempt on the president, vice president or their families. Or cabinet members and others requiring the highest level of executive protection. Or if there's a suspicion of financial or electronic crimes including fraud, identity theft and hacking with catastrophic repercussions that could threaten our national security. And I can't imagine how any such unwanted events might apply to the frigid Langley campus right now.

Focus. Focus. Focus.

My nerves are singing like violin strings as I drive toward my headquarters. Around a traffic circle, and up ahead, the white vacuum spheres loom larger, lined up like gigantic ostrich eggs. I feel the pressure of time, not looking forward to an all-nighter in Mission Control, and the threat of almost everyone being sent home indefinitely interferes with everything. All because of feuding politicians, and for that matter, I don't care to make a list of everything I must get done before the government shuts down.

Assuming that happens, and it almost never does. But the specter of it is damaging on its own, the researchers in their usual uproar because who wants to be locked out of his or her office? I know I wouldn't. But one of many advantages in working for NASA Protective Services is that's not going to happen to us. Not usually. And never to me.

Once 1232 has been evacuated, I may not be able to work inside as a scientist, but that doesn't mean I can't access the building during routine patrols.

In other words, pretty much whenever I

like and for whatever reason I might decide. The same is true of my protective services HQ and our next-door neighbor, NASA Fire and Rescue. There's nothing to stop me from coming and going as I please, and when I turn into the parking lot, I'm surprised to find it empty except for the small fleet of army-green Polaris ATVs.

"Where the hell-o is everyone . . . ?" Muttering as I tuck my truck in the chief's empty spot where his Harley-Davidson was earlier.

Leaving the briefing when Fran and I did, he's probably safely home by now, and good for him. Because there are no heated grips and seat, no batwing fairing that would make me want to ride a motorcycle in this cold. Grabbing my gear bag, I lock my truck, and gosh darn it's freezing.

"Brrrrr . . . !"

Hurrying along the sidewalk, I maneuver around patches of pet-friendly salt toward the back entrance of our two-story modern red brick and blue-tinted-glass building. Scanning my smartcard to unlock the front door. Hurrying inside and stopping in my tracks.

"Hmmm."

Doesn't seem anyone's home, and I'm not surprised based on the empty parking lot.

But the alarm isn't set, and I stand perfectly still, on high alert. Looking around the lobby inside our blue world. Blue carpet. Blue-upholstered reproduction furniture. Walls displaying the blue NASA logo, "Meatball," as those in the know call it, and rocket launch and space photographs with wispy white clouds and oceans of lapis blue.

Doing a high recon, my counter-intel instincts kicking in. Aware of any shiny surface that might reflect the slightest motion of an intruder lurking about in here. Including autonomous surveillance devices, because these days I have to worry about more than humans. Not so much as a twitch of anything or anyone caught in glass doors and partitions, or in the big flat-screen TV turned on with the volume off in the sitting area.

And that's odd, too, the channel on a NASA live video feed of the two US astronauts currently on the International Space Station. Its commander, Peggy Whitson, and Jack Fischer are setting up cable harnesses for the installation of the presumed Low Earth Atmospheric Reader (LEAR) at 2:00 a.m. tomorrow. Less than 9 hours from now, and I've been routinely monitoring the NASA live feeds on my phone. So far everything is nominal and a go for the doubleheader.

The resupply launch from Wallops is on track, the rocket on the pad, stolid and iridescent white in stormy weather. And in outer space, the SpaceX Dragon and the Station rendezvoused yesterday, the cargo capsule safely berthed, its payload in the process of being unpacked and stowed. It's an astro-rodeo I've been to many times before, except this one is different. And hardly anybody knows it.

LEAR is tricky business, and I find it an eerie irony that I'm watching the very astronauts who are about to install it in outer space. Reminded that I'm assisting in a falsehood about the true nature of the instrument rocketed from Cape Canaveral two weeks ago, the cargo capsule orbiting earth ever since until captured by the Space Station's robotic arm.

During the EVA, this same arm will carry Commander Whitson and the alleged nerdy scientific instrument to a research platform attached to the Station's shiny metal structure. Except LEAR isn't LEAR, and it won't be observing or measuring anything about Earth, the moon, Mars, deep space, not anything anywhere. Not exactly.

What the public is told and what's actually true can't always be the same, not with our military, not with NASA, and I pause for a moment, watching the astronauts talking to each other and to Mission Control, saying things I can't hear. Probably dealing with Houston exclusively for the pre-prep setup going on inside the Station's US lab module.

But during the actual EVA, it will be Rush sitting in the hot seat. He'll be in Langley's Mission Control, overseeing the installation of a top secret multibillion-dollar instrument that, trust me, isn't typical, normal or expendable. It's not exactly some high school science project that's about to be sling loaded half the length of a football field and plugged into a platform while orbiting the earth at 17,500 miles per hour.

I can't help but find it slightly unreal that this is what's playing silently on TV right now. Since it's just my freakin' luck that in the face of the government shutdown and storm warning, I have a rocket launch and spacewalk happening simultaneously. That's a lot for essential NASA people like me to manage when everyone else has been sent home.

If the furlough happens as threatened, then at midnight the Langley workforce will be reduced from some 3,600 to no more than 50 of us holding down the fort. The same will be happening at every NASA center, including Wallops Island and Ames. But what's nagging at me aren't the big items on my list like rockets and top secret instruments.

I can't figure out why the TV in our lobby is set on the International Space Station network at all. The channel is always on CNN or Fox, depending on who gets his or her way about what we watch on any given day.

Who's been in here?

Finding the remote control on a table, I turn off the TV, and wander over to a section of blue cubicles we reserve for visiting law enforcement agents and interns. No sign of anyone, and when there are no human distractions, I'm unpleasantly struck by the similarity between high-density work areas and milk crates or egg cartons. Glancing at what's out in plain view on top of desks, deposited in wastepaper baskets, pinned on partitions. And from there I move on to do a high recon inside the break room, the restrooms.

Using my skeleton key of a smartcard to check various areas I pass, stepping inside the Office of Emergency Management, OEM, where data walls are busy with live feeds from hundreds of surveillance cameras at the gates and on campus. Big flat-screens are busy with news correspondents mutely explaining what's happening on the streets and in outer space, and with weather reports, and skirmishes on the Senate floor.

I pause to watch for any update about the government shutdown, and it appears the political chaos is status quo. I'm not surprised that the emergency communications center we share with Fire and Rescue is swamped. For a moment I watch a real-time video feed of dispatchers and operators overwhelmed with calls. It's rush hour, and one traffic mess and mishap after the next. But I don't see any alerts I ought to know about beyond politics and storm alerts.

Satisfied all is clear and secure, I leave the OEM and shut the door, headed to a long hallway of investigative workrooms and offices. My steel-toe shoes hushed by blue carpet. Just me, myself and I. Nobody else home, and yet I can't shake the feeling that something's not right. For starters, the TV was set to NASA's International Space Station channel when it never is unless something dramatic is going on. Far more perplexing than that is why the security alarm wasn't set.

"What moron didn't do that?" Under my breath.

I hope it wasn't the chief but can't imagine he'd be that careless. A Massachusetts Institute of Technology graduate with a background in military policing and intelligence, Elroy Rogers has a PhD in astrophysics. His preferred ride is his iron horse Harley-Davidson touring bike, white with Screamin' Eagle pipes and a custom silver-studded western saddle seat. Naturally, nicknamed Trigger, and no doubt it and Dr. Rogers blasted out of here not all that long ago. They might have been the last to leave.

But our illustrious chief is anything but sloppy. No way he neglected to set the alarm, and I'm beginning to wonder what's happened to everyone. Doors I pass are locked for the day, and I understand the top brass, branch executives and contract management shoving off by this hour. Especially with a furlough looming, but not every single special agent, no one left standing except me.

Where is everyone?

As if there's nothing going on when I know that couldn't be further from the truth. All of us are chronically backed up, and I sit down on the carpet in the hallway, resting my back against the wall, realizing how much of today I've spent on my feet without a break. I try Fran's cell phone.

"Miss me already?" she says in my wireless earpiece before I can utter hello. "Was getting ready to call you."

"Good, because I'm confused." Keeping my scan going, and one thing NASA doesn't lack is photographs, mock-ups and models of all its toys and those who use them.

From my vantage point on the floor I can scan the entire empty hallway, painted in a soft gray tone, both sides arranged with large photographs of vehicles tested in various wind tunnels, including vertical-spin and high-temperature ones. Everything from NASCAR race cars to hypersonic jets and spacecraft, and I find it a shame what we tend to take for granted around here.

Me included. It's easy to think space capsules, satellites, moon habitats, robots and the like are normal when they're your wallpaper.

6

I explain that I'm sitting on the floor inside our headquarters with nobody home.

There are a number of inexplicable things going on, I let Fran know. Including at least two black Suburbans with special antennas and signal jammers roaming the campus. Maybe following me.

"You're *sitting in the hallway*? Huh? What for? You get in trouble with the teacher again?" her voice in my wireless earpiece, and I can tell that she's still driving, probably headed home. "And I'm *sure* you're being followed because there's a plot behind every bush, isn't that right, Aggie?"

Fran's usual dig at my no-stone-unturned way of doing business, accusing me of inflating the smallest thing into a full-blown Agatha Christie mystery.

"Just making sure there's nothing inside our headquarters that shouldn't be here," I reply from my seat on the carpeted floor.

Both sides of the hallway are a gallery of more poster-size NASA photographs, these of astronauts in their Extravehicular Mobility Units, EMUs. A jargony term for their puffy white spacesuits and Simplified Aid For EVA Rescue, SAFER, "jet packs." Seeming tiny and fragile with nothing but handrails and shiny braided stainless steel wires to keep them from floating off from the half-million-ton Space Station, flaring in the blackness like platinum in the sun.

All around me are photographs of walking on the moon, of splashed-down crew capsules and the Space Shuttle. But I admit to having a soft spot for our spacecraft orbiters, satellites and probes like Cassini, Viking and Galileo. I can get quite attached to the gold-winged antenna dishes we deploy as our explorers and spies, sending them on endless one-way flights to cruise planets, moons, stars. Our creations but not in our own image, that's for sure. Doing as instructed without stupid questions or attitude.

Never shirking their responsibilities or complaining. Or in a mood. Out to lunch. Taking a nap. Ditching their orbit for a better one. Our autonomous astro-envoys do what we decide. As long as they're not hacked.

"I worry you're getting really weird," Fran in my ear. "Excuse me, I meant *weirder.*"

"When I walked in a few minutes ago, the TV was on and the alarm wasn't set. You got any idea why?" I ask.

"That's bad. Have you checked who was the last to leave?"

"Not yet. I intend to get to the bottom of it and write up whoever did it. We can't have people coming and going with no thought of setting the alarm," I reply. "Last I checked, we're some of the lucky ones who don't get furloughed. Where is everyone?"

"It's almost suppertime, Aggie. In case you're not looking at the clock, and I don't know about *everyone.* But Kim and John had to leave early today, both of them not feeling so hot. That bug going around, the same thing Easton had a few weeks ago. And Butch and Scottie are out on a DOA . . ."

"Excuse me? What DOA and why don't I know about it?" Unzipping my gear bag.

"Cool your jets. Maybe you weren't called because it's a sensitive situation and not for everybody's ears," and she's just going to keep picking on me.

My punishment for witnessing her moment of weakness in the tunnel, and nothing new. When she's had one of her phobic

90

attacks and I have to help her out, the aftermath is predictable.

"Ha-ha, very funny." I take off my steel-toe sneakers.

"I got the call not even two minutes ago from the Hampton officer first on the scene," Fran puts all snide kidding aside. "I was getting ready to let you know that a NASA outside contractor appears to have committed suicide."

"Oh boy." I never like to hear something like that. "Awful," and I almost add, *Especially this time of year,* but think better of it.

Fran doesn't need a reminder that death and destruction never take a holiday. She's not the same after what happened three years ago, and the closer we get to December 24, the darker her mood.

"Wanted you to be aware in case you hear something about it," she's saying. "Hopefully it won't be on the news before we can notify her next of kin."

"This didn't occur on campus, obviously," working my feet into my boots. "There's no way I wouldn't be aware of a death inside one of our facilities." *Unless nobody's telling me anything anymore,* I can't help but wonder.

"Thankfully, no," her voice in my ear. "Not here. At Fort Monroe. She was renting one of those upscale apartments in a building that used to be barracks during the Civil War. Living alone."

Tying my bootlaces in double bows, and I don't like the sound of this, already getting an unsettled feeling as my thoughts slam back to the stolen badge complaint.

"Fort Monroe is where an outside contractor claimed her car was parked when her badge allegedly was stolen out of the glove box yesterday afternoon," I remind Fran.

"It's a big place, and a whole slew of our contractors rent houses and apartments out there." She doesn't want to hear about the missing badge again. "Furthermore and to my point, there's nothing suspicious about the death so far. She even left a note."

"Or someone did. How'd she do it?"

"Hanged herself with her laptop charger cord. That's the word so far."

"And who found her? Since she supposedly lived alone."

"A wellness check," Fran says.

"Huh?" Makes no sense. "Why would Hampton PD pay a wellness check to her apartment? Did someone call in a concern?"

"A coworker did. On NASA's emergency number a little while ago, asking if we could get an officer to run by her apartment. That no one on her team had a key, and the woman hadn't shown up at Langley today and wasn't answering her phone. I can get the recording, some genius boy she worked with who sounded about Easton's age. He mentioned she'd left work yesterday not feeling well, and that was part of the concern. I got a Hampton officer to run over there and check."

"How did he get in?"

"The door was unlocked. I guess she was making it easy for us."

"Or someone was. Who's the victim?"

"She's not necessarily a *victim* . . ."

"If she killed herself, she's her own victim if nothing else. The name of the woman I interviewed yesterday was Vera Young," and I spell it. "A 54-year-old electrical engineer."

Silence.

Then, "Crap. Well that's her all right. A 54-year-old electrical engineer temporarily relocated to the area like a lot of people," Fran passes on what little she knows so far. "Part of a team based in Houston, on contract with NASA to work on robots that will assemble shelters in space, like on the moon or something."

"Habitats, storm shelters, inflatable airlocks. The work going on in the Structures and Materials Research Lab," I tell her.

"And as you know, that lab happens to be in Building 1110. Which is next door to 1111 and joined to it by the Yellow Submarine tunnel."

Getting up from the carpet, I begin to pace, definitely not happy about anything I'm hearing.

"I know you don't take all this quantum stuff as seriously as I wish you would," I say to Fran over the phone. "But after I'd finished running diagnostics down there in 1111-A yesterday, I responded to the stolen badge complaint in the very lab you're talking about. One building away, directly next door. Structures and Materials is on the south wing of 1110's first floor."

"What did Vera Young have to say when you interviewed her?" Fran says as I shake out my legs, stretching them. "I've not read your report yet. Was a little too tied up with the briefing and almost being suffocated in a bunghole tunnel."

"Her story is she went home yesterday around 11:00 a.m. with a migraine, and neglected to lock her car," I reply, stretching my lower back, stiff from working out in the fitness center early this morning. "Late in the day she tried to return to campus, and at the main gate opened her glove box, discovering her badge had been stolen."

"Sounds like BS to me."

"Her smartcard accesses 1110," I add, "and theoretically could get someone through the airlocks of 1111-A. Don't you see why this bothers me, Fran?" I'll just keep pushing my point until she acts like she cares.

"Aside from the fact that everything bothers you. But you'd have to know the secret combination to open that secret Yellow Submarine door and enter your secret tunnel, right? And you said nobody knows it."

"I never said that nobody does. And I'm always concerned about people getting critical information they're not supposed to have. Like smartcards and security codes." I pick up the steel-toe sneakers, my hard hat and gear bag. "But yes, the submarine hatch is largely inaccessible, thankfully. And as you've mentioned, we canceled Vera Young's badge the instant she reported it missing. But I don't like that she left midmorning and didn't attempt to return to the campus until almost 5:00 p.m."

"You know how some of these people are. No common sense. Not a lick."

"She said she headed back to Langley after her headache was better," I continue to relay what Vera Young claimed to my face.

"She told me she intended to work late. That she was behind in her projects. In summary, we have a window of around 7 hours when someone could have used her smartcard inappropriately before it was canceled."

"But easy enough to check if you interrogate the electronic history of everything her card might have accessed yesterday afternoon while she supposedly wasn't on campus." Fran's had enough of what she views as perseverating and I consider being thorough.

"Don't worry, I will." Pacing up and down the hallway, and it feels good to move. "Among other things, it bothers me that she was paranoid and defensive," I explain. "I didn't like her story then, and now I really don't."

"In the meantime, if Butch and Scottie come back with anything of concern, we'll head right over," Fran says. "Or if we find out she allowed someone to *borrow* her smartcard."

"Let's hope not. Maybe send me any info you have next time you're stopped at a light or when you get home." I hold my badge over the scanner outside my office door. "I'd like to see the suicide note. Which reminds me, who's responding from the ME's office?"

"Joan."

"Good." I'm relieved to hear it, and we end the call as I open my door.

Joan Williams is the lead death investigator for the Tidewater District medical examiner's office, a bloodhound, and the one I always want to show up. Plus, we're friendly with each other, and that's always helpful when you want information or assistance. I walk into my office, setting my gear in a chair as my landline begins to ring.

"Now what?" Stepping around boxes and piles of stuff I've yet to sort through or properly store, making my way to my desk.

Maybe someone calling in reference to the possible suicide. Or yet another disturbed person abducted by aliens. Or convinced that walking on the moon was fake news. That evolution and climate change are, and all science-loving infidels are going to hell. The list is endless and getting longer as social media, extremism and vitriol stoke the vulnerable population that Fran calls TLCs. As in "the Looney Tune Crazies."

No room to spare in here, and I bump past the table piled with tactical body armor, boxes of ammo and my handcuffs. Almost knocking over my level III active shooter police shield, more beaten up than it used to be after riot training in the Hampton Coliseum the other week. Reaching for my phone, noticing that caller ID is blocked, the number coming up as *Unknown.*

"Captain Chase," I answer.

"It's Dick," my former commander General Melville says right off, and it enters my mind that there's no reason for him to assume I'd be in my office right now.

"Are you spying on me?" Kidding but not really, and completely baffled that he would reach out.

I wouldn't have bet on it after the way he treated me earlier, and I wonder what's going on. Because nothing about his demeanor toward me today has felt positive or warm. I switch the call to speakerphone.

"Very funny," his unamused voice inside my office.

"Nope, not funny considering the source. Let me guess. You used an app probably very similar to the one I have, and saw my ID number pop up in 1195C."

"Be careful what you give me."

Except it's not quite accurate that I gave him the app in question, although I did develop the first generation of it while working under his command in Colorado

98

Springs.

"Just to be clear, I only *helped* develop the app you're using, whatever version it is by now," I remind him.

"Yes, that's *literally* correct, making me think of that nickname of yours that Liz came up with . . ."

Liz is his wife, and she didn't come up with it.

"Concretia. And you're the one who started calling me that, thank you very much," I reply. "Anyway, you know how I am about not wanting to take credit I don't deserve."

"Am I on speakerphone?"

"Inside my completely empty department, all the inmates having fled the asylum, it would seem. There. I'm shutting my door just to be extra private. I hope the rest of the briefing went okay." Stepping around a chair, squatting in front of the gun safe.

"Yes. In fact, some of us are still talking. We're about to wrap it up."

"I'm really sorry I had to rush off." Entering the combination on the keypad. "That Fran and I did."

"And what did you discover if anything?" Dick's voice pleasant but cool.

"It's curious. There's no evidence of a malfunction with any of the sensors in

99

1111-A, but one of them definitely detected motion. Got no idea why," I reply, and I have to wonder what I might have done to displease him. "There are other complicating factors that I find concerning, as well. Including someone who supposedly committed suicide, an outside contractor whose badge allegedly was stolen yesterday. Guess where she worked? Building 1110."

"That doesn't make me happy."

I open the gun safe's galvanized steel door. "I know you understand my worries, Dick, especially with that particular section of tunnel and what's inside. You know how I feel about any utility area that's accessible to a variety of people who don't have top secret clearance. Or any reason to be around such technical vulnerabilities."

"Yes, yes, I understand the way you think since I'm partly to blame for it." What he says couldn't be nicer, but his demeanor doesn't match his words.

"Is everything okay? You seem distracted." My way of saying he's acting more like a stranger than the man who mentored me for years and is an old family friend.

"There's too much going on as usual. I was hoping you might give me a lift back to the air force base before I have to get ready for another dinner I don't want to go to. We could catch up for a few minutes. As you may have heard me mention at your briefing, I've got to fly out of Newport News in the morning."

"I believe you said you were driving to DC," I reply, and I have the unpleasant sense that he's testing me for some reason, supplying erroneous details I feel compelled to correct.

Because he knows I will.

7

"Sorry," he says. "That was an earlier draft of the itinerary, some days it's hard to keep up. But you're right, tomorrow is DC. Listen, I really do want to hear what's going on with you, how Houston went, as we've not talked since the interviews."

"We actually have. Once," I remind Dick of what he's supposedly forgotten. "Right after my week at JSC, and as we speak there's still nothing new to report. Houston remains quiet. And I guess if it's quiet a whole lot longer, I'm going to suspect that things didn't go as well as I thought."

"And what's happening with Carme? Is she being good karma or bad?" His usual pun, only he doesn't say it with any humor or warmth. "What do you hear from her these days?" and I find it disconcerting that he would bring her up.

"Not much," I reply uncomfortably because my sister's silences have become longer and more troubling.

"How about anything at all? I'd settle for that. Is she doing all right?"

"She's been off grid," I admit, waiting for Dick to weigh in, but he's gathering information and not inclined to give it.

"I don't know where she is right now, but that's not unusual," I go on to say. "I assume she's alive and well, otherwise I have no doubt you'd know."

I wait. But he won't bite.

"Because I have to believe you'd tell me if the worst happened," I add.

Another pause, and Dick remains silent over speakerphone. Anybody walking by would assume I'm talking to myself. Which I'm known to do on occasion.

"You'd tell me, right?" I'm starting to feel scared that something horrible has happened to my sister.

"Yes," he finally says quietly, a little softer. "I would."

"I've not heard from her hardly at all since seeing her last month," I'm relieved by what he said but not reassured as I stand in the middle of my office, uncertain what to do. "And usually I take that to mean she's involved in something she can't talk about. Or won't. Because she's not in a position to. Period."

Waiting for his response again.

When there isn't one, I continue, "Not that she's been very communicative for a while, certainly not since she was home last. The second week of November, after our interviews and she flew out, returning to her deployment. Wherever it was. Or is."

Dick doesn't indicate an answer. Not a word or a sigh. Nothing one way or another about where Carme might be deployed, and if she's reasonably safe. He doesn't say he knows. He doesn't say he doesn't.

"I assume she's okay," I keep pushing. "That we're talking good karma. Not bad," and he won't take the bait.

Instead he finally says, "I'm wondering if either of you have heard from Johnson Space Center about what they're thinking or intend."

"I don't know about Carme, but I haven't, not yet," loading a clip into my Glock .40 cal. "It could be any day, I suppose. Depending on what happens with the government shutdown," racking back the pistol's slide. "If we end up furloughed and for how long," chambering a hollow-point round, and he really can't expect me to believe that if there was news from JSC he wouldn't know it before my sister and I do.

Maybe I'm idealistic, but I assume a

former astronaut who heads the newest branch of the military, Space Force, would know what's going on with NASA. Especially as it pertains to the Langley twins, as we're now called at JSC, and maybe that's the problem. Maybe Dick does indeed know what's going on with the astronaut review committee, and it's put him in an awful quandary.

He could be sitting on information that will change my destiny forever, make or break my heart and dreams. My default is to conclude the latter based on his negative affect. No wonder he's been distant and now wants a ride. He needs a moment alone in person to let me down easy. As gruff as he may seem today, no doubt he's kindly motivated.

Making sure I hear it from him, my former boss, the very person who encouraged and groomed me to be a cyber ninja of the first order, a Master of Space. He's going to tell me I didn't make it to the next round. That neither Carme nor I did. But then again, that's ridiculous, my gloom and doom based on nothing more than insecurity and fear.

I'm hypothesizing without the benefit of real data. Reaching a conclusion without doing the math.

And I know better. And he would expect

more of his protégé than that.

Stop it.

I warn myself to keep in mind what I'm always preaching to my sister, to Fran and pretty much anyone else who will listen. Pay attention to the details. It's the little things that will kill you. I know that better than anybody and can't afford to lose my focus or my cool. Never again. Not for any reason.

You know better!

Yes, I do, having learned that lesson in the hardest way, and I sound like the most reasonable person on the planet as I tell Dick it was excellent seeing him today. And I'm very pleased he thought enough of me to call. It would be my honor to give him a ride. I'll head out ASAP and meet him at NASA Langley headquarters, Building 2101.

"Give me 10 minutes max," I say to him as I take slow quiet breaths, restoring order and clarity the way I always do.

Focus. Focus. Focus.

Being deliberate, one thing at a time. Holstering my pistol. Attaching it to my belt. Next my badge. Then my handcuffs. Before reaching inside the tall narrow safe for my HK416 assault rifle, which has a nasty habit of toppling over because it's too big to lie flat. Propping it up in back. Gently closing the door. Making sure it's locked. Thoughts settled now. Better. Much better.

"Look for me in a white pickup truck at the front entrance," I hear myself saying calmly, confidently to Dick. "All I've got to do is lock up swabs in the evidence refrigerator, and I'm good to go."

"You took swabs of something inside the tunnel?"

I explain it as I look around my office, making sure I'm not forgetting anything before heading out. But there's not much to forget. This facet of my career requires far fewer textbooks, journals, tools, technologies and heavy mental lifting than what I do the rest of the time when I'm not as armed and dangerous.

Mostly what I keep in here is what one might expect of a federal special agent. Gear and weapons, and a desk with computers, facing the corner windows, angled so I can scan Langley Boulevard and its surrounds while my back is never to the door. On the credenza is the bottomless box of deactivated visitor credentials that need to be returned to the Badge and Pass Office. Plus, the in-out basket for reports awaiting my review. But I don't bother with as much on paper as I once did.

The one small bookcase is crowded with

thick security protocol and procedural manuals, and a *Webster's Dictionary* left over from high school. That's about it, but I still scratch out plenty by hand and keep a fat notebook full of graph paper for my calculations. The wall-mounted whiteboard is currently occupied by my protractor-perfect diagram of a recent motor vehicle accident in the technical library parking lot.

Inside the two locked filing cabinets are archived copies of my investigations, interview transcripts and equipment inventories going back to when I was a teenage intern. On a shelf is my collection of challenge coins. And next to it my only personal photograph, Carme taken in 2016 not long before I left Colorado Springs, helmet tucked under her arm, grinning next to a Pave Hawk attack helicopter in Syria.

No need to have a picture of our parents, would seem rather awkward since both of them work here. There's nothing else in my office that would tell people much about me, and I don't believe in revealing more than necessary. As little as possible is my mantra. Even if I didn't feel that way, there's no room for "I love me" clutter, and grabbing my backpack and gear bag, I walk out into the hallway, locking up.

Across from my door is another one with

a fail-safe keypad of push buttons under glass, making it possible to get inside if there's a power failure. Scanning the door open, I enter an area few people are allowed to access, and not simply because of the evidence stored. Tucked in a secure area in a back recess is our Secret Internet Protocol Router Network, SIPRNet, the Department of Defense's means of safely exchanging sensitive and top secret information electronically and over the phone.

But what I care about as I walk in is the stainless steel refrigerator near the gun-cleaning room with its workbench, compressed air and lingering scent of Eau de Hoppe's gun oil, as I like to joke. Retrieving the clear plastic evidence envelopes from my gear bag, I make sure they're properly dated, labeled and initialed as I deliberate how best to store the swabs of what looks like blood.

Moisture and bacteria are the enemy of DNA, and it will be ruined if left in unbreathing polyethylene. I decide to transfer the swabs to individual small paper envelopes, sealing them inside a larger one that I secure in a locked drawer of the locked refrigerator. Making one last foot patrol around the department, including the restrooms, before returning to the lobby, and I look and listen.

Interrogating the app on my phone the same way Dick tracked me down, checking on any smartcard ID codes that might indicate someone has forgotten his badge or is still inside. Not a sign of anyone, only my code popping up for this locale. Setting the alarm, I walk back out into the frigid night, remote starting my truck in the lot.

It's half past 6, the wind blustery as I drive the short distance to Building 2101. The temperature continues to drop, and by this time tomorrow the nor'easter is supposed to roar in from Canada, creating blizzard conditions along the Eastern Shore from Maine to the Outer Banks.

Haze shrouds the moon and stars, the air moist and freezing cold, and I disagree with the weather forecast. I believe the snow is going to show up earlier. I somehow always know when it's coming, and I wonder if we're going to end up scrubbing the resupply launch at Wallops. Should the weather turn bad enough, it will be quite the ordeal lowering the rocket from its vertical position and tucking it back into bed.

The dark shapes of trees rock in the wind as I pull up on 2101, our new headquarters of curvy glass and metal cladding. Everyone around here refers to it as the Cruise Ship because that's what it looks like, especially when lit up at night as it is right now, and I imagine Dick on the top floor with the center director and other distinguished guests. Possibly he's in the same secure breakout room where I was briefing everyone earlier.

Keeping the engine running, I sit behind the wheel, parked by the bright entrance. Waiting behind tinted glass, watching people leave, contractors and NASA staff paying little mind to my big white police truck, assuming they notice. Because if I'm honest about it, there can be truth in stereotypes, and many NASA folks and those of their ilk live in a perpetual *Far Side* fog.

Pushing instead of pulling on doors. Crossing streets without looking both ways or in any direction. Oblivious to emergency lights, sirens and people wearing guns. Overloading circuits by plugging in too many devices and starting small fires. Not to mention the dings, scrapes, fender benders and misplaced vehicles, the wrecked and lost bicycles.

All perpetrated by the same magicians who flawlessly plan space missions, launch probes and telescopes to the sun and Saturn. And with surgical precision land rovers on such inconvenient heavenly bodies as Mars, Venus, the moon. With a few deep impacts on comets and asteroids like Eros and Itokawa.

I don't include myself in this eccentric lot as I may notice odd minutiae that others don't. And yes, I can be reclusive and OCD. I can be a lot of things I'm not necessarily proud of, but I have excellent situational awareness. A good example is the two black Suburbans with government plates that were behind me when I drove away from 1111 not so long ago.

The very sort of protection detail that I'd expect Dick to have, and yet here I sit, waiting to give him a ride that I know for a fact he doesn't need. I send him a text, letting him know I'm out front waiting as I puzzle over what he really wants. Anxiously rubbing my thumb and index finger together, reliving what I felt at the time it happened. And then earlier today when Dick touched my hand the way he did, causing a jolt of fear and shame.

He doesn't need my executive protection or a lift. The commander of Space Force could have his choice of government vehicles and military escorts until the cows come home, his safety and transportation not dependent on little ole me. My former boss isn't impulsive or sentimental, and he must have something important, possibly confidential, in mind.

He doesn't waste his energy on just any-one, and I rub lightly round and around, feeling the scar, the healed flap that's partially numb. While I wait for him.

Sitting down on the white tile floor, slippery with blood, out of breath, my heart pounding through my chest. Having made a god-awful gory mess as I wait for him to come.

Better he gets here before the others, imperative that he does. Has to be just us. As bad as it is, it must be just us. No one else can see me in such a state, can discover the darker side. At least he already knows I'm flawed. That I don't predict and prevent everything correctly. If at all.

Hurry!

Haven't always seen the bad thing coming. And look what's happened from day one.

Please hurry!

Three strikes, you're out. He'll be hard on me. Not as hard as those under him would be. Can't live it down. Always so careful. Known for it. Annoyingly, ferociously careful. Waiting for him, the flesh pale and bloodless where the blade went in.

Dead.

Numbly imagining the consequences. And how I'm going to explain it. As I detect footsteps in the corridor, brisk with heavy purpose. Recognizing the sound of him headed this way.

"Sorry, sorry." Unlocking the door.

There's no excuse. Don't know what else to say. Except I didn't mean to ruin everything.

". . . It's okay, Calli . . ."

". . . Was trying to clean the mess . . . Should have been more careful . . ."

"Okay, easy, Calli. Easy. I'm going to help you up . . ." Dick's voice coming from above.

"So stupid, so stupid . . ."

"Easy does it. Easy . . ."

Lifting me effortlessly, bright-red blood all over his uniform shirt and the tops of his boots.

8

Checking the time. As usual I'm early.

I told him 10 minutes and it's been 8, and while I wait, I send Rush Delgato a text:

How are things looking?

As far as I know, all is a go for the EVA at 2:00 a.m., an activity that won't be affected by our weather on the ground, doesn't matter if the rocket launch is scrubbed. They're not related, just happening at once, and I'd feel better if Rush could keep in closer contact, as we've not communicated since early yesterday. Let's just see where he is. Or isn't. And I reopen the app on my phone that tracks people by the chip in their smartcard.

If he's on campus, I'll know. And he knows I'll know. I'm always kidding that he can run but he can't escape the long arm of the law. *Hmmmm.* When I enter his badge number in the search field, it comes back empty handed. It would seem he's not here right now and hasn't accessed any of Langley's 200-plus facilities today. So, unless he's wandering around outside in the Arctic blast, he's likely not on campus.

I type another text:

Happy BDay almost. Don't be depressed. Old dogs can still learn . . .

Changing my mind, deleting the part about depression and old dogs. He probably won't think it's funny, might ignore me more than he already is. Tomorrow my sister's boyfriend turns 40, and the last time Carme and I were together, she mentioned Rush wasn't happy about what was coming up and best not to pick on him too much. "Even if he deserves it," she quipped. So, I'll be careful what I say. But I have a little something to give him at the launch, a birthday surprise I found while trying on boots at Oak Tactical last month while running errands for Mom in Williamsburg and Toano.

Totally up his alley, a pen made of an aerospace composite that writes in all conditions (upside down, underwater, in microgravity), equipped with a carbide-tip glass breaker. Only in an homage to Rush's lagniappe Louisiana roots, I threw in a little something extra. Doing what NASA does best, transforming the wheel instead of reinventing it, and I'm still debating whether to tell him about the cool sensors I implanted.

Some in the pen itself. Others spun into the engineering-grade of polylactide I used to 3-D print a gently magnetized carbon nanotube sheath, black with a non-reflective matte finish. A hip and handy way to park his new patent-worthy writing tool while working around anything ferrous down here in Flatland. Or perhaps up there one day in the weightlessness of outer space. In either place, no Velcro required, and I open my door as Dick appears in 2101's steely glass entrance.

Busy typing one handed on his phone, he pushes his way through the door, long legged and wide shouldered in air force camouflage. The 4 embroidered stars on the front of his shirt are the only sign of his formidable rank, his tan desert boots skipping briskly down the steps as nimble as a cat, his breath steaming out in the cold.

A tactical backpack slung over a shoulder, he follows the walkway toward my truck, where I stand sentry, politely waiting, not hurrying to greet him. Making no friendly move whatsoever. Certainly not a hug. Not even saying hi as I open the passenger's door. He's the commander of Space Force, and I'm treating him accordingly, his demeanor this day making me stand on ceremony and be wary. As if we'd never met.

"Good evening, sir." Willing my right hand to stay down by my side, the impulse to salute as I did during my air force days overwhelming like a phantom pain.

Nodding at me, he pockets his phone, the fixed smile on his strong clean-shaven face more tense than cheerful, the set of his jaw hard. Carrying his APECS camo parka instead of bothering to put it on, and he'll tell you he runs hotter than most. Especially when he's unhappy.

"Hmmm and uh-oh." *Something's up, all right.*

"Thanks for doing this, Carme." Calling me the wrong name as he climbs in, and I'm never happy when anyone does it.

Least of all, him. I feel slapped and belittled, but he'd never know it. Besides, it doesn't matter what I feel. I can keep it tucked inside just fine.

"You mean Calli." I slide behind the wheel, easygoing as I shut my door, my eyes watering from the cold. "You know how insulted Carme gets if anyone thinks I'm her."

"I sure do. My apologies to both of you," he makes matters worse. "It's been one hell of a long day."

Setting his backpack on the floor between his feet, he grabs his shoulder harness. Pulling it across his chest, trying to find the buckle, stabbing for it in the blackout.

"Sorry for how dark it is." I lean close enough to detect the vague woodsy scent of his aftershave.

Close enough for him to smell my hair. That's assuming I wear a scent of any sort, and I don't. Not even the White Musk cologne and lotions that Carme has me pick up for her at the Body Shop, remnants of her fragrance all over the place. In medicine cabinets, on the kitchen desk, and in the converted barn, where our bedrooms, offices and the workshop are.

"Excuse me, don't mean to crowd you . . ." Suddenly self-conscious, getting heated up and awkward as I lean against him, fumbling with the shoulder harness, neither of us able to see what we're doing. "You know how I am about interior lights inside vehicles." Guiding the metal tongue, locking it in with a sharp click. "I prefer not making myself a more visible target than I already am." Resettling behind the wheel, the space between us cool and empty again.

He refolds his parka in his lap, and it doesn't escape my notice that he keeps his right hand tucked under it.

"What were you saying uh-oh about?" he inquires.

"Oh, don't mind me. You know how I mutter and mumble. But I have to say that you don't look very happy, and I'm worried you found my briefing frustrating. Because I know I did," I reply, hoping his frosty mood is about that and nothing worse. "If you want me to be perfectly honest."

"I always want you to be perfectly honest." Staring straight ahead, the glow of streetlights illuminating his square jaw, hawkish profile and short silver hair.

What my mom calls his Dick Tracy handsomeness. Which is ironic when you find out that his name is Dick and he has a daughter named Tracy.

"That's really all I ask, really all anyone can ask," he says, and for the first time since I've known him, it crosses my mind that he's questioning my integrity.

Maybe that's why his behavior toward me has been so off today, it occurs to me, and I'm stunned.

"You know how I feel about telling the

truth, the whole truth," he says, sitting tightly coiled as if about to spring into action.

But overwhelmingly what I sense is his displeasure and disappointment. As if I've betrayed him somehow. Done something wrong. And he doesn't know me anymore.

"It's one thing I can always count on when dealing with you, whether I like it or not. You tell the truth, naked and unvarnished," he adds.

"Except when I can't." Finding a break in traffic, I pull back out on the main drag. "At times I can't, depending on what I've been entrusted with, same as you. Even if nothing that might concern me is anywhere near your level."

"At times you can't," he repeats. "I don't believe I've ever heard you say that to me."

"I've never had to keep secrets from you under any circumstances I can think of." Headed to the closest gate that will take us onto the air force base.

"Including now?"

"You see? You're questioning me, and I have to say with all due respect that I'm unclear why the subject of my honesty has come up. And of all times, now. You know better than most how I feel about co-incidences." As I hope with all my might that whatever's going on with him has nothing to do with Johnson Space Center.

Because I'm back to that worry again, only with a vengeance this time.

"You sure?" He stares at me in the dark.

"Am I sure of what?" I can't get warm, and yet I'm sweating through the armpits of my shirt.

"You sure this isn't one of those times you can't be perfectly honest?" Dick says.

"Perfectly honest about what?" I can feel his eyes looking me over carefully. "What might I know that would be off limits to you, necessitating my being deceptive or outright lying?"

"Nothing, I sure as hell hope." He looks back out the windshield at the dark campus, squinting in the glare of oncoming headlights. "It's critically important we trust each other now more than ever. Just remember what you and I have always talked about. Which is what?" he quizzes me again.

"It could be a lot of . . ."

"What do we always say, dammit? About communication?" he cuts in.

"That it's all there is between us and the great abyss."

"Which is why our adversaries want us blind, deaf and dumb, and guided by lies," he adds, reminding me of how much I miss working for him.

Remembering all the what-if scenarios we'd mull over and explore as everyday normal. Like what if fake news precipitated an attack, causing massive casualties? Or if wandering "friendly" satellites with robotic arms were programmed clandestinely to go on the offensive in the nanoblink of a command? Or if a swarm of killer drones was deployed from the nose of a rocket? It could be any manner of technologies that might disable or hijack our own satellites and other spacecraft in near-Earth orbit and beyond. Rendering us helpless in ways more damaging than any bomb.

"Blind, deaf and dumb, yes indeed," I agree with him wholeheartedly.

Because he's singing my song. And I'm singing his. This is the mission we partnered in. To defend our defenses. To predict and prevent an unwanted event before the thought takes form.

"If you want to know what would be most effective," I say what I always have, "take a look at what's already been done. Take a look at nature. That's your best model. And when an animal attacks, what does it do? It goes after the face, the eyes, the mouth, the ears."

"Not just animals. Any smart predator will do that," Dick says.

"No matter how powerful our missiles or guns, without the ability to communicate, to receive and transmit, we're no match for the enemy." Paying close attention to my driving, I watch the slow-moving strand of bright-red taillights ahead. "This is the rest of what I was going to say today before I had to bail because of the detector alert. It's what I'm always preaching. Except it's more like crying in the wilderness or screaming wolf, if you want to know how I feel most of the time."

"People like you and me live in an invisible world." Dick says this constantly. "What we see is *not there* to the masses, which is good if you don't want panic in the streets. But critically bad if you want to survive and live freely, if you don't want our planet to one day be a scorched rock like Mars. Your average person never thinks about what might happen if and when Russia or China or both decide to take out our satellites, our space stations and telescopes, our rovers and rockets."

"Or worse, take them over to turn on us," my remark followed by another one of Dick's silences.

As I drive slowly, I can barely make out

the shape of NASA Langley's water tower, red and white swirled like a tulip against the dark horizon. And the tall stack of the trash-recycling steam plant, its black silhouette quiet for the night.

"I mean, what could be worse than fighting against your own training and invention?" I add. "What could be more horrible than having what you created betray and hate you?"

"I don't know," he says. "Why don't you ask God?"

"I don't need to, and we already have the problem anyway, the massive and intractable problem of stolen intellectual property," I reply. "The most insidious enemy we do battle with every day, and the very thing I was worrying about during the briefing. Why do you think I wasn't thrilled? Because nobody listens."

"I think everybody was listening. Whether they took it to heart is another matter," he replies. "It's what we always say about the forest and the trees. You have to see both to get the complete picture, and most people don't. A lot of them don't see either one."

"Which is why I spend a lot of my days feeling the way Chicken Little would if he knew the sky really will fall because it has before." I'm resting my right arm on the console between us as I drive, and Dick startles me by reaching for my hand.

Taking it in his and gently squeezing as he explores the topography of my right index finger again. Touching the scar the same way he did at the briefing, only more carefully now that we're alone in the dark. And maybe I'm figuring out what he's doing. Better put, maybe it couldn't be more obvious.

"I'll sure as hell never forget that day." His demeanor is instantly more relaxed and familiar.

"I won't either. It was pretty stupid." Freeing my hand from his, placing it on the wheel because I'm not sure what to do with it now.

"I thought I'd walked into Helter Skelter," he says, and it did rather much look like the scene of a massacre. "Don't worry. I won't ask you to slice open stale bagels again."

"They weren't stale. Just frozen in the middle. You want to tell me what this is about?" I ask, and it's a toss-up whether I'm more indignant than hurt. "First, it's misinformation as if you're quizzing me in an episode of *Mission: Impossible* . . ."

"Ouch. I'd like to think I'm more finesse-y than that."

"Calling me Carme isn't exactly subtle. And now for some reason you seem to feel a need to check out facts including my, quote, 'unique identifying feature.' Seriously, Dick? Is this our new secret handshake? Feeling my scar? A scar that for sure my twin sister doesn't have. Do you not know who you've been talking to today? After all we've been through, do you not know me?"

9

"I'm not trusting much at the moment, Calli," he admits, his attention fixed straight ahead as I drive through the windy dark.

"Nor should you or any of us now or any other time, I suppose," barely creeping along Langley Boulevard, the traffic bumper to bumper. "But why would you assume I might be Carme? What would possess my sister and me to play a juvenile trick like that on you of all people? Not that it would be possible, as I've not seen her in almost a month. But I wouldn't anyway. And why would you call me the wrong name? Why would you test me?"

"You two used to swap places with each other when you were younger."

"The operative phrase being when we *were younger,* as in grade school, and high school occasionally." I'm stung that he would think so little of my judgment and maturity. "As in kids, teenagers. Why would you assume she's in the area? Because if she is, it's news to me. Not that I have any idea of her whereabouts. She might be in Colorado Springs with you, for all I know."

Silence.

"Or North Africa or the Middle East," I add. "Why would she be in Virginia, why would you assume that?"

"I try not to assume anything," he says.

"Is that why you have your gun in your lap? Because you can't assume you can trust me?" Dismayed by the emotions threatening to flare.

"Why would you think that?" he says quietly without moving in his seat.

"I don't know. Maybe there's some other reason your right hand is under your parka, and has been since you walked out of HQ and got into the truck?" I reply pointedly. "I also noticed you were doing something on your phone as you were coming down the steps, probably another app that's reading the analyzer in your backpack. I should know, since I've got one in my gear bag. A good one."

"I have a feeling mine's better."

"I have no doubt that's true since your budget might be slightly bigger than mine," I reply. "And gosh only knows what you're trying to read or figure out. But if you really do have a gun, then you're in violation of the law because no weapons are allowed on the NASA campus unless you're sworn police. And I am. And you're not. I could turn it into a felony if I wanted."

"I can only hope you'll be fair." Drolly.

"In fact, it would be within my rights to cuff you and bring you in." I couldn't be more serious.

"How awful if you had to toss me in the clink," he deadpans.

"I'm not kidding, and in case you didn't notice, you're not the only one armed and dangerous. Word on the street is I'm pretty much an Annie Oakley. So why don't we just agree right now not to shoot each other as I'm driving you back to your room?"

"I think that's a fine idea."

"Good."

"Now that we've agreed to a cease-fire, I have a riddle for you," he adds. "What are the two biggest problems you don't want in an aircraft, a spacecraft? Think forest and not the trees."

"Obviously, loss of control and loss of signal. You don't want either one. And they come in pairs, one almost always leading to the other, and you're . . ."

"Screwed," only that's not the word he uses to finish my sentence.

I look out at the picnic and recreation area, the historic wind tunnel and other landmarks where Carme and I used to play while we were growing up here. Barely moving toward the traffic circle, and with the bad weather report and threat of a furlough, a number of people already have buttoned up their offices, not hanging around until we're officially closed at midnight.

Sensible and makes my life easier, but the normal staffers aren't who I worry about. It's the die-hard researchers we have to chase off with a stick. That would include me if I weren't the one carrying the stick, and it's a hard, heavy one at the moment. Harder and heavier than usual, as if made out of ironwood. I could crack a skull with it if I'm not careful, and I feel the slow burn of a bad mood heating up.

That's what happens when someone creates chemistry, and Dick has created it. I wish he hadn't. But he has.

"If we lose the ability to communicate with an asset and can't control it?" he continues to confide now that he doesn't outrageously think I'm Carme pulling the wool over his eyes. "Whether it's our new super rocket or a human being equally capable of doing great harm . . . ?"

"We're screwed." Because I feel I am.

Trying to ignore the ache in my gut. Slightly nauseated as if I'm hungry and not. *Please don't throw up.*

Driving with my left hand, self-consciously rubbing my right thumb and index finger together, and Dick and I are quiet. Inching along until the traffic tapers off dramatically when I hang a left on West Durand Street, toward the air force base. I don't want to be insubordinate. But no way I'm letting him out of this truck without an explanation for what he's been implying and why he's been acting this way all day.

As the silence continues, he knows better than most that when presented with a void, eventually I'll fill it.

"Okay," I have to say. "Obviously, something's happened. Something serious. So serious that a minute ago you weren't sure who you were sitting with inside this truck. And possibly haven't been sure who I am since you arrived on the Langley campus. Even though I've acted the same as always and wore the flight jacket you and Liz gave me."

"I'm glad you still have it."

"I would never part with it," I reply, and it's the truth. "Tell me what you can. You know I'll help. I'll try, at least. Just level with me, whatever it is. No matter how much I might not want to hear it, Dick."

"You're correct in saying that something serious has happened. Yes," he replies quietly, grimly.

"How serious is serious?"

"Unprecedented, frankly, in terms of potential damage. Welcome to our brave new world. Where nothing's what it seems."

"Nothing's what it seems?" I bounce his own words back to him. "That sounds about as bad as it can get. What exactly are we talking about?"

"I can't and won't say. You'll have to deduce from me what you will. But understand up front, Calli, that I'm not at liberty to satisfy your curiosity no matter how unbearable."

"Unbearable?" My suspicions stampeding again. "I could have done without hearing that."

10

We've reached the sturdy brick Durand Gate with its barriers and tire shredders, the security forces less friendly over here on the air force side. Not that our protective service officers are warm fuzzies, either.

"*Unbearable* is a strong word." I slow to a stop.

"Yes, it is." Dick takes off his lanyard and badge.

"With personal shadings," I add.

"Both correct and not."

"Let's hold that cryptic thought. See this MP coming up?" As I watch his approach. "He's always such an a-hole. Better get ready."

Lowering my window, I say good evening to the unsmiling military police officer in his camouflage and beret, his M4 carbine slung across his chest, his Beretta 9mm on his hip. The name tape on his uniform reads Crockett, and based on that and the unusual accent I've noted from our previous encounters, I've pegged him as being from Tangier Island. Whatever his pedigree, he goes out of his way to give me a hard time whenever he can.

Don't ask me why. But if anyone in my custody or company doesn't display his or her credentials fast enough, MP Crockett is going to lower the boom. He might make a comment about my truck, insisting on running a mirror under it to delay and hassle me further. Or point out the beginning of a crack in the windshield that needs to be fixed instantly or else, costing me additional toil and trouble.

Dick drops his badge in my lap. But before I get a chance to hand it and mine out the window, MP Crockett has his flashlight on, practically blinding us. More aggressive than usual, as if I've done something to really piss him off this time.

"Playing musical cars tonight, ma'am?" he snipes in a cold flat tone.

"Excuse me?" I have no idea what he means.

"I need to check your registration, ma'am," he goes on severely, and I'd almost be disappointed if he didn't make sure it's current.

Because he does it every time, and I open

the glove box for the hard copy, knowing full well he won't stop there. Even when he's less angry than he seems right now, he's always a jerk.

"I'm talking about the stickers on your plates, ma'am. And I'm going to need to check the undercarriage of your truck. Both of you need to step outside."

"Whatever you say, Officer." Making a big point of handing him our badges. "But first, here you go."

Directing the light on our lanyard-tethered IDs, and silence. As it dawns on MP Crockett that while I may not matter in the food chain, it's probably not the best plan to bully a 4-star general by making him stand outside in the brutal cold. While you inanely check the undercarriage of my NASA police truck for explosive devices, stowaways, fugitives, who the hell-o knows what.

"Have a good evening! Sir!" He foolishly snaps a salute at Dick, making him a target if the wrong person is watching.

Returning our badges, the thoroughly rattled MP waves us through.

"That's probably one of the biggest reasons I'd like to be a general someday," I say, driving away.

"Sounds like a good enough reason to me." Dick is his old self again but more somber than I've seen him in a long time. Maybe ever.

"Considering my promotional trajectory crashed and burned when I left the air force as a captain?" My usual self-deprecating humor, as if all is fine. "I don't think that particular MP back there is ever going to be more threatened by me than he is right now."

"You never know." Dick stares at the winter-brown grass of the Eaglewood Golf Course and its driving ranges, where I've hit my share of balls very badly. "I'm not about to ask or tell you something out of school, Calli," he says. "You just heard me say it loud and clear."

"Copy that. I heard you." I try to smile but can't pull it off. "I admit you're making me nervous. Saying 'nothing is as it seems,' and now something 'out of school.' As in personal but not?"

"Yep."

"Oh boy. Deception and personal in the same breath. Then you have something to say that involves me. At least sort of, it seems."

"I'm afraid so," he answers, and my stomach tightens as if I'm about to be punched.

No matter what else might be going on, he wanted to see me face to face tonight to inform me that I didn't make the cut. I'm not the right stuff to be an astronaut. What else would it be? It's been the better part of a month since Carme and I concluded our weeklong interviews at Johnson Space Center. We're expecting to hear any moment whether we made it to the final round.

Down to the last 50 out of an original pool of some 17,000 who applied to the Astronaut Candidate Program, and with each day that passes, I'm more nervous and worried. Fran's not wrong when she complains that I've been more tightly wound and edgier.

Unlike my sister, I have emotional strings that play strongly, loudly, and I wish I didn't. It's hard not to think of all the times my father has cautioned me about getting my hopes up. Don't live ahead of yourself. Or spend what you've not been paid. Or make decisions based on what hasn't happened yet.

"I've gotten some feedback about your visits to Houston," Dick starts in, confirming what I suspect.

At least I think he is, and I assure him, "You don't need to spare my feelings." Paying close attention to my driving, always on the alert for deer around here.

"I never have when it comes to shooting straight with you," he says as I notice something moving in the dark, a jogger out in this weather up ahead on Dodd Boulevard.

Probably a man based on the height and long powerful stride, broad shouldered, head down, moving relentlessly along the fitness path. In stealth black that I note is non-reflective as he passes through the outer reaches of lamplight in swirling fog. Turning off on Andrews Street toward Air Combat Command, the vertical wind tunnel and Back River. Running as if it's nothing in this bitter cold. Springing around icy patches, sure footed and directed.

"But I suspect that what I'm about to tell you isn't what you're anticipating." Dick is looking down at his phone, typing something with his thumb. "You might think I came here to give you answers. And I didn't. I can't give you the news you're waiting for, Calli. I'm sorry I can't tell you. Good or bad."

"Then you're not here to inform me I'll never be an astronaut." It may be the hardest thing I've ever asked point blank.

"I'm not here to tell you that," is his non-answer as I turn off on a narrow lane leading to officers' housing.

He isn't going to allay my fears. He won't say yea or nay either way, and I'm reassured while at the same time gripped by dread. Driving slowly along a poorly lit narrow lane. Following it to the private enclave of handsome buildings tucked back behind trees.

The irregular moon slips in and out of clouds above slate roofs, and if you didn't know where you were, you might think you're in an early 20th-century English village.

I park behind Dodd Hall, where with rare exception only high-ranking guests the likes of generals and admirals are privileged to stay, the Tudor-style building one of the oldest on base. I've escorted enough command staff and other VIPs to be familiar with the layout of the two floors, each with 4 large suites offering any amenity a guest might need. A full kitchen, laundry soap, ironing board, coffee maker, minibar, even a desk with a SIPRNet classified phone.

It's always quiet and private back here, and rarely are there many guests. Judging by the empty parking lot, Dick might be the only one tonight. But I'm not surprised and would expect as much. The weather prediction alone is enough to make most people cancel plans to visit Virginia's Eastern Shore, and they have in droves with more to follow, no doubt.

Should the storm gain strength, Governor Dixon will evacuate all low-lying areas at risk, including this peninsula. That possibility in addition to the furlough threat as politicians continue to duke it out, and who in their right mind would want to come here now? Yet none of it deflected Dick from showing up with virtually no notice, and as we sit inside my truck fogging up the windows, I have to ask myself why.

If he has sensitive questions for me, he could send a classified communication. Or easiest and most practical, pick up that SIPRNet phone and call ours at police HQ. He knows how. We've communicated over SIPRNet countless times, and as I continue thinking back to his demeanor at the briefing, he was wary then too. I attributed his behavior to the situation, those present, and the fact that we'd not been face to face in three years.

Not since I abruptly left his command in Colorado Springs about this time of year in 2016. But I also was preoccupied earlier today, making my case about cyber vulnerabilities and protection, hammering home my usual point that the best defense is the best defense. Which sounds like a misspeak or a typo but isn't.

I threw down the gauntlet, issuing a bold challenge to Dick and the NASA Langley, NASA Goddard and Wallops Island directors, in addition to the police chiefs, military officials, DC suits and everyone else present this afternoon. I told them that if I were the adversary, the first thing I'd do is find a way to hack into NASA. From there it would be dealer's choice of what I'd penetrate and violate with the ultimate goal of neutralizing our national missile defense system while crippling the North American Aerospace Defense Command, NORAD.

That would be my first strike at taking down democracy's high-value assets, and I'd go on from there knocking out radar and satellites, ultimately rendering all defenses useless. This would leave America and our allies wide open for attack, I stated for a fact, and my Armageddon awareness, insights and strategies aren't anything Dick hasn't heard from me before. He seemed attentive enough but was plenty distracted, stealthily glancing down at his phone and answering messages.

At no time was there any reason to think he wanted to talk to me or see me tonight. He didn't mention he might ask me to drive him anywhere. And it wouldn't have occurred to me in my wildest dreams that his coming to Langley unexpectedly on his way to DC during a major storm and furlough threat might be related to my sister or me. Or both. But now I have to wonder.

"Maybe you'll let me ask you a question," I say to him as I turn on the defrost. "Just one, how about it?"

"Depends on what it is."

I try to think of the best way to phrase it as it occurs to me to take off my shoulder harness, now that we're not moving. I adjust the defrost fan a notch as the glass begins to clear.

"I realize you're here for meetings on your way to DC," I begin cautiously. "I was pleased you wanted to attend my briefing, that you would take the time and be interested. Especially since we've not seen each other, only talked on the phone and emailed now and then since I left."

"You've always had an open invitation to visit us," he says. "We've encouraged you and Carme to come skiing, snowshoeing, hiking, whatever. You're always welcome."

"I'm sorry we haven't . . . and thank you. But what I'm trying to say," I continue awkwardly, "is I was looking forward to today, but then we saw each other and you didn't seem particularly happy. Or friendly, to be honest. In addition, I've noticed a

Secret Service detail cruising around, possibly following me, one of the vehicles a watchtower for electronic countermeasures, I'm pretty sure."

I wait for him to comment, and of course he doesn't.

"And that's not typical around here unless the president, vice president, someone like that is visiting," I go on. "And no one is. Except you. And normally even the commander of Space Force wouldn't require a Secret Service protection detail that includes a signal jammer to neutralize such things as improvised explosive devices, including ones possibly delivered by drones. So, I'll just go ahead and draw attention to the elephant in the room and ask what's wrong. Because something is."

Pausing again, waiting for him to fill in the blanks, and he's not going to help me out.

"You brought up Houston and my sister," I keep going because I must. "I get the sense there's something on your mind, and I hope I'm not being presumptuous to say . . ."

He holds up a hand to stop me, "I'm not going to explain myself to you."

"Yes, sir. I understand." I can't help but bristle.

"For God's sake don't 'sir' me, Calli. We

know each other too well for that." Taking a deep breath, and loudly, slowly blowing out.

"You haven't been acting as if we know each other very well," I tell him in no uncertain terms. "And I'm wondering what I did . . ."

"You didn't do anything, and sorry. I don't mean to be impatient." His jaw muscles clenching. "But I'm not here to give you news about your future, okay? I don't want you thinking it or running down the field with something you might imagine that's totally wrong. Or maybe isn't wrong. But either way, it's not up for discussion or debate at this time, and I'm sure you know what I'm getting at," he says, and I do.

He's referring to Carme's and my status with the astronaut selection committee.

"I'm not going to give you information on that. It's not why I'm here," he says. "Let me say it again. *It's not why I'm here,*" slowly and with emphasis.

"Obviously, it wouldn't require the Secret Service if you're here simply to tell me whether Carme and I made the cut or not," I remark. "Or if we should be contemplating other career paths for the future . . . ," my voice trailing off because I simply can't imagine it.

Or maybe I won't imagine it, refuse to, I

think stubbornly. Maybe I won't accept that I'll never be an astronaut. Maybe there's nothing else for me, and I take a deep quiet breath, willing myself not to get emotional.

"I'm not telling you that, and please don't bring it up again," Dick is saying. "Period. End of message."

All this while he's taking in everything around us as if he might be watching for someone while speaking in a way that makes me halfway wonder if we're being monitored or recorded. But I'm not about to hint that such suspicions would cross my mind when I'm in my official NASA Protective Services vehicle having what I assume is a private and confidential conversation with a trusted mentor and family friend.

"You don't need to explain," I hear myself saying to him as my uneasy thoughts collide. "But let's get to the most important stuff first. How are Liz and the kids? I think about them often and hate how quickly time goes by. Hard to believe we've not all been in the same room in three years." Anything to lighten the mood and soften him up.

"Great," he says, "everybody's great. It looks like her cooking competition show is going to get renewed for another season."

"Yes, you mentioned that earlier, at the briefing. Fantastic news but I'm not surprised, and I hope you'll remember to pass along my congratulations."

"Makes it hard that she has to try out everything on me first," he says distractedly.

"Having tasted her sinful renderings, yes. That would be difficult," I agree. "But you're not the only one with the problem. My mom watches her, and guess what I end up eating?"

"I need to start hitting the gym harder." Pressing his hand against his washboard belly.

"You and me both." Knowing I haven't had a washboard belly since I moved back home, and most of it is Liz Melville's fault.

Her *Kitchen Combat* pits first responders and the military against each other in a cooking war, and is one of many reasons why I'm not in better shape. No matter how much I run or lift weights, it's no contest when my mother gets going in the kitchen with the deep fryer and dutch oven.

"The collateral damage of Mom watching Liz's show and trying out everything is I can't always . . . ," I almost say *button my pants* but catch myself, thank goodness.

I don't need to be talking to the commander of Space Force that way, especially under the circumstances. It's not like he's at the house, sitting on our front porch, or

I'm hanging out with his family in Colorado back in the good ole days. Eating amazing food. Throwing back his lethal cocktails.

"Anyway, how unfair that Carme and I are twins but don't have the same metabolism," I should be quiet and quit while I'm ahead. "She never gains an ounce, and all I have to do is look at a cookie or a Big Mac. Or Liz's baked brie."

Silence, and it's significant that Dick hasn't asked a single question about my NASA parents, whom he's known for years, going back to the Air Force Academy, when my sister and I were nothing but a dream. He's not so much as asked how I'm doing, his attention fixed on what he perceives as his agenda, his mission.

Shifting his position in his seat, he stares at me for a long moment, and I feel it coming.

11

"When you were in Houston for your first-round interviews, it was after Carme had been there for hers," he starts in, the headlights shining across the parking lot illuminating Dodd Hall's brick-and-timber back entrance.

"As you know better than anyone, the policy is to keep twins separated. We weren't together, weren't in the same groups. She was the last week of October. And I was the week after that, almost exactly a month ago," I add, and it's hard to believe that much time has passed.

"I'm wondering what you might have heard about her."

"What I might have heard about Carme?" I'm instantly defensive.

"If you heard any comments about her."

"I've not met the other candidates who were in her group, so I haven't talked to anyone who . . ."

"Might you have heard comments, gossip from anybody at Johnson Space Center?" he persists. "Maybe from someone who might have been involved in the interview process? Or witnessed it? Or overheard something?"

I realize how quick I am to say no. To want to, at least. When the truthful answer isn't that simple, and I have a bad feeling I might know what he's fishing for.

"Since you showed up exactly a week after she was there," he pushes his point, "others might have mistaken you for her. Perhaps they made remarks. Maybe you overheard things about what Carme might have been observed doing or saying while she was there."

By now I have no doubt what he's after, information about an incident involving my sister at the local watering hole, Woody's. I heard about it from one of the bartenders when I showed up a week after Carme had been there and he thought I was her.

"As you're aware from personal experience," I'm explaining to Dick, "we're not easy to tell apart even if you know us well."

"Witness when I first got into your truck," he says.

"Except that's not why you called me Carme," I won't give him an easy pass.

"That was just another one of your tests."

"What happened, according to the bartender at Woody's?" And of course he would know about it.

"From what I understand, it was Halloween night, and Carme showed up as J-Lo," I launch in. "Our favorite cliché, right? In the old days, we'd go out together, both of us as J-Lo. Anyway, I show up in Houston a week after my sister's interviews not knowing anything about what happened Halloween night. Let's just say I got quite the reception when I walked in."

"Because the people there, or some of them at any rate, thought you were Carme," Dick infers, or maybe he knows.

"Trust me, it wasn't positive, not hardly. Not that I'm unaccustomed to people mixing us up," I make the understatement of the century. "But I was blown away by the confusion and upset caused until everyone understood that I have an identical twin."

"The incident involving Carme occurred on Halloween night, that's correct," Dick confirms. "She and the candidates in her group had dressed in costume for happy hour as part of a team-building exercise."

"I heard a story about her having to tell some woman to eff off after a confrontation in the parking lot." I feel my mood darkening by degrees as what I've dreaded begins to creep closer.

What did you do? My silent voice bounces off the inside of my skull. *What did you do!*

"What else did you hear?" Dick is asking.

"Only that she made a scene over 'some local redneck dude' who wouldn't leave her alone. And I quote."

"Where did you hear that? Who are you quoting?"

"The devil herself, Carme." I smile despite it all. "I asked her about it after both of us were back in Virginia and before she left again," I reply as if there's nothing disturbing about her behavior, as if I might even find it amusing.

When I absolutely don't. I'm unnerved in ways I can't begin to explain, and was when I heard her bizarre account the first time.

"I see," Dick says. "Then you really know only what she told you."

"That's correct," and I don't like that he's implying the obvious. "I realize there are two sides to every story," I go ahead and say it.

Giving him a chance to comment, and he doesn't.

"I'm passing along what was conveyed to me," I add, "and that's all."

I wait, and he volunteers nothing.

"It sounds like it's not all," I then say dismally.

"It wouldn't appear so." He looks at me, his somber face set in deep shadows as we sit in my truck.

The defrost is going, the surrounding area what I call *gently lit and secluded.* A nice way of saying much too dark and deserted, no one around but us. It's always private and isolated when tucked back here, but tonight it's starkly vacant like a moonscape. Every place I go seems like that, with people leaving and businesses shutting down.

Chaotic politics and an approaching whopper of a storm, either one bad enough on its own, and it's as if the world is about to end. Or already did and nobody told me. I can't remember feeling this desolate. Not since we found out Mom was sick and I had to leave Dick's command, had to give up the military when it wasn't what I'd planned since day one in my goal-directed life.

"Are you aware of what happened to that so-called local dude?" Dick asks. "And what your sister might have said about him? And whether they might have had a history?"

"No."

"Had they ever met before that night, according to her?"

"I'm not aware of much. She and I talked

153

about this only once," is my response.

"Do you know anything at all about him?"

"I don't."

"I'm wondering if Carme might have mentioned whether he had a Texas accent, for example." Dick's voice is clipped like the soft snaps of a whip. Just enough to smart.

"I have no clue. She didn't say."

"How about any accent, including a British one?" he asks, and I shake my head no. "Then she didn't fill you in beyond calling him a local redneck."

"Pretty much," I remark, and whatever's coming next can't be good after a windup like that.

"His name was Noah Bishop," Dick informs me. "And he wasn't local to Houston or Texas. Not native to the US either, as you might have gathered."

"Was?"

"As in past tense," he says.

"In other words, dead."

"I'm afraid that's the suspicion, although thus far unconfirmed. Noah or his remains aren't to be found anywhere, it seems. As if he vanished without a trace."

"Including an electronic trace?" I suggest, and Dick's not going to touch it. "Who is he? Or was?" I ask.

"A 36-year-old aeronautical engineer with one of the aerospace giants."

"Which one?"

"PSS," Dick says to my amazement.

Pandora Space Systems is one of the more voracious competitors for government contracts. I might go so far as to call it predatory, especially when it comes to the Defense Advanced Research Projects Agency.

DARPA's focus is emergent military technologies, and what that boils down to is Pandora (as most of us refer to it) is involved in projects as off grid and cloaked in secrecy as they get. But more to the point, the multibillion-dollar aerospace company is where Vera Young was employed, working as a contractor with a team of researchers out of NASA Langley's Building 1110.

Choosing not to share this with Dick yet, I'm obsessed with sending Fran a text, clueing her in that the alleged suicide is growing more disturbing by leaps and bounds. But it will have to wait. I don't dare touch my phone right now, giving my former commander my complete attention as he explains that Noah Bishop was at Woody's Halloween night. And for some reason Carme decided to get in his face in the parking lot.

"This isn't what I heard," I reluctantly reply, and a part of me doesn't want to know the truth. "I'm not aware she started it, and that the confrontation was with the guy and not his girlfriend. The way I heard it, he kept hitting on Carme until she put him in his place verbally. Telling him to back off . . . Only knowing my sister, those weren't her words . . . At which point the girlfriend walked up . . . Well, I think you know the rest."

But Dick isn't about to indicate what he knows or doesn't.

"Supposedly the girlfriend then lit into Carme, never a smart thing to do . . ." I don't bother finishing what I'm saying, already knowing that's not how events unfolded.

It sounds contrived as I hear myself repeat what Carme told me when I eventually asked. In fact, it sounds so poorly scripted that I halfway wonder if my sister was pulling my leg or mocking me with such a confabulation. I say nothing more, waiting for Dick's response, and not getting one. We sit quietly, just the sound of the gusting wind.

Staring out at the bare branches of pecan trees and crape myrtles lining the sidewalk, thrashing and grabbing at the air like claws. The black sky thick with fog and clouds.

"I get it. That's not how it went down," I break the silence.

"It wouldn't appear so," he answers. "Not that we know much except witnesses saw Noah drive away after the confrontation."

"And Carme?"

"For a while she was inside drinking beer with her team," he says. "But she didn't leave with them, apparently called a ride-sharing service, was seen being driven away in the front seat of a white Jeep Cherokee."

"Someone driving his personal car for hire, and I'm always telling her I wish she wouldn't do that. She shouldn't be sitting in front either. But you know how she is."

"I'm not sure what you're saying," Dick replies, and he's fishing again.

"I'm saying she's never been the worrier I am, and I'm not telling you anything new. Carme's afraid of nothing. And nothing's going to hurt her, isn't that the way she is? And that's only gotten worse."

"Since when?"

"Last spring, I started noticing things were getting a little more out of bounds with her." I find discussing all this acutely uncomfortable, and I look away from him, out my side window. "Everything at a higher pitch, a higher volume, at times more ramped up than I've seen her."

I lower the fan at the distant sound of a dog barking and baying somewhere in the dark, and I open my window a crack, listening.

"Did you ask her about it?" Dick says, and I can feel his eyes on me, watching carefully.

"You know how that goes. Everyone notices a change except the person involved." I'm aware of the redwood paling around the back of the guest house next door, and nearby, the big boxy shape of a backup generator.

No lights on, dark as pitch all around, and I listen to the dog going at it frantically. Could be a beagle or some kind of hound, and I hope it's simply outside on a quick potty break. No domesticated pet would fare well in these temperatures.

As Dick is saying, "Then she was unaware her behavior seemed different."

"When I've brought it up, she's defensive about it. As indelicate as it is to say, I even wondered if something's going on with her hormones. Or her thyroid. Or something else chemical."

"When people are defensive," Dick says, "usually that indicates some degree of awareness. What the hell is that dog barking about?"

"And why is it outside in this weather . . . ?" The words no sooner are out of my mouth than the barking stops. "There, thank goodness," waiting, listening.

Not a peep, and I roll up my window.

"Has the driver in the white Cherokee been questioned?" I get back to that. "And what about a plate number and security cameras? When Noah Bishop left earlier, are we sure he was alone? We sure he wasn't followed? Or surveilled?"

"This isn't something we'll get into now, but he definitely drove off alone," Dick says. "There was no girlfriend with him that night or probably any night. I don't believe he's into girls. Or was. Security cameras at the hotel show he didn't return, and he hasn't been heard from since."

"And that was a little more than a month ago."

"Affirmative."

"How is it something like this hasn't been in the news?" I'm not sure I believe it.

Most upsetting and inexplicable is why my sister felt she couldn't tell the truth. Why would she hide that the so-called redneck dude hitting on her was gay and has since vanished in thin air? I don't understand why

159

she would misrepresent the facts. As close as we've always been, finishing each other's sentences, thinking the other's thoughts, sensing moods and events no matter how far apart. Since when does she feel a need to deceive me?

"It's not been in the news because it would be most unhelpful," Dick says as if it's that simple. "Noah is someone of interest for a number of reasons, and was before this happened. Before he disappeared."

The way Dick says it makes me feel he's personally acquainted with this man. And I find myself picking up one of those sotto voce vibes that I get all the time, another quirk that's best left unexplained to almost everyone. But I sense a powerful undercurrent of truth that will reveal itself in time if I'm patient and pay close attention. If I use my head and focus. If I refuse to feel what I feel. Which is mostly pain and pure dread.

"Whatever's happened to Noah Bishop," I decide, "well, I certainly hope he's all right. And what I can't help but wonder is if it might be possible he *chose* to disappear?"

"Anything's possible," Dick gives me another non-answer.

"Where is he from originally besides the UK?"

"London, a graduate of Oxford, dual US

and UK citizenship, living in Los Angeles for the past 15 years. That's where he was visiting from when he encountered Carme at the restaurant. Worked out of Pandora's facility on the West Coast. But the headquarters is in Houston, and they also have offices in DC, London, Buenos Aires, Singapore, and so on."

"I know they're extremely competitive," I reply. "Well on their way to being a serious contender with behemoths like SpaceX, Blue Origin, Virgin Galactic."

"Noah was working out of the West Coast plant, where much of the autonomous vehicle research and assemblage is done. They're also completing a launch complex north of Santa Barbara, in addition to exploring the use of Wallops Island for East Coast launches, which you may have heard about."

"I've not heard much," I reply. "They do a good job of staying out of the news, their big target the military. Especially the high-risk bench-test technologies that can be pretty *out* there. Like DARPA stuff. What exactly did Noah do for Pandora?" I ask.

"Sensors, robotics, that sort of thing. Much of the work classified, obviously."

"If it's DARPA, yes. Top secret and then

161

some," and I'm about to come out of my skin.

Even if one believes in coincidences, which I don't, it's a stretch for me to assume that the disappearance of one Pandora researcher and now the sudden death of another within a month of each other are normal or random.

12

"And you think Carme did something to Noah Bishop," I go ahead and say it. "You think she 'disappeared' this guy."

"She's capable." Dick stares straight ahead at the back of Dodd Hall in the glare of my truck's headlights.

"So are you. So am I. So are a lot of people we know. That doesn't mean anything."

"I think there are way too many questions and not enough answers."

"Have you asked her?" I push harder. "Why don't you just ask Carme what happened on Halloween night?"

He reaches down for his backpack, setting it in his lap, signaling it's time for him to head to his dinner.

"Is she a suspect?" I don't quit. "I mean, seriously, Dick. What are we talking about here?"

"There's no evidence she did anything to

163

him," he finally gives me something helpful. "But I need to talk to her."

If he hasn't, there's a reason, all of it adding up to something much worse than it sounds. A major problem that he's not about to spell out to me. He's concerned enough that he might have come here from Colorado simply to have this moment. To catch me off guard, making sure I have no time to mount a defense for myself or my other half.

"Look, she's definitely been hotheaded, aggressive, I'm not going to deny it even if it would make her most unhappy that I said anything. Carme's always expected unwavering loyalty no matter the cost."

"Even if she's in the wrong."

"Her being wrong has never been a big part of any equation unless it's something silly. Like a bet, a question on *Jeopardy!* . . . Nothing remotely similar to what we're talking about now, Dick." And I feel utterly dejected, hollowed out. "I've been assuming her moods are related to the stress of her deployment. Mom, Dad, all of us have been aware that she's not herself, is inconsistent. You know, something seeming off."

"Give me an example." He digs in a pocket for his room key.

"What comes to mind is after our interviews and right before she flew out to return to her deployment, she started an argument. Was pretty nasty, swearing a blue streak about one thing or another, and that's not like her. Didn't used to be like her. She knows I'm not a fan of crudeness and cursing. Then next thing I know, she shows up with a 6-pack of my favorite beer as if nothing happened."

"To control and manipulate you," he states it as a fact.

"I figured she felt guilty. Because she'd been so unpleasant. It was like someone turned on a switch. And then turned it off."

"How long ago was this? When you had the argument."

"Mid-November."

"Overall you're saying her behavior has seemed more extreme." He settles back in his seat, and what I'm saying seems to be of keen interest to him.

But it's not making him happy, and I feel his gravity.

"At times, yes. Vacillations in her behavior that I began to notice last spring, as I've said. Subtle at first." I do my best to be objective.

"For example?"

"For example and in general, one minute she's worried she's hurt your feelings or

165

thinks you don't love her anymore. Then suddenly she couldn't care less, is ramped up like she's on steroids. Which she isn't."

"And you know that for sure?"

"I can't say what I know for sure. But it's been my belief that she's not into drugs of any kind. And hardly drinks, at least she didn't used to."

"And now?" he persists. "What have you witnessed?"

"It's not fair to say, having not seen much of her this year," I falter. "But over recent months she's gotten a shorter fuse and doesn't back down when maybe she should."

"Including with you?" Staring intensely at me, my heart pricked by a cold needle of fear.

"Well, she can be tough sometimes." I'm speaking very quietly and with difficulty. "I almost never hear from her."

"How has your fuse been? Shorter than usual or the same?" It seems an odd thing for him to ask, and immediately I feel on guard.

"My fuse?" I reply. "I don't believe I'm the one getting into scraps in parking lots."

"I'm asking how you're feeling, Calli."

"Pretty much status quo except for worrying about my future, if I'm being completely honest," and there I go saying that again.

"And we know how much we value complete honesty. Tell me what you've noticed about your sister's drinking." Dick won't let it go. "Since you brought it up."

"Only that it's more than it was. But erratic. When we were together last, she would go several nights and be her old self. Then suddenly want to party, and you know, get plastered."

"Did she tell you she was plastered the night of the confrontation with Noah Bishop?"

"She didn't say . . ." As I catch something out of the corner of my eye, a light blinking on inside one of the second-floor suites. "It would seem that someone else is staying here after all."

I direct Dick's attention up to the east wing, to the light around the edges of the drapes drawn across three windows facing us. He barely looks, isn't interested, and I think of the dog barking and baying a little while ago.

"I'm pretty sure I was the only person here this morning," Dick then comments.

"You're definitely not alone now." I also have no doubt that his air force security detail would be aware of anybody else staying in the same lodging house as him.

There's no military police presence back here, scarcely eyes or ears. No alarm system or cameras, no motion sensors on the grounds or dead bolt locks on the doors. The commander of Space Force can't possibly be left unattended and at the mercy of whoever might decide to check in. I don't care if Dick is armed to the teeth.

"Your room number?" I ask him.

"608."

"Someone is upstairs on the opposite end of the floor from you." As I stare up at the lighted room, watching for any sign of movement, a shadow moving behind the drapes. "Someone who came in off Dodd Boulevard, through the front entrance, was dropped off, I'm assuming, since there's no parking in front. And it wouldn't be housekeeping at this hour. Possibly a guest who doesn't have a car. Not everybody does. You don't, for example."

But Dick isn't interested in other guests or where they might park, and I can't imagine how awkward it is for him to interrogate me about someone both of us have put on a pedestal and care deeply about. Now here he is quizzing, prodding and probing to get the answer he needs. And desperately doesn't want. Which is if it's possible Carme is connected with the disappearance of a Pandora Space Systems engineer who happened to be in Houston while she was there last month.

Perhaps even more pressing is where she is now. Difficult as it is for me to fathom, I sense that Dick may not know. He may not be aware of anybody who does. If that's true, then things have gone from troubling to bad beyond belief. He fumbles to release his seat belt, and I don't help him this time.

"If you think of anything, get in touch." He opens his door. "Should you hear from Carme, I must be informed immediately. Please. As I'm sure you've gathered, Calli, it's very important."

"Is she AWOL from the air force?" I grip his arm, and he hesitates but doesn't answer.

But if he doesn't know where she is, then the air force doesn't. Maybe nobody does, and my sister has vanished without a trace like Noah Bishop did.

"Without knowing anything more," I hear myself saying as frigid air blows inside my truck, "as things stand right this moment, how damaging is what you've told me in terms of Houston? Or more bluntly, in terms of Carme's chances of ever becoming an astronaut. And if she's messed up somehow, what might that mean about me?" Not an easy thing to ask, but I have a right to know.

"I don't want the committee making a final decision until I can bring her in to talk," as Dick climbs out of my truck. "I hope you'll let her know she needs to do that," he says as if assuming I'll be communicating with her before he does.

I lean toward the open door, looking up at him, trying to read his face. But he won't give me his eyes.

"That works both ways," I try to make him look at me. "I know you're not obligated to pass along any information. I respect that. But it's Carme. She's my twin sister."

Nothing from him as he stands in the cold next to the open door. Staring off at everything except me.

"Is she going to be all right?" I'm starting to feel shaky inside. "I mean, you'd tell me if . . ."

"You're going to have to trust me a little bit, and I've gotta go. My dinner date will be here to pick me up in 20 minutes," he says with a stiff smile that chills my soul. "Well, not the secretary of state himself, but close enough. Stay safe. I know you know how." As he closes the door.

■ ■ ■ ■

I watch him cut through my headlights, headed to the deep-set back entrance, thick oak, arched and bordered in brick. Still carrying his parka draped over an arm, his knapsack slung over a shoulder, and inserting his keycard, he disappears inside. I wait until his upstairs light flicks on, always careful not to leave guests until I'm certain they're safely in their suites.

Lodgings like these have no doorman, security, front desk or other services, nothing more than housekeeping if requested. You'd better hope you don't find yourself locked out with no car or phone, especially if not properly dressed. The only options are hoofing it to the nearest guard gate or a mile to the Langley Inn for another key. Even that won't save you if you've locked yourself out with no badge or ID.

I stare up at the lighted window, wondering who else is staying on the second floor. Opening files in my memory, I can see the exact location of the suite after climbing the two and a half flights of stairs. Counting the carpeted wooden steps as I see them in my mind, as if I'm climbing them one at a time. Starting at the back door landing, 24 steps leading to the second floor. Then three doors down to the left in the corner, suite 600, the numbers stainless steel against dark stained oak.

I'd be foolish to trust whoever's staying within reach of Dick until the data tell me differently, and at a glance it makes little or no sense that a complete stranger could have slipped in between the cracks. I can't think of a worse breach of security than someone with ill intentions staying under the same roof as a 4-star general who has the ear of the president. An assassin or pretty much anyone could attack Dick at every twist and turn of the creaky old floors, I don't care how adept he is with his Beretta.

Saying his hall mate is an innocent guest with no connection to him, it's also hard to imagine what rational mortal would check in the night before a major storm. One runs a serious risk of being evacuated or getting stranded here. And why was the drop-off at the front entrance and not the back? Most high-level people staying at Dodd Hall use the rear door.

It's more private, there's a parking lot, and if your passenger is a recognizable VIP like General Melville, you don't have to stop to let the person out on a busy road for all the world to see. The only obvious exception is when it's raining or snowing, the front sidewalk and entry covered by an awning. But there's no precipitation tonight. Plus, the wind would be more brutal in front of the building because of its exposure to the water.

Whatever the case, I find it odd that Dick acted stone-cold indifferent to whoever might be staying in the same building with him. In my logical way of reasoning things out, that suggests he already knows who it is. Possibly a security detail but I've not noticed any big SUVs in the area, not on the roads or parked off to the side. Certainly not the two Suburbans I noted barely an hour ago.

Most puzzling is that Dick would trust me with sensitive information about my own flesh and blood. Let's start with that, because it goes without saying that it can't be expected that I'll be totally objective. No matter my best intentions we're still talking about my identical twin. Yet in the same breath he basically lied about who's staying on his floor in an air force officer's lodging house. That's assuming he knows who's in suite 600.

Of course, he does.

Leaving the AFB, I drive along Wright

Avenue, then Dodd Boulevard, heading back the same way I came. Traffic is heavier now, a lot of people leaving work, running errands or getting the heck out before the storm hits.

Never make assumptions. He might not know.

What I don't see are people walking, jogging or out with their dogs, the temperature dipping into single digits, the windchill below zero. I keep thinking about the barking I heard a little while ago, uncertain why it nags at me, bothers me at a deep level beyond my obvious concern about any animal freezing to death. Gosh, I hope not, and now that the idea is firmly planted in my head, I navigate and keep up my scan accordingly.

Passing the Command Surgeon, then the Langley Chapel, the conference center, the headquarters for Air Combat Command, all of the buildings handsome brick and timber. Cruising main roads and side streets, one end to the other, I wend my way back to the Durand Gate, searching for anything or anyone at risk out here. Gliding past the big white tanks of the fuel farm, F-22 hangars, the frosted fields blinking red with runway beacons, the empty fitness path snaking alongside to my right.

I follow the rocky shoreline, the river a void without a single light on the horizon. Driving with my window cracked, I listen for the dog. Hoping no creature great or small is lost or abandoned in this weather, and I imagine one of the neighbors in permanent base housing taking out his or her pet. A beagle, a basset hound, something with a deep throaty baying howl that carries.

I feel unduly worried about Dick, even scared, or maybe I'm projecting my feelings about my sister onto him. Sometimes knowing a lot about psychology can be a real detriment, doing more harm than good when I'd be better served taking things at face value. Like MP Crockett, for example, as I deliberately slow to a crawl at the Durand Gate, making sure I lock eyes with him, neither of us smiling. *Go screw yourself,* but he can't hear me or penetrate my bulletproof affect.

Not that I actually would swear at him or anyone if avoidable. I'm quite decided about my use of language, believing words are like computer code, once executed they have a life of their own. Compared to most people, including my twin sibling, I probably come across as a Goody Two-shoes from the 1950s with my use of euphemisms, spoonerisms and made-up expressions.

I don't curse, cuss or turn an ugly phrase unless I really mean it, and you'd better hope I don't. I'm not all that nice when sufficiently riled, and the tall gangly officer with his big teeth and Old World brogue-ish accent isn't a worthy opponent. Although it would be a lie if I said I'm not secretly enjoying myself right now. It must be killing him that I was driving a famous 4-star general all by my lonesome with no assist from him or his comrades.

It also wouldn't escape anyone's notice that Dick doesn't ride in the back seat as if I'm nothing more than an armed driver. He sits up front like a colleague, a friend, and MP Crockett no doubt can't stand that I keep such company to begin with. A lowly protective service agent like me.

A female to boot. And here I am spending private time with someone who thinks nothing of dining with the secretary of state. Or attending White House briefings in the Situation Room.

13

MP Crockett's disgruntled stare follows me in my mirrors.

Jerkoff, I think without so much as a facial twitch, startled by my sudden solar flares of anger, reminded of what Dick said just minutes ago:

"How has your fuse been? Shorter than usual or the same?"

How ironic that he would ask me about my moods today of all days when I'm getting increasingly aggravated and not 100 percent sure why. As if it's not coming from me but from elsewhere uncontrollably, and I've experienced emotional power surges like this before when something is wrong.

Big-time wrong. Usually wrong with Carme, and it certainly would seem that something is. Not to be selfish, but in addition to my fears about her welfare and future, I also have to worry about mine, explaining why I asked Dick about JSC. For research purposes, identical twins are an asset to the astronaut program. Comparisons can be made to show the physical and psychological effects of traveling and living in space, and Carme and I are considered an attractive package, to hear NASA people talk.

But that was then and this is now. Who's to say that Dick isn't preparing me for the disastrous news that my sister and I didn't make it to the next round? Not just one but both of us, it gnaws at me as MP Crockett vanishes from view in a swirl of exhaust.

Picking up speed past the base hospital and emergency room, then the exchange, I head to where Sweeney and Armistead Boulevards meet at the end of Runway 8.

The roar of F-22s taking off shakes the air, and I check my phone, doesn't matter that I know better than to multitask while driving.

Just because I'm well versed in what will do you in doesn't mean I always heed my own advice. It all depends, and I'm surprised to see that Fran called repeatedly while I was with Dick, my ringer set on silent mode. I try her back, and when she answers, I hear voices in the background, recognizing one of them as Special Agent Scottie Ryan. Then a male voice belonging to Butch Pagan. He's saying something about opening the front door again, doesn't want "too much air blowing in and disturbing anything."

"You're on speakerphone and I'm alone," I say right off. "What's going on, Fran?"

"Seems like I'm the one who should be asking you that. Are you okay? Where the hell have you been?" She's full of her usual bluster, but I detect her stress. "I was beginning to think you'd dropped off the edge of the earth."

"The earth isn't flat, as it turns out. So, that's not likely," I reply, and she's at the Fort Monroe scene.

Has to be, suggesting something about the alleged suicide isn't sitting right with her. Or sitting less right than it was, and I'm not surprised based on what Dick just relayed to me. In fact, I'm plenty freaked out.

"I'm on my way, have some intel that makes the situation at hand of concern . . . ," I start to say cryptically.

"What intel?" she interrupts. "And please pass it along because I sure would appreciate anything that might help explain exactly what we're dealing with out here."

"Are you familiar with Pandora Space Systems?"

"Only that Vera Young worked there. And

that they're a huge aerospace company with a lot of military and NASA connections."

"They do a lot of classified work for our government, including DARPA, and one must always be concerned with spying," I reply, on LaSalle Avenue, squinting in the glare of oncoming traffic. "Don't forget about her so-called stolen badge."

"Oh, I haven't forgotten. That's what I'm trying to say. Turns out you were probably right to get hinky about it. Hold on, I'm walking outside." The sounds of Fran's booted footsteps, a door opening and banging shut, and what she really wants is to smoke.

Not that she makes a habit of it after quitting several decades ago. But if she's lighting up in a subzero windchill after responding to a scene she expected to be garden-variety ordinary last we talked, then without additional input from me, she'd already determined the situation is trouble. That's putting it mildly as I think of Noah Bishop and wonder where my sister is right now.

"What else?" Fran's voice booms out of the speakers in my truck as I drive.

"I've made the important point for now." I steer her as far away from Dick and Carme as I can. "Suicide or not, we need to explore any possibility that Vera Young's death could be connected to yesterday's incident. In other words, could it be a cause and effect? And has anybody checked to make sure her badge hasn't been used unauthorized? I haven't had a chance to run a search of her ID number, to interrogate the security system . . ."

"Well, Scottie did, and that's another puzzle. She deactivated the smartcard yesterday at 5:33 p.m. But somehow it wasn't deactivated after all." What Fran is saying makes me feel exponentially worse. "Or got reactivated, don't ask me how."

"You've got to be kidding." That bad feeling at the back of my neck.

"Do I sound like it?"

"It's not possible the card reactivated on its own. Have you asked Scottie if she's *absolutely sure* there wasn't some sort of glitch?" I ask. "Or that she actually did what she intended, that the system saved the change?"

"Swears on her own life that she took care of the card the minute it was reported stolen yesterday, and that the status was changed to *inactive*," Fran insists.

"But what you're telling me is the card was still *active* as of just a little while ago," I make sure, thinking of the sensor alert in 1111-A that seems inexplicable.

181

"She says yes. It was still active," Fran's voice confirming.

"This is bad, really bad." I'm not going to sugarcoat it. "Either the ID wasn't deactivated after all, or something far more nefarious is going on."

"I guess you can drill down into the metadata or whatever and see if something was tampered with," Fran says with little enthusiasm, likely thinking such a thing isn't possible, and she couldn't be more mistaken. "I sure hope not, but again, what's the truth about her badge, and why is she dead? Have you had a chance to look at the call sheet I sent you? And the suicide note?"

"Not yet. I'll take a look when I'm not driving."

"You want to fill me in on what you've been doing since I talked to you, what . . . ? Forty-five minutes ago?" she then says. "Not answering emails or your phone. Off the radar. Where have you been and with whom? You get abducted by aliens? You sure you're okay? You don't sound happy."

"I'm headed to a death scene," I almost snap at her, and that's not like me. "What's happy about it? Especially this one?"

"Something's happened since I saw you last. You're in a funk, all right." Fran cares about me enough that she's not going to stop until I confide what's wrong, and I can't.

"It's not important now, we'll save it for later," I tell her, and the truth is it's not something I can talk about with her ever.

As close as we are and as much as we've always shared, I can't possibly divulge what Dick said to me. Although Fran wouldn't be completely shocked. I'm not the only one who's noticed that the fluctuations in my sister's behavior have gotten increasingly turbulent and unpredictable. Fran's heard me mention it in the recent past, and it settles over me coldly, horribly that I can't say a word or make allusions about what I've learned. Not to my closest friend or anyone.

Including Mom and Dad when I see them later at home. Or to Carme herself, and it crosses my thoughts that I almost hope she doesn't contact me anytime soon. I won't know what to do if she does, and I don't think I've ever felt so alone.

"Where am I supposed to be headed?" I talk hands-free while driving fast. "The only address I have is Fort Monroe."

"The apartment's in the renovated barracks near the Jefferson Davis memorial." Fran's voice inside my truck.

"There are a lot of renovated barracks.

Which ones?" As I cross Back River, water on either side of me in the dark as if I'm going full throttle in a boat.

"I don't know if the particular barracks have a name," she says. "I'm looking out here in the tundra and don't see one. Off Bernard Road, just head toward the light-house."

"The address would be helpful," I answer, and she gives it to me.

"You'll see all the cars," she adds as if I don't know how to navigate around here. "How far out are you?"

"About 15 if I step on it. Is Joan there yet?" I take the exit for East Mercury Boulevard, flipping on my emergency strobes, flashing blue and red.

"She pulled up a few minutes ago," Fran says, and I'm passing other drivers with impunity.

Nobody's going to stop my police truck. Not to give me a hard time, a ticket or for any reason, and the more I think about MP Crockett, the faster I drive. My replay of his demeaning antics toward me are like dirty rotor wash I need to fly out of before I crash-land. It takes a lot to anger me. I'm not one for fits of pique. It's rare I raise my voice, and unheard of for me to slam a door or throw things. But I could do some real damage with the mood I'm in.

Rubbing my right thumb and index finger together. Passing Hardee's, jolted by nostalgia that almost brings a mist to my eyes. Like so many places around here, the burger joint has been in Hampton for as long as I have. Rubbing my scar, images flashing of school friends in the parking lot back in a day when life was simple and innocent compared to now. When it felt safe.

I can see my sister and me sitting inside Dad's rebuilt '68 Camaro as if it were yesterday, eating french fries, drinking soda, talking about girl stuff and boys. Watching people while we plotted and planned our futures. Most of all, looking up at the moon and stars, imagining ourselves there and beyond.

Rubbing and rubbing in little circles, feeling the looped indentation on my finger pad. Better now. There was a time when there was no sensation at all.

Slow down, slow down, slow down. Deep, deep breaths. Soothing myself the only way I know.

Envisioning the river and weathered wooden dock. The huge oak tree with its rope swing long enough to slingshot you to Oz. And the ducks and geese flocking in the emerald-

185

green grass. Going out on the boat. The sun high in the big blue sky. The weather severe-clear, fighter jets screaming over runways on the other side of water white capped from the wind.

The sights and sounds are there. Then gone. As I'm swept away by a turmoil of emotions far too strong for me to tolerate. I can't go home again. Can't transport myself there with my mind, not this time. As I sit on my bed, the top sheet as tight as a trampoline.

". . . I feel bad I'm not there with you right now." Dick is kind over the phone, and I detect the pain in his tone as I'm keenly aware of my physicality.

I experience my reality not virtually but miserably, held fast by the gravity of my offi-cer's quarters some 2,700 kilometers, or 1,700 miles, from Hampton, Virginia. Unable to fathom feeling soothed or happy ever again. Listening to my entire world crashing in. Staying surprisingly steady. Not shedding a tear or complaining. Inside my spartan room. With its one window over the twin bed. And the antique wooden apple crate, where I park my coffee and Beretta.

The bookcase crammed with textbooks from grad school. Lots of training manuals. Com-puters, signal analyzers, a gooseneck lamp on the desk. The ergonomic chair piled with body armor, other gear.

". . . I'll track down Carme, but wanted you to hear it from me first . . ."

Dead calm, no reaction at all, as if something in me has shorted out. Listening.

". . . I'm sure you want to talk to your parents. And of course, talk to Carme. But not right away. For all her toughness she isn't all that strong when it's emotional stuff. As you know better than anyone . . ."

Staring wide eyed through the dusty glass. The sun burning small and bright like the white dot from a magnifying glass. The distant Colorado mountains snow covered and dazzling in the morning light.

". . . She's going to have a harder time than you . . ."

A harder time because she can't handle being needed by anyone, I think loudly but wouldn't dare articulate or telegraph. A harder time because she'll resort to evasive tactics next. Ducking, dodging like she always does. Unable to help being that way. Dick knows her too. Almost as well as I do.

Telling me he'd appreciate it if I'd give him the chance to talk to her first. "To directly pass on to your sister what your father told me. Because he promised your mom . . ."

Just like Dad always does.

". . . Assured her she didn't need to . . . Well,

you get it, Calli . . ."

Get that as usual Dad said he'd take care of it.

". . . He wanted me to be the one who told both of you . . ."

Just like you've always done.

". . . I told him I'd do that, and he didn't need to worry about it . . ."

Just like you've always done, I keep thinking to myself as Dick explains how hard my father is taking it. Couldn't make the call himself. As if I need to be told that.

No explanation required for why Dad won't call his daughters, his only two children. Someone has to carry that torch for him, has to lead us along the darkest of ways. He's not going to be the messenger bearing bad news, certainly not this bad news. Never has been. I've always known what he can and can't handle. And under different circumstances it would be me making the call to my sister.

I'm thankful that Dick would spare me from that. As I listen to him on speakerphone. Alone inside my stark quarters.

". . . Listen, Calli, I wish no one had to be called. And I understand if you're not up for giving me a hand this morning . . ."

Feels like one of his tests, prodding and probing to see if I measure up. Checking to make sure I'm strong enough.

". . . If you'd like, I can get someone else, no problem . . ."

Thanking him for being so thoughtful, telling him not to worry. No biggie. Nothing I can do right this minute anyway. But it explains the fevers and fatigue, I hear myself say. And better to catch it now than later. Stoically putting a positive polish on my mom having cancer. While telling him I'm A-OK and will see him at 0800 hours.

Showing him once and for all that I may not be my fighter-pilot sister. But I'm here to serve and won't let him down. No matter what, nothing will stop me. Not even the most devastating news of my life.

Can't seem to catch my breath. Can't stop thinking about it.

Focus. Focus. Focus!

14

"Slow down," muttering to myself repeatedly as I ease my foot off the gas, wondering what Carme would say if she could see me now.

To hear her talk, I'm too passive, tolerating far more than I should. She doesn't hesitate to make cracks about the way I drive, park, pass, or fly a plane or helicopter for that matter. I don't take risks unnecessarily, always one to handle powerful machines sensibly and respectfully, and I'm dismayed by the uproar I'm in.

I don't understand what's got me in such a state except that I can't abide bullying, and I furiously envision MP Crockett again. But neither he nor anyone else is an excuse for my being out of sorts to the point of recklessness. Tires squealing, I accelerate past an old clunker chugging along as if there's no tomorrow.

Whooping my siren to make my point.

Glaring in my rearview mirror at the offending driver, some little old lady who barely can see over the steering wheel. *People like that are a menace on the road,* it flares aggressively but not out loud, and I take a breath. Telling myself to calm down. To stop acting like a hothead, a primitive savage. It's not that poor old lady's fault or anybody's problem but my own, for heaven's sake.

As it begins to occur to me why I'm in such a state, why my fuse might be shorter than usual, to pick up on what Dick asked earlier. His question isn't hard to answer. It's just hard to look in the mirror, and one doesn't have to be an expert in human factor psychology to pinpoint the problem. But what I'm feeling about my sister is beyond conflicted and downright ugly now that she's managed to introduce real trouble into our world.

What have you done? Asking this repeatedly as I drive, the chiaroscuro of pitch darkness and glaring lights playing tricks on my eyes. I hate it when hurt and rage creep up my throat, threatening to hack their way into my self-control. That I can't allow. When I let my guard down, I've seen what happens.

"We're still taking photographs and video,

making sure no stone's unturned before doing much else," Fran continues to explain over the speakers in the dash. "Trying to figure out what in Judas Priest would make somebody do what this lady did. Like self-flagellation . . ."

"What is?" Watching what I'm doing, flying along in the frigid dark, the wind buffeting my truck.

"Or a hair shirt. You know, people who cut and starve themselves . . . ," she's explaining unhelpfully.

"What are you talking about?" I have no idea.

"Punishing herself," Fran says. "And what she wrote in the suicide note fits with that."

"Let's first make sure she wrote it," I make that point again.

"There's no reason not to think it so far, but I've got to admit I'm not feeling good about her so-called stolen badge, really not feeling good right about now. She reports that yesterday, as you've been beating the drum about, and you were right to do so, as it turns out. Because next thing she hangs herself? You'll see when you read the note. It's obvious that she was feeling pretty worthless."

"Many people are when they decide to take their own lives, assuming that's what this is. And I'm making no assumptions at all. Including that something is *obvious*," I reply. "Tell me about her car and if you've located it."

"A 2018 Lexus SUV, silver, parked in front. A lease."

"Anything unusual?"

"When I pulled up, I had the plate run, but we've not searched it yet, not really gotten to it," she says. "I did shine my light through the windows, and nothing caught my attention. Now the scene inside the bedroom isn't what I'd call normal, not by a long shot," she adds, and I'm on Stilwell Drive now, just past the Division 5 state police headquarters.

"I thought the first responding officer said he didn't notice anything strange," as I flash red and blue through darkness and water, the Hampton River on my left and Mill Creek on my right.

"He meant he didn't notice anything that made him think something other than suicide," Fran's voice again. "But hey, it's not like he got very close or was even aware that the bedroom reeks of chlorine. In fact, you can smell it the minute you walk in the front door."

"And you're sure the source is her apartment?" Winding around a frosted playing field, the soccer goal posts missing their nets.

"Oh yeah."

"And the explanation?" Slowing down, the glowing eyes of deer literally caught in my headlights. "Because there's no swimming pool around there. Maybe some kind of cleanser? And what do you mean, the officer didn't notice an odor? It must not be very strong."

"It's actually overpowering, but this particular officer has no sense of smell."

"Well that's not safe for a cop . . ." Watching the deer scamper off.

"Polyps in his sinuses or something. I keep telling him he's got to get it taken care of, but yeah, he didn't notice. Now that I'm here enjoying the full experience, what I can tell you is we're talking about chlorine bleach. All over her, from head to toe. And it's not a pretty sight."

"That would be excruciatingly awful, the fumes alone, not to mention what it would do to your eyes, mouth, throat. And we're supposed to believe she did this to herself?" Creeping ahead in my truck, ready if the deer decide to bound across the road. "We sure this wasn't done after the fact by somebody else? What does Joan say?"

"She just got here. But so far, no indication of defensive injuries, nothing at a glance. What it's looking like is liquid bleach might have been part of the suicidal ritual, that's the theory of the moment. We haven't located the bottle, whatever it was in . . ."

"Hold on a minute . . ."

"I know, I know. Believe me, I know what you're going to say," Fran's voice cutting back in, loudly. "How did it disappear?"

"It doesn't make sense to pour bleach all over yourself. Then dispose of the bottle off site," I'm emphatic. "Then return to the apartment and hang yourself. All this while you're suffering from severe chemical burns. And where did the bleach come from to begin with? You've looked everywhere? Laundry room, under the sink, the trash . . . ?"

"Like I told you, I can't say where it might have come from," Fran's disembodied voice.

"Maybe there's a receipt. When I interviewed her yesterday, she claimed to have stopped off at Walgreens on her way home."

"There's a lot to dig through and even more questions, but don't be so quick to discount that she did this to herself," Fran's response. "Sort of like people who shave their heads or paint their faces before recording themselves blowing their brains out."

"No, it isn't like that. This sounds more like self-mutilation, self-torture."

"Well, you brainy NASA types aren't exactly average, so I wouldn't expect you to snuff yourselves like everybody else," Fran has to get in that snipe at least once this night.

"I've got my chemical suit in the truck, but what about the hazmat trailer?" I ask.

"It's en route so we can decon when we're done. Anyway, I could have done without an effed-up scene like this one, that's for sure. Especially right now with everything else going on. I hope you've got a strong stomach," and at least Fran's not phobic about blood and guts, is perfectly fine with dead bodies no matter their horrific shape.

Decomps aren't a bother, and I've watched her wade in after floaters as if it's just another day at the beach, the entire time deliberating over where and what we should eat after clearing the scene. Autopsies are easy, doesn't matter who or what, and I find it stunningly illogical that she doesn't flinch when it's babies or kids.

Yet she can't drive through a tunnel alone if at all, and swears she'll never again own a vehicle that has a trunk.

The Tahoe got run-flat tires, and so did my

truck, after Fran picked up a nail and almost died three years ago. Depending on how she tells the tale, and there are many versions of what actually happened that Christmas Eve after I'd left Colorado and moved back home.

"Any sign of the media?" I raise my voice over the noise of the heater fan and the engine.

"No one's shown up here yet," her voice loud from the dash. "But that reporter I hate so much just tried to call."

"You hate all reporters."

"This one in particular. *Calendar Boy* who thinks he's God's gift."

"He left me a message, too, but not about this. I assume he's unaware of what we've got out here?" I sure hope so because we don't need Mason Dixon rolling up.

"I don't know. I didn't answer and won't call him back," Fran says.

"Probably best to ignore him."

"You do know it will get harder now that his show is going regional, the entire South-east. Leah heard something about it," she says, and our international visits coordinator is a closet fan of Mason Dixon, I don't care what she protests to the contrary.

"Let me guess," as I drive, and there's scarcely anyone on the road the closer I get to Fort Monroe. "She heard him bragging about it *on his own show.* In other words, self-promotion and not necessarily reliable."

"All I can say is that according to the all-knowing Leah, he'll be moving his studio to DC. Apparently, has gotten permission to be part of the White House press corps, if you can believe that."

"Bad behavior seems to pay well these days," I reply, and my emergency strobes are reflected in the plate-glass windows of a gas station I pass.

Like so many other businesses, lights out, nobody home.

"Not that I listen to his show or care," Fran's voice bristling with sarcasm. "But you can rest assured the only reason he got this newest gig is the obvious. The same way he's gotten everything else. Calendar Boy couldn't get hired to write fortune cookies if it wasn't for his doting uncle Willy."

"I wouldn't go that far, and it's not a good idea to underestimate anyone, least of all Mason. He's not stupid, and a lot of people love him. Granted, it's mostly women and gay guys," I add.

"Talk about a conflict of interests, and don't think the other reporters I know around here aren't pissed," she continues as if she couldn't resent him more. "The governor deliberates evacuating us, and who breaks the story? Next, he'll *officially* declare an emergency and confirm he *for sure* is evacuating us, and who do you think will get *that* scoop as well? And on and on it goes."

"Which is probably how Mason found out General Melville is here," I decide. "The governor could have reason to be aware. Or maybe someone around him does."

It wouldn't surprise me. Governor Willard Dixon has the challenge of overseeing a commonwealth that not only shares a border with Washington, DC, but includes NASA, the air force's Air Combat Command, the largest naval station in the world and the Pentagon. Just to mention a few major targets should an adversary decide to divert a plane or missile and send it slamming into critical Virginia infrastructures that could cripple our government or military defenses.

"Listen, Fran, I think we should be very careful." I wind up our conversation with what shouldn't need to be said. "Something's going on, and I have a bad feeling we're not even close to knowing what it is yet."

"No joke." And she disconnects, leaving me to the sounds of driving through the wind and cold on my 16-inch run-flat tires.

199

At least it's my lucky night when it comes to hitting all the yellow lights, speeding along, my strobes rolling full tilt. On Mc-Nair Drive my truck is a juggernaut of brilliant blue and red, flashing past the marina and the yacht club, the boats dry docked and shrink wrapped for the winter. Then around the bend, the 9-story Chamberlin looms in the dark, the once-famed beaux arts hotel now a posh retirement home.

I notice few cars in the parking lot, barely a third of the apartments lit up, and I wouldn't blame people for leaving while they can. It's no fun in this cold if the power goes out and the roads are flooded, and I can see the former guard gate up ahead. One I've been through countless times since I was a kid, unmanned now, not a whiff of an MP to flirt with or evade.

I don't ease my foot off the gas, driving a little too fast through the walled entrance, entering the largest stone military installation ever built in the United States. I probably won't get used to how Fort Monroe feels today, tame in an empty echoing way. None of the thriving mission-driven energy, the real estate and all that goes with it repurposed and pricey for the greater Hampton area. As is true of many monuments to a grander past, the 565 acres and historic edifices have been converted into private homes, condos, recreational facilities and tourist attractions.

But that wasn't the case when my sister and I were coming along. The army base was still active then, decommissioned only 7 years ago while we were in graduate school. The absence of a military purpose and presence is a shock I won't get over, and as much as I don't always like repurposed historic sites, that doesn't mean I don't appreciate the point.

Better to put the place to good use. Better to return it to life, and in the process hope the public comes to know about what's gone before and why it should matter anymore.

15

I know my old stomping grounds like the back of my hand, could serve as a tour guide for their every attraction.

Starting with the most popular, the fortified casemate where the imperiled president of the Confederacy, Jefferson Davis, was imprisoned in 1865 at the end of the Civil War. Everybody loves a good tale of humiliation and punishment in an unheated jail cell that's now a museum, I suppose. But that's never moved me much.

What I love are the memories held in crumbling ramparts and parapets, the cannons, earthworks, bulwarks and nature trails. Even the RV park and old stone church would have a tale or two worth listening to could they talk. As would the parade ground with its ancient live oak trees, the miles of beaches, the fishing pier and the pet cemetery. All of it is quite spooky at night even when one isn't responding to a death scene.

I can imagine the appeal to Edgar Allan Poe's morbid creativity when he was stationed here from 1828 to 1830. It wouldn't surprise me while he was tossing and turning in his army cot if he suffered night terrors about a heart beating beneath the floorboards. He very well might have thought about murder because I know I did when wandering about with Carme. Trying to outdo her with my creepy mysteries that would have sent most kids fleeing home in terrified tears, their hair standing on end.

Except she doesn't frighten easily if at all, not going back as far as I recall. Mostly what we did in this water world of ruins and huge guns was play sports and our fantasy games. Then in high school it was drinking and carousing, especially with hot boys we'd take to the pet cemetery for a romantic scare. It's not an exaggeration to say that during the base's active years, Carme and I never lacked for a friend with an officer's blue sticker on the family car that would get us through the guard gate. Bootlegging booze in suntan lotion and water bottles, and brazenly flirting with the military cops, who flirted right back.

Except to be honest, my sister's the one who did all that. But I can't plead innocence, always eager to go along for the ride. Nothing stopping us locals from turning the place into our own personal resort or private club that included unlimited access to boats, fishing, tennis, bowling, a campground, a gym and athletic fields. I see it all like a movie, memories sparking like mad as I follow the water-filled moat from inside the perimeter.

The remains of stone barracks and buildings are skeletal and weathered gray like old bones, equipped with the barest of modern conveniences. Nothing much more than safety railings and infrequent iron lamps. Following the familiar signs pointing out historic sites, and I can recite the posted descriptions verbatim. The Old Cistern, first noted on a map in 1834, a source of water for the garrison . . . The 12-pounder Howitzer, a bronze fieldpiece made by Richmond's Tredegar Iron Works in 1862 . . .

The Rodman gun, smooth bore, weighing 15,800 pounds . . . The arsenal, specializing in seacoast gun carriages . . . The Engineer Wharf, where Jefferson Davis landed as a prisoner . . . And coming up on my left, tucked behind winter-bare trees and a plugged cannon, the casemate where he was confined in failing health before being moved inside the fortress. Finally released on bail some wretched 5 months later.

Across the moat the Old Point Comfort Lighthouse burns strong today, a safe beacon for sailors on the Chesapeake Bay, and a lookout used by the British during the War of 1812. And next ahead, the single-story redbrick former barracks where Vera Young is dead. The street in front is lined with Hampton and NASA police cars and trucks, and the unmarked windowless black van from the Tidewater medical examiner's office. I park behind Fran's Tahoe, texting her that I'm here.

Grabbing my gear bag, I climb back out into the dry-ice cold, the night restlessly empty. Just the sounds of the wind. The thud of my door shutting. My boots as I walk around to the back of the truck. Lifting the tailgate, I open a storage locker to retrieve my tactical chemical clothing and full-face respirator. Can't be too careful these days. Law enforcement and military operatives like me have a lot more to worry about than chemical spills.

In general, chlorine bleach isn't what we fear, but we're far more concerned about horrors like anthrax, ricin, sarin gas and carfentanil. But we can't be certain what we're dealing with until tests are run in the labs. Even if it turns out that the chemical is nothing worse than what one might find in most laundry rooms, I don't want it on my skin. I don't want the fumes, and with a chirp of my key, I lock up beneath an overcast tarp that covers the moon and stars, completely obscuring them.

Across the dark void of the moat, the lighthouse burns through a moiling fog that will form rime on whatever surface it touches. The cold pierces my thin clothing, and I can't stop thinking about Dick's reaction or lack of one to the old flight jacket with its stiff brown leather that's beginning to crack in places, the elastic cuffs sprung, the patches faded. The obvious explanation is he might not have been sure who was wearing it. Carme or me.

But after putting me through his trial by ordeals, he knows darn well who I am. And yet he said not a word about the special gift he presented to me in front of Space Command. Helping me put on the vintage jacket for all to see as if he were passing on a special mantle. That's what I wanted to believe anyway when I left active duty and Colorado, when I left Dick three years ago almost to the day.

It was never supposed to be for good, the plan written in the stars that I'll serve with him again under very different circumstances. As an astro-acrobat installing antenna dishes on the moon while making sure no adversary destroys or hacks into them. As a cyber ninja flying through space on a tether of technology, repairing a telescope orbiting the sun a million miles from Earth.

Maybe doing a little satellite wrangling along the way, tracking down and tethering rogues and runaways that might create havoc in our telecommunications and defense. Or checking out an interstellar visitor like the cigar-shaped 'Oumuamua passing through, maybe landing on it to take a sample or two. It was a given that I would return to Dick's command when fully trained and ready, but it's best not to get caught in a loop about him or Carme right now.

I'm distracted beyond belief, lecturing myself nonstop as I cross the street, headed to the silver Lexus SUV parked by the curb near the brick walkway. Now's not the time to obsess over the unreality of my former boss sitting in my truck only moments ago, informing me that my identical twin sister, my other half, my other self is a person of interest in a disappearance and possible suspicious death.

Worse, I'm supposed to report to him immediately should I hear from her. As in *Aye, aye, sir, Captain Chase reporting for duty,* and I'm unsure what to make of that. Or if I would comply. If I could bring myself to choose fidelity over family. Because so far, I've not done a very good job with that. Always bending the same way when those winds blow, moved by what I love.

That's why I'm not in the air force anymore. Why in the minds of the MP Crocketts of the world, I'm nothing more than a nerdy scientist whose hobby is to moonlight as a security guard.

The flap is attached by nothing more than a delicate tether of skin. The flesh white and bloodless. Dead. The way I feel.

Drained of life, about to faint. Trying not to look as Dick applies pressure, his arms around me, his powerful hands slippery with blood that's soaking into the camouflage cuffs of his sleeves. Like the doctor taking care of Lincoln after he was shot, it bizarrely occurs to me.

Holding my right hand over the sink, palm up, applying pressure to the fingertip filleted to the bone. The pad with its looped and whorled fingerprint all but amputated, hanging by a thread. Feeling him against me and the throbbing pain he's causing. But I don't squirm or throw up. I don't resist the slightest thing he does.

"It's going to be fine, Calli," he keeps saying that and my name, and I think about what I've done to myself, to him and everyone.

Blood drip-drip-dripping, splashing in stellated round drops, bright red against white porcelain.

". . . This is going to sting a little . . ."

Trembling against him as he pours Betadine, dark reddish brown like liquid rust, and it doesn't sting. Not even a little. But rather burns like hell fire. As if I'm being tortured with a red-hot poker, and it's all I can do not to arch my back and shriek. But I keep it to myself. Not flinching or uttering a peep. Not showing any visible indication of what I suffer.

Except for the shaking, inside and out. About to collapse as he holds me up. My body trembling like something in the agonal throes of dying. Mortified that I can't stop.

". . . Deep, deep breaths, Calli. Try to hold as still as you possibly can . . ."

Bracing me from behind at the sink, his arms around me, holding my hand, cleaning the wound as gently as he can.

". . . I had to be trained as a medic to go into space, but that's not saying you'd want me giving you stitches if avoidable . . ."

Talking to me soothingly as if I'm a child.

". . . That's not going to work anyway, sutures aren't going to do the trick. I'm opting for adhesives, but no guarantees about that either. Not sure it's going to take, just being honest . . ."

All the while I apologize for the trouble I've caused. For ruining the morning and possibly my life. All from obeying orders. From doing exactly as I was asked. At a time when I wasn't in the proper frame of mind to conduct business as usual. But I showed up as commanded, salutes and all, only to pull a stunt like this. As if things weren't bad enough.

"I'm sorry, sorry, sorry. All it took was a second while my mind was somewhere else." I wouldn't stop saying it as he applied the Steri-Strip bandages, pain blotting out the sunlight flooding through the windows in the break room.

Blanking out such shameful memories and thoughts, I really can't afford distractions, can't indulge my weaker self by succumbing to them. What I must do now is concentrate on the mission. Do my job. Get over myself.

"Focus, focus, focus," my breath smoking out each time I mumble and mutter.

Ears cold bitten, eyes watering, I approach the driver's door of the leased Lexus, mindful where I step, always on the alert for hazards like ice and frostbite in this kind of weather. Keeping up my scan for the infrequent vehicle going past in the wintry dark, making a note of every license plate, the wind gusting and groaning, evergreens and bare trees rocking and thrashing, dead leaves sailing and skittering.

I set down my gear on the pavement, and shine my tactical light through the silver SUV's windows, contemplating what Vera Young told me when I interviewed her late yesterday about her alleged stolen badge. I mull over her claims about driving away from Langley midmorning, headed home with a migraine, making sure I knew it was her routine the minute she'd leave the NASA campus to take off her lanyard with its attached ID. She wanted me to know that she was extremely careful. So careful that she never wore the badge while getting gas, stopping at the store or running other errands, she told me emphatically.

It seemed her every concern and motivation were unrelated to her personal safety. And that's odd. I thought so then. More so now, wondering why a woman living alone wasn't more mindful of physical threats. But mostly what I sensed from her was paranoia about the top secret technologies she was hired to work with and protect, in addition to fears about professional rivalries and sabotage.

Without saying it in so many words, she sent the message loud and clear that Pandora Space Systems has a zero tolerance for imperfection and indiscretions of any nature. No surprise since the company is known for being relentlessly competitive, and unforgiving of negligence or mistakes, the work environment as stressful as it is exciting. Maybe not a hostile workplace but close enough, and Vera seemed quite anxious and upset when I was with her early yesterday evening.

Weighing out loud the consequences of the problem she "accidentally caused," as she must have put it half a dozen times. Apologizing profusely about her badge, about being "inattentive," blaming it on her migraine, and as I'm thinking this, I'm envisioning her written statement. I home in on the red flags waving their same warnings, only much more brightly, impatiently this time:

". . . I'm extra careful about my NASA badge and appreciate the responsibility that goes with being granted such a privilege . . ."

First red flag: When I was with her, I got the feeling that she didn't appreciate the privilege at all. She seemed put out for having to live away from home, resenting that she was stuck in the boonies with a team of considerably younger researchers. She was none too happy, I might add, when I showed up with my list of questions.

". . . As I drove through the guard gate, leaving the campus, I took off my badge, never wearing it in public because no one needs to know my name or where I work. I don't wear it in photographs and never leave it easily accessible to anyone . . ."

Second red flag: She was appropriately mindful, and yet would opt to leave her badge inside her vehicle? Ever?

". . . I arrived at the drugstore around 10:15 and before going inside, collected my badge from the passenger's seat and secured it in the glove box . . ."

Third red flag: Why not tuck the badge inside her purse or coat pocket?

". . . I remember this distinctly because my wallet fell on the floor, and had I not noticed, I would have ended up in the store with no money . . ."

Fourth red flag: This extraneous detail is like a geofence around a part of the narrative that becomes problematic for her. She doesn't want to talk about getting out of the SUV and what she did with her badge. Most likely because she's outright lying, and therefore quick to skip ahead to 11:00 a.m., when she walked into her apartment and climbed into bed. Staying there the rest of the day, or so she said.

"... Finally, at around 5:00 p.m., I was feeling well enough to return to Langley. To be honest, I wouldn't have bothered were I not so far behind in my projects, with a storm and government shutdown predicted. When I reached the main gate and opened the glove box for my badge, to my genuine surprise and upset, it was gone ..."

Fifth red flag, I don't really trust it when people use words like *to be honest* and *genuine.*

"... I realized it must have been stolen and immediately reported this to the NASA police."
Vera Young, 12/2/19

16

I also don't like it when someone instantly assumes theft, no questions asked.

Why was she so quick to believe that her badge was stolen instead of the more likely scenario that she lost or misplaced it? It went through my mind when I was talking to her that she *wanted* people to think the ID was stolen, and I envision her incident statement form.

I see it in my mind as clearly as if it's in front of me, the page half-filled with her handwriting, tiny and flattened as if the words are too shy to raise their hands in class.

Pretty typical for a lot of NASA-type introverts like me, and what Vera wrote as fact might be perfectly plausible were her statements not rife with deception. I don't accept that once she arrived home, not only did she leave her badge in the glove box, but she failed to lock the SUV.

That would be the only way someone could steal anything from it without smashing a window or having access to the fob or the radio frequency signal necessary to command the vehicle to release its hatch, hood, doors. Plus, a would-be thief or spy after her badge would have to know she was home sick yesterday afternoon, her SUV parked here at Fort Monroe, the badge tucked out of sight in the glove box with doors unlocked.

What a stroke of luck, except I don't think so. Even if such a thing were possible, it still wouldn't account for the SUV being unlocked again today. Only this time its negligent driver is dead inside the apartment, a cord around her neck, doused with a caustic chemical like chlorine bleach.

"Uh-uh," I'm shaking my head.

Added to the implausibility, I don't know of many people, especially those from major cities like Houston and Los Angeles, who leave their cars unlocked. Not unless they're fleeing an earthquake, wildfire or assailant. Granted, if Vera had a migraine, she wouldn't have been thinking as clearly. Or maybe she was in so much pain it was all she could do to get inside her apartment. Maybe I could accept that she forgot to lock her SUV yesterday, but how does that explain the rest of it?

What about today?

I ask myself this again, unable to imagine her explanation for what I'm seeing as I probe with my flashlight. Cupping a hand around my eyes to reduce the glare while holding my breath so I don't frost up the glass. Zeroing in on the center console, on the cup holder closest to the gear shifter. All but certain that what's glinting in the light is the keyless remote, meaning not only was the SUV left unlocked, but someone could have driven off in it.

"Makes no sense," muttering under my smoky breath, my lips frozen, eyes and nose running.

Unzipping my gear bag, I root around, and *rats,* I'm almost out of clean gloves.

I pull on a fresh pair, my hands getting numb, my fingers wooden and clumsy as I open the driver's door. The handle is biting cold through the thin sheath of purple nitrile, and I can't do anything more than look. Not only am I without the proper protective clothing, but as underdressed as I am for the weather, I couldn't last long enough to conduct the most rudimentary search. Not even close, and I'm getting colder by the second as I find myself faced with more questions than before.

Starting with why Vera Young would leave her Lexus unlocked and the key inside. Especially when it's not even 24 hours after she claimed someone had stolen her badge from the glove box while she was home sick yesterday. When was the last time she was in the SUV, and where did she go? Did she drive somewhere today before supposedly dousing herself with bleach and wrapping a computer cord around her neck?

Speaking of, where's the computer or device that goes with that cord? In other words, is the weapon (a ligature) indigenous to the scene, and what might I find in her electronic files? And what might her GPS tell me, or did she navigate by using an app on her phone like Waze? Most of all, I want to know who she was close to, her admirers and rivals. Who were her romances and bad endings? I recall her mentioning an ex-husband and several grown children.

Apparently, she has a sister who also works for Pandora Space Systems but isn't here at Langley, isn't part of the lunar autonomy robotics team in Building 1110. Is too senior for "roll up your sleeves" work like that, Vera said, more or less, and it wasn't hard to figure out that she didn't think it fair she was being farmed out to the East Coast for long cold months on end.

But if she were having trouble with any-one, she gave no indication. It occurs to me I need to talk to this upper-level sister of hers, see what she might have to say about Vera's life and why it's brutally ended. I remember she mentioned this sister's name in passing, an unusual one. Neva. As in Eva with an *N,* and darn it all, I wish I'd spent longer with Vera yesterday.

I wish I'd asked her a lot more questions. But it never entered my mind that she might be a candidate for suicide. And I still don't think it, not unless the evidence gives me no choice, and so far that couldn't be further from the case. Predictabilities, prob-abilities and equations that don't add up are dancing crazily through my head, and if I close my eyes, I almost can see the data flowing by on the backs of my lids.

I'm also fast turning into a block of ice, and shutting the driver's door, I take off my exam gloves. Stuffing them in a pocket of my jacket, I sense something, an energy touching my awareness. Similar to white noise only what I'm picking up is slow and rhythmic like a heavy surf in the low-frequency range of a bass guitar, the A string at 55 Hertz (Hz). But nope, not quite, more like an octave lower at 31 Hz, like a B string.

As opposed to the 440 Hz produced by the note that violinists tune their instruments by, and I feel the music of a living being. It's invisible spectral energy thrumming in the dead quiet cold. I feel it in the brown grass, bare trees, thick shrubbery and water surrounding an endless row of low brick apartments. And I worry I'm being watched, feeling eyes on me like heat.

Possibly an animal getting closer to human habitation because of the extreme cold. Maybe a deer. But I don't see anything or anyone even as the sensation persists. Having no idea where the energy might be coming from, I'm careful how I maneuver myself. Unsure where to turn my back. Mindful of the Glock 27 subcompact pistol on my hip.

A .40-cal hollow point is chambered and ready to find its mark with an extra 8 rounds for good measure if someone does the wrong thing, and I'm thinking what I always do. Please don't force me to shoot, because I will. There's never been a question that if needed I would kill to defend myself or someone else. Hopefully, that won't be called for tonight, and I open my mind like a dish antenna, seeing what I pick up. The unsettling sensation persists, and I can't pinpoint the source or know if it's imagined.

I shoulder my bags of gear, starting out for the walkway while taking on the mindset of a predator.

I tell people to consider it an instructive and adrenaline-boosting game if they wish, but don't mistake it for entertainment or a fun distraction while out to dinner or running errands. The paces I put myself through as a matter of routine aren't for everyone. Not unless you want to lose what innocence you had left.

Ignorance really is bliss, but in my book looking at the world through the eyes of an opportunistic a-hole is necessary for survival, not to mention peace of mind. Once snakebit by reality, you can't make it unreal, and as I approach Vera Young's apartment, I ask myself what a violent individual would notice and assess about the former brick barracks where she lived. Most glaringly are the perennials in front, tall and plenty thick enough to hide behind.

But there are other ways just as easy if the goal was to keep her on the radar. Driving or jogging by, making sure to change the routine constantly. Or using a high-powered telescopic lens from the concealed vantage point of tree canopies, this time of year the evergreens, the huge spruces and hemlocks. Also fire escapes, rooftops or nearby rental units. Maybe someone was watching, possibly stalking her. If so, why? Are we talking NASA or Pandora related, in other words, professional? Or personal and someone she knew? Or a stranger? What about erotomania?

Or sexual homicide, which is what I fear. It could explain the bleach. For sure, sodium hypochlorite isn't going to do anything helpful to blood, semen, saliva, and it wouldn't be the first time that toxic chemicals have been used by killers in an attempt to eradicate DNA. It's also nothing new for a violent crime to be staged in hopes of throwing the police off track.

Adrienne Shelly, the actress who wrote the movie-to-Broadway hit *Waitress,* is a tragic example that instantly comes to mind. In 2006 she was found hanging by a bedsheet inside her New York apartment shower, the suicide scene faked by the real killer, a construction worker on a job inside her building. There are other terrible stories, and it's been my experience that the most common answer very often and tragically is the obvious one.

The wrong person in the wrong place at

the wrong time. If only certain paths never crossed. More often than not, offenders look for low-hanging fruit, for an easy opportunity.

The sharp stench of bleach wafts up my nose with each wet sound of the mop. The airman in his camo BDUs going about his duty cleaning up. No expression on his young clean-shaven face, no aura of disdain or distaste. As if it's normal to be confronted by blood that's been dripped, smeared, spattered and tracked everywhere inside the break room.

The mop head's long cotton strings leave feathery trails on the gory tile floor, the water in the bucket turning deep pink. Sloshing, slapping wetly, and I'm aware of my rapid shallow breathing, aware of Dick leaning heavily against me, tearing off a strip of adhesive tape. Pain throbbing in my finger to the beat of my pulse, pounding like a bass drum as I worry.

"Please don't let me lose part of me," I silently pray to whatever out there might decide to listen. "I'm sorry for being stupid. I won't ever be again." Not a word of it out loud.

Pain and fear throbbing as I burn with shame, the pungent odor of chlorine, the sounds of water lapping and plashing. Returning me to the river, to the dock at the edge of the yard on the day the world stood still. How my mom describes it. Don't know what Dad has to say, doesn't talk about what he and the police decided. Or what Fran's father had to say when he dropped by the house that night.

I can see the moon shining on wind-ruffled water as if it's yesterday. Walking through newly mown grass, smelling wild onions, the air clean and cool. Turning around at the sound of a car engine, small rocks popping under tires, headlights shining.

Dust billowing from the police cruiser on our driveway, headed to the barn as Mom emerges from it, running toward me, demanding I come inside. Demanding I tell her and Dad what happened, that I explain to them and the police what I'd done.

Yelling and in tears, her long hair down and flying everywhere, as the cop car parked and she clutched me by my shoulders, digging her fingers in. Hugging me so tight I was lifted off the ground.

It would seem Vera wasn't as security minded as she should have been. I can tell that already by her ground-level apartment with no motion sensor lights or alarm system, and you wouldn't have to recognize her silver Lexus on the curb to suspect she's in. All you'd need is to know which apartment is hers, number 110.

You could tuck yourself out of sight behind dense boxwoods and arborvitae. Peering inside her windows to your heart's content in broad daylight or middle of the night, and chances are the neighbors wouldn't notice. Not when they're staying indoors and out of the brutal cold or leaving in droves before a major storm makes landfall. But no matter what, it wouldn't be hard to spy, doesn't matter if the drapes are drawn as they are right now.

The fabric isn't heavy enough to black out the shadows of people moving inside when the lights are on. Someone interested could determine when Vera was home. In which room. And if she were alone. Added to that, the lighting in this well-heeled residential development isn't exactly 400 watt and closely spaced like a prison yard. The graciously spread-out iron lamps I pass are intended for gentle nonintrusive illumination that doesn't ruin the view and keep residents awake.

It's always quite dark around here at night no matter the time of year or weather. But pitch black or high noon, it doesn't matter if there are no eyes and ears. And I suspect there weren't in the greater Fort Monroe area earlier today, based on the empty buildings and parking lots. The low-lying streets and alleyways have been shut down and blocked off with traffic cones and barricades. Sandbags are piled in all the right places to prevent flooding should the monster nor'easter hit dead on, hardly anybody out and about in this neck of the woods.

Folks around here are old hands at life on the water, at going with the flow, taking the good with the bad, and I estimate that at least a third of the peninsula residents drove away long hours ago. We don't need permission or an invitation in this idyllic part of the world that we call home. No official evacuation order is required for the locals to seek higher ground, taking pets and vehicles out of harm's way.

The apartment's front door is unlocked, and walking in, I call out, "Hello, hello!" Not wishing to startle anyone or get shot.

Stopping just inside, I'm instantly aware of the pungent chlorine odor, sharp in my lungs, stinging my eyes. Setting down my bags, I'm pulling the door shut when Fran yells for me to leave it open a crack.

"It's good to get some fresh air circulating now and then." Her voice is muffled as she checks inside the dishwasher on the other side of the apartment, which is two small

rooms with the total square footage of a
cracker box.

17

The kitchen and living area are combined into a single open space, the wide-board heart-of-pine flooring and exposed brick walls going to the 1820s. To the right of the refrigerator is the bedroom, and through the half-open door, I can see a stretcher.

"You won't believe how bloody hot it gets in here." Fran turns my way, pushing up the clear plastic flip-up visor of her full-face respirator, what looks like a stealth-black motorcycle helmet with a Bluetooth-integrated intercom system that makes communicating with each other easy.

"That sounds like a problem I'd like to have." My lips move frozenly, my hands uncooperative as if they belong to someone else.

Crouching, I unzip my equipment bag as Fran lifts a stainless steel knife out of the silverware rack, holding it up to the light.

"Dishwasher wasn't run," she reports

loudly. "Nothing in it except a knife that looks like it has mustard on it."

"Maybe used to make the sandwich left in here," Scottie Ryan offers, busy checking for evidence near the fireplace while Butch Pagan films.

Everyone is in level-A dark-gray chemical suits, and over these go our tactical vests and weapons. Plus, heavy rubber boots, gloves, respirator helmets, and I happen to know from experience that it doesn't take long to get fed up slogging about, sweating profusely and breathing through a charcoal filter while worrying about contaminating evidence.

The smallest task becomes a cumbersome chore when you're insulated in unbreathing synthetic fabrics and rubber, fogging up your visor, and trying to handle delicate forensic tools like measuring devices, thermometers, tweezers, scalpels. But then I've yet to meet a scene that was a vacation, most of them deplorable with no access to food, water or a toilet we can use.

Not to mention filth and critters, extreme cold and heat, sickness and stenches. The list is endless, nothing on it good, and the challenge is to resist difficult distractions. To pay attention when conditions are abysmal. Not letting discomfort get the best of you. Block it out.

Focus. Focus. Focus.

"Okay, that's it." I can't take it anymore, shutting the front door before I get frostbite, putting my respirator on right away so I can better communicate.

"You may not believe it, but in 15 minutes you're going to have sweat running in your eyes," Butch apologizes as I begin taking off my boots. "And the bigger problem's going to be driving home later in sweaty clothes. Even when the hazmat truck gets here, I can decon, but I've got nothing to change into, will have to put on the same sweaty BDUs I got on under this shower curtain I'm wearing right now."

"Or drive home in all of it," I suggest to him. "Which is what I'm going to do."

As he photographs the inside of the fireplace, and from here it looks like a working one but unused. No screen or logs, the andirons bare, and I notice a silver laptop propped up on the antique cast-iron mantel.

"Ditto about putting on sweaty clothes," Fran's voice in my helmet as she opens a cupboard, looking a little bit like a combination of an astronaut and a character in *Avengers: Infinity War.* "Even my socks are wet. But I got to admit, when I went outside to take a few puffs a little while ago? It actually felt good, so comfy I could have taken a nap."

"That's what people say before they die of hypothermia." Leaning against the front door in my stocking feet, I work my feet through the legs of my front-entry protective suit, some 5 pounds of antistatic butyl rubber and a fluoropolymer material with sealed seams that won't leak.

It zips diagonally across the chest like a tactical wetsuit, and has padded shoulders and knees with cleverly placed pockets. Next up are my hazmat boots, more butyl rubber, pull-on with thick tread worthy of a snow tire, and already I'm warming up.

"The fumes in here are worse than they might be because the place is so small, about 800 square feet total, I'm going to guess," Scottie lets me know. "So you really do need all this crap on as miserable as it is, and also for the record going forward? This is my first scene at Fort Monroe, and it's tough in more ways than one."

"Worse than ever under the circumstances," Butch chimes in.

"What they're saying," Fran's voice, "is if you gotta pee, there's no place to go around here. Especially when nothing's open."

"The bushes are always an option," Butch says, "explaining why Scottie keeps toilet

231

paper in the back of her truck."

"It's called thinking ahead and taking care of business."

"That's exactly what it's called. *Taking care of business.*"

"Except not happening in this weather."

"Unless we're talking about freezing your ass off."

"Let's not talk about it at all. I was doing just fine until you had to bring it up."

"When it's this cold, yellow snow hangs around for a while . . ."

On it goes, back and forth, and Butch and Scottie do this a lot, carping and picking at each other like sibling rivals or frustrated lovers. In their late 20s and triathlete strong, they often are confused for brother and sister, with their straw-blond shaggy hair, fair skin and blue eyes. None of which is visible at the moment, just glimpses of their upper faces through scratched plastic as they work side by side like astro-CSIs in all their gear. Taking video and photographs, dusting the coffee table for prints.

As I watch them, I can't help but feel pleased that they're processing the scene the way they've been trained by Fran and me, the same way archaeologists excavate a site of antiquity. Working one layer at a time, preparing for every contingency because there's no going back. A single act of carelessness, and the ancient vase or skull is crushed. And if you don't dust for prints or swab for DNA when you should, chances are it will be too late by the time you realize your mistake.

My rule is to treat every death as a suspicious one, and I look around while pulling on my rubber gloves, scanning for signs of what might have gone on in here not so long ago. Something that might make me think of a burglary gone bad, a home invasion or attack resulting in a struggle. I don't see blood, not anything that strikes me as out of place. But that doesn't mean I'm picking up positive vibes. Because I'm not.

"Jeez Louise, what took you so long?" Fran walks over to me, reopening the front door to the arctic chill. "Not to worry, we've been keeping track of changes in temperature in the bedroom where she's at," indicating the door ajar in the far wall, where I can hear someone moving around.

Hopefully, Tidewater's ace death investigator, Joan Williams, is busy looking at the body and will have something helpful to say by the time I get to her. But that won't be for a while. I know better than to walk in there right now, and it's going to take all of my self-control to resist.

"We've got our forensic bases covered," Fran is saying. "Better to supply a little air-conditioning than have sweat dripping in your eyes and not be able to see what the frick you're doing. This is twice today I've almost gotten heat exhaustion because of you."

"I might understand the tunnel," over my helmet's intercom as I put on my ballistic vest. "But how is this my fault?"

"Somehow that's how it will turn out." Her face is shiny and hot behind plastic, wet ringlets of hair plastered to her forehead, and it's creepy when she talks.

The respirator's filter is twice the size of a hockey puck. Meaning it's impossible for me to see the lower part of Fran's face as I listen to whatever it is she has to say. It's almost as if she's communicating by telepathy, speaking without a mouth, and I find this disconcerting.

"You okay?" Staring at me. "I got a little worried when you weren't answering your phone."

Her blue eyes study me carefully, and I don't look forward to the exchange we're about to have because she won't be happy with my answer.

"Suffice it to say that I was detained

234

unexpectedly and unavoidably," I reply cryptically. "General Melville wanted a ride back to his quarters."

"And why pray tell would *Moby* need you for a ride?" Her pet name for Dick Melville, and not necessarily said playfully or with affection.

Intractably threatened by him, she wouldn't admit in a thousand years that for someone so accomplished and tough, she can be woefully insecure and yes, jealous. In her mind, Dick outranks and outshines her in every way imaginable, and she'll tell you he's another one who thinks he's God's gift. An accusation she makes about a lot of attractive, powerful people, I might add. Including her somewhat estranged husband, Tommy.

And also, Carme. Even at her most humble and gracious self, my sister is going to intimidate a lot of people, especially Fran, and that's the root of the problem. My oldest friend and mentor can't handle that Dick and my sister have all the power. They really do. Not her. Because they have power over me. Enough to prompt me to throw in my lot with them and leave Langley and all involved forever.

Without looking back. Or missing Fran. Or thinking about her again, period. That's the way her phobic mind processes what she perceives as data, at any rate. Doesn't matter what's true or rational. I know this is how she feels, regardless of whether she doesn't say it, denies it or tells me I'm full of crap.

"He wanted me to give him a lift so we could catch up since we'd not seen each other in three years," I find myself explaining to her, on the verge of defensive.

"What about his security detail? What did he do, ditch them?" her voice challenges inside my respirator helmet. "What was so important that he'd go to all the trouble to tell his detail to get lost? I mean, what freakin' 4-star general does that? Makes no sense, in fact sounds kind of suspicious, if you ask me. What did he *really* want?"

"We'll talk about this later." It's not up for debate, and I don't like the innuendo. "Before we do anything else," I point at the pale-blue Tyvek shoe covers over her rubber boots, "I need a few pairs of those. And plenty of gloves. And for you to fill me in on what you know so far."

I intend to gather all the data I can before walking in, no matter how curious I might be. And I *am* curious. Not just a little, but insanely, insatiably, even if I don't let on, don't give the slightest sign of the magnetic

236

force pulling at my attention. It's hard to explain, but I'm tactile and sensuous with an exploratory drive that keeps me from taking another person's word for it, from sitting still and being complacent.

I have to see something for myself. I have to look, hear, taste, touch, and that's the compulsion I'm feeling. It's all I can do to restrain myself from at least catching a glimpse through the open doorway leading into that chlorine-pickled bedroom. Grateful no one, not even Fran, has a clue what's going on inside of me.

It isn't obvious, and I make sure of it. I can't let anybody pick up on my inner match of impulse versus will, each grappling for control and determined to overrule. My parents are always saying that my greatest gift is also my fatal flaw, feeling empathy among other potent emotions. What they're really getting at is the dirty truth that unlike my sister, I'm too sensitive. Too quick to assume responsibility and blame. Too tuned in to everything and everyone.

Too inclined to make it my responsibility to find what's lost and fix what's broken, to encourage and heal, to satisfy and soothe. Don't ask me where such traits came from because I'm not sure I know. Although genetics plays a role. Also growing up the way I did in the shadow of my ambitious overachieving twin who never suffers from self-sacrifice or doubt.

Carme doesn't know what those are, doesn't begin to feel the way I do. Never has, but no big deal. Fortunately, at the age of 28 I'm disciplined by now at resisting the usual temptations, having learned in the military the importance of not giving in to my high-voltage impulses and passions. Before that, during my earliest days of interning, Fran taught me to keep my limbic flares and surges to myself. To quash my reactions and temper my strategies.

Most of all, to sit on my desires, and probably the most overwhelming one bar none when pulling up on a scene of injury or death is to zero in on the human factor first thing. Translated, we're wired to make a beeline to the victim no matter how dead and gone or for how long. Our most primitive instincts compel us to stare, study, circle the mauled or deceased, and by the time we're done, we're not going to be objective and open minded anymore. Certainly not about witnesses and evidence.

Not really about anything, and to show up on a death scene with my mind already made up about what happened is rather much like setting out on a cross-country flight without factoring in airspace regulations and fuel stops. Or having sex before knowing the first thing about someone. Or planning the wedding before getting engaged. In other words, unwise. Yes, stupid. Or as Spock was always saying on *Star Trek,* "Illogical."

Cheating, taking shortcuts, your wish is your reality. Rushing to the coveted prize instead of honestly earning it. Garbage in, garbage out, and the result is as predictable as quantum computing at its worst. The output is changed by the input, and the correct answer depends on who wants to know. Therefore, it's critical what data you take in and when, and to avoid raising questions you're not prepared to ask.

When everything depends on everything else, the more you can observe and preserve in advance, the more objective you're going to be when you finally reach the end goal. Whether it's a rocket launch, the top of Mount Everest or a dead body hanging from a closet door. The purer your method and reasoning, the less likely it is that the great nemesis of precision and fairness will have its way with you. The less likely you'll fall prey to what every self-respecting colleague of mine fears most of all.

Bias.

Which compromises computations and weakens our defenses, leaving us vulnerable to malfunction and destruction. Because the most treacherous enemy is the one you think you know and understand. The one you trust and love. The one whose darkness threatens your very light, the heart and soul of your very power, and you're none the wiser. Your subjectivity, your bias has rendered you blind, deaf and dumb. You see what you want to see instead of what's there.

One of the great ironies is our defenses are knocked out most efficiently by our own personal beliefs and learning, by our own programming and wiring. As Mom used to say, *"We're our own worst enemy."* Bias is masterful at carrying itself convincingly, nimbly, glibly, even lovingly on the legs of the preacher, teacher, colleague, friend, mentor, or worst of all, the significant other or family member.

If you ask me, the kryptonite for all humanity is bigotry, prejudice, us against them. Well-intended people blinded by rivalry and ambition or love and the bonds of blood.

Overpowering and being the decider of who's in and who's out. Dividing people into groups. Making lists and assumptions. Deciding I'm okay and you're not.

18

"I'll tell you what I'm telling everyone." Fran hands me shoe covers and a box of exam gloves, size XL to fit over our cumbersome rubber boots and gloves. "Anybody who comes in here, we need to make sure they're not allergic to bleach or have some preexisting respiratory problem."

"Absolutely," I agree, and already my face is hot inside my helmet.

"Or aren't the sort to fake it, to malinger, right?" she says next.

"How are we supposed to know that, exactly?" I have to ask. "What polygraph are we going to use for laziness and greed?"

"Ha-ha, very funny. I'm just putting it out there in case you have reason to worry about someone coming in here and trying to take advantage of the situation," her voice goes on as if she's hijacked my thoughts. "Everyone's to cover up from head to toe the same way we are. What we don't need is a lawsuit on top of everything else."

"Copy that." Working a pair of nitrile exam gloves over my rubber ones, my hands cold and stiff. "We're very lucky she didn't pick something really awful like hydrofluoric acid. Which there's plenty of where she was working in 1110, and also in the materials labs and so on because some of the scientists use it for etching, metal cleaning."

"I don't get why you'd do any of this to yourself," Fran stares at the bedroom as Joan walks past the doorway, holding a camera. "Me? I'd just take pills. Not that I have enough of anything to do me in. Well, I probably do, but it would hurt like hell, and I'd probably wake up brain damaged." She actually thinks about it for a second. "Never mind, don't want to go there, but I sure wouldn't do what she did."

"*If* she did it." I continue to explain as Fran's attention bats about like a moth, "My point is, considering where she worked, she had easy access to any number of corrosives used in the labs, used in pyrotechnics at the gantry, used for a lot of things. Sulfuric and nitric acid come to mind. And hydrochloric. All of which make chlorine bleach seem like aromatherapy by comparison if your intention is to damage your own dead body and everyone who gets near it."

"We can be grateful for small favors, I guess. Because imagine working around hydrochloric acid. Jeez." Gloves off, Fran is busy scrolling through whatever's landing on her phone. "One thing's for sure, it's going to be a bloody mess to clean up as is. Not literally *bloody.* Most of it not our problem, but how are you supposed to collect evidence with bleach everywhere?"

"Very carefully." I lean against the front door, balancing on one leg at a time, pulling the Tyvek shoe covers over the lower part of my boots. "Also, are you aware that her Lexus is unlocked, the keyless fob in a cup holder on the center console?"

"Say what?" Fran is definitely startled, and I hope she doesn't get defensive next.

"When you were checking out her SUV, did you by chance try the doors?" I ask as diplomatically as I can.

"Like I told you, I looked through the windows with my flashlight because I didn't want to touch anything yet," she answers with an edge.

"I don't blame you, same thing I did. The only reason I tried the doors is because I noticed the fob inside." That's not exactly true but close enough to keep her feathers from getting ruffled, if I'm lucky.

"So, the answer is no, I didn't try them,"

she huffs and puffs, nudging me out of the way. "Gotta keep the air flowing in here. Lord, I hate chlorine, don't think I'll ever go to a swimming pool again."

"I'll make sure not to tell Easton that." As I avoid the frigid air seeping in, images from childhood flashing in my head, Carme and I swimming at Fort Monroe from the time we were old enough to wear water wings.

Which was probably until we were three and got comfortable with our faces in the water. Our parents would bring us out here to Fort Monroe's YMCA when time allowed. But if we were really fortunate, we might get the extra treat of the heated indoor pool at the former Officer's Club. But only when family friends would take us there. Neither Mom nor Dad were members.

"And you didn't notice the key in the cup holder?" I'm going to keep probing even if Fran blows up at me.

"I didn't, and that's kind of weird. Was it hard to see?" She's more baffled than defensive, thank goodness.

"Not with my flashlight," I reply candidly. "It wasn't hard, especially if looking through the window of the driver's door."

"Okay, I don't know why I didn't see it. Obviously, it had to be there if I looked through the windows not even an hour before you did."

I don't say anything, and sincerely hope she's right. Because I'm fast reaching the point of believing there are no hard-and-fast rules, that all bets are off. In a nutshell, nothing's normal about what's going on, and I'm beginning to feel that nothing will be again.

"But how does it make any sense that she would leave her key inside?" Fran gestures toward the bedroom as if Vera Young can hear us. "Unless she was *hoping* her car would get stolen."

"If we're talking suicide, why would she care what happens to it after she's dead?" I reply dubiously.

"Maybe she didn't want someone to have to be responsible for paying out the lease."

"I'm not saying that's impossible, but I have a strong feeling that's not going to be the explanation." I begin to move around, headed to the fireplace, to the plaster-and-exposed-brick wall where a thermostat is mounted, set on 70 degrees Fahrenheit, the actual temperature in the room 61.

I'm digging in my gear bag for a notebook and pen when Fran's cell phone sounds its Spider-Man ringtone, her phone instantly slaving to the Bluetooth intercom.

"Sorry, gotta take it," Fran loudly lets us know. "What's up?" she answers her son, Easton.

"About to have supper . . . ," his tiny voice.

"Well that's good, but you've probably figured out I'm tied up for a while, got a case to deal with. You and Aunt Penny go ahead and eat without me . . ."

The Aunt Penny she references is my mom, whose real name is Jane. She was called Penny as a child because she's so thoughtful, as in "a penny for your thoughts." Or equally apropos, she's like a bad penny, always showing up. So the stories go.

"Well aren't you lucky . . . ," Fran's voice through our respirator helmets' intercom system.

Subjecting us to that special voice she reserves for her Little Mr. Sunshine, as she calls him, especially when he's cranky.

"Make sure you save some for George . . ."

That's my father.

". . . And you'd better leave some mac and cheese for Calli and me, okay? And yes, the fried chicken . . . ," Fran goes on.

I stop by the coffee table, making rough sketches in my notepad, visual prompts that later will help me recall with photographic clarity what I'm seeing as I scan my sur-

246

roundings. Standing on the edge of the braided rug, I jot notes and draw whatever catches my attention. Waiting for what might land on me unexpected, uninvited. Imagining myself as a two-legged spectrum analyzer before I sweep the place with a real one.

I'm curious about signals while already having a good idea about some of what I'll find. Wi-Fi. Cell phones. Radios. Any beacons including the lighthouse on the other side of the moat. No telling what else, but taking into account who this woman was, what she knew, was working on and all the rest? I plan to poke a stick at it, so to speak. See what's invisibly all around us that might be a witness, a snitch, a tattletale.

". . . Well you know what I say to that. No Spider-Man until after supper and homework . . ."

"No fair . . . !" Easton's shrill chirp.

I tune out their phone conversation, letting my intuition run wild before I muddy my cognitive waters with thoughts and deductions that might prove baseless and biased. As I flip pages in my notebook, making comments and sketches, it's obvious the apartment came furnished.

Nothing I'm seeing would be worth moving all the way from Houston, and I've noted similar arrangements in other Fort Monroe rentals. The green corduroy sofa and matching side chair, the nested glass end tables, the walls arranged with prints of Colonial Williamsburg in the snow and similar Virginia themes.

The cherry coffee table is a reproduction, and nothing is on it except an empty bottle of Tsingtao Light beer, and a plate with the remains of a ham sandwich. Wheat pita bread, chopped lettuce, a lot of pico de gallo and mustard, an unusual combo that reminds me of my sister. She thinks everything is improved by salsa fresca, although what I'm looking at doesn't exactly qualify as "fresca" anymore.

Could I smell anything through my charcoal filter, I'd detect the faint foul odor of food turning bad, and I lean closer to the white plate with its several bites of sandwich. Drying and beginning to wilt and rot, the food has been sitting out for a while, several hours at least, possibly giving us additional clues about what went on and when.

For example, one might suppose most people don't start the day with a sandwich and beer. Certainly not NASA-level scientists, but the bigger mystery when contemplating someone facing imminent annihilation is why bother with a last meal at all. I'll never understand fantasizing about what to eat one final time on death row or before committing suicide. I couldn't swallow a bite if my . . . about to say *if my life depended on it,* but I guess that's a bad choice of words under the circumstances.

Not that I can put myself in another mortal's shoes with total accuracy. But it's difficult to imagine staying home from work intending to torture and disfigure yourself with a caustic chemical before committing suicide. Yet at some point in the midst of this it's time for a snack? And further, you've got a hankering for your favorite beer and a sandwich prepared to your liking?

But then again, there's really no playbook for such desperate acts, and believe me, I've heard my share of depressing accounts that on the surface don't make sense. Why go about business as usual while plotting and planning to shoot yourself or jump from a building? Why put on makeup and fix your hair? Why leave a hateful recording blaming everyone? Saying this is what they get while in the same breath promising to slash your throat in the bathtub to minimize the mess?

I can say with great confidence that it's nearly impossible to know why people do what they do. Just when I think there are no more surprises, I get one.

"Have you looked inside the refrigerator yet? Or checked the trash. For other beer bottles, for example?" I ask nobody in particular, my voice and breathing loud inside my helmet.

I walk into the kitchen in all my rubberized and filtered gear, and the shoe covers over my hazmat boots would make papery sounds on the hardwood floor if I could hear them.

"I took a quick glance," Butch's voice as he films away, and I'm starting to get a headache. "A lot of vegan-type stuff like miso soup and tofu. But also normal food."

"Would that include ham?" I inquire pointedly. "Is that what you mean by *normal*?"

"And mustard, fresh salsa, beer," Scottie jumps in. "The pita bread's in a basket next to the stove."

"Anything like that we're going to dust for prints and swab for DNA, just in case," opening the cabinet under the sink, finding the trash. "Or bring into our evidence room, better yet, if justified. That way no one's working in Antarctic drafts and noxious fumes. Or worst of all, these chemical suits." I'm already sweating, and it seems impossible I was all but frozen a few minutes ago.

"You're thinking she's not the one who

made the sandwich," Butch decides, and his eyes look irritated behind scratched plastic, his cheeks red and hot.

"We want to consider all potentials while we've got the chance." I pull out the trash can, lined with a garbage bag and almost full. "But let's do a quick systems check first. How are you guys feeling? Any ill effects?"

They give me a thumbs-up, saying no problem, and no big deal. Reminding me of how much fun it is getting sprayed with oleoresin capsicum and other fiery chemicals as part of our training. Sitting in a gas chamber, you'll learn in a hurry if your respirator isn't seated properly, only making that mistake once. Neither of them has been on a scene like this, none of us has.

I suggest to them that we do the best we can in these unpleasant and hazardous conditions. Not to feel pressured or rushed, and that we'll seal off the apartment when we leave. Other than the hazmat team cleaning up the spill, we'll keep everything exactly as is for as long as needed.

"That way, if we need to get back in because of other information that comes up, we can," I add, fogging up my face shield. "In the meantime, let's collect everything that might be relevant. What about a Walgreens receipt? When I asked about it yesterday, she said she didn't have it with her. That it was here at the apartment."

"If it is, I've not seen it yet," Scottie's voice over the intercom inside my helmet. "I assume the point is to prove she really went to the drugstore on her way home, as she claims in the suicide note."

"If it's really a suicide note, but yes, we need to know if she stopped anywhere at all and what she purchased," I explain.

"Bleach, for example," Butch suggests.

"Right, but where's the bottle?" Scottie brings up that glaring problem again.

"You'll want to go through the trash very carefully." As I watch Fran by the front door, still on her phone, but she has her helmet off now, and we can't hear her. "If you'd rather bring it into the evidence room, as I've said, dealer's choice. But that's what I'd recommend because the conditions in here certainly aren't optimal. I'm sure Fran would agree."

But she's not looking in our direction, fidgeting with her pack of cigarettes and talking to Easton. I can tell she's fitting for a smoke, and that motherhood isn't her favorite thing right about now.

"We're going to want a stat alcohol level

to see if she was drinking beer before she died." I'm going down the list with Scottie and Butch. "And are her stomach contents consistent with a ham sandwich?" I explain, and my interest in what she might have eaten and when go beyond figuring out time of death.

I also have my other thought, not a pleasant one. But if it turns out she died by a hand other than her own, then clearly someone else was inside this apartment with her. Should that turn out to be the case, it's not unheard of for a burglar or killer to raid the victim's refrigerator after the fact, fixing a snack, leaving detritus similar to what I'm seeing on the coffee table.

"Let's package the sandwich, plate and all the fixings in the fridge, anything touched. Including the knife from the dishwasher that might have mustard on it. And the beer bottle comes in," I'm telling Scottie and Butch. "In the off chance the DNA might not be the dead lady's, obviously," as I look around for any sign of a migraine.

19

At a glance, there are no prescription bottles, no over-the-counter medications.

Nothing that might tell me the person living here suffered from sick headaches, the special kind of misery my mom is plagued with from time to time. But I'll have to wait and see what else turns up, and my attention wanders back into the living area. To the small brick fireplace that was coal burning when the barracks were built after the War of 1812.

I'm curious about the laptop computer, wider than the old iron mantel and unsafely propped up. I wonder why it's there. It would seem a strange and perilous place to use a computer or park one. There's no evidence a fire has been built in recent memory, so nobody was standing there for warmth or the sound of crackling logs. Then why not work at the kitchen counter or leave the computer there? Why not the couch?

Or the bed or desk in the other room? I have to wonder if the laptop might have been left conspicuously where it is, perhaps deliberately with first responders in mind. Maybe someone wanted us to notice it and puzzle the way I am. And I stare across the room at Fran leaning against the front door, gloves and respirator off, on the phone with her unhappy 6-year-old son. And I shove up my visor because she has her helmet off.

". . . You're going to do what she tells you, now aren't you?" she's saying to Easton. "Being unpleasant isn't going to help me change my mind, now is it?"

Fran watches everything and all of us. Doesn't matter how out of sorts, agitated or phobic she might get. One makes a huge mistake assuming she misses much, and I catch her eye.

"Have you looked?" I point a bulky gloved finger at the laptop.

She shakes her head no. "Computers and cyber crap are your department, Aggie."

"Thanks for that, Sherlock," I smack her right back.

But Fran seems none the wiser, back to Easton with a sigh, "Okay, okay, but only for tonight. I'll let you skip the *peas,* as long as you tell your aunt Penny *peas* and thank you very much . . ." Shooting me a wink and a thumbs-up in appreciation of her own pun, not a new one, by the way. "Yes, you'll stay there until I'm done just like always. Of course, you won't be by yourself . . ."

"What about you? Either of you look at this yet?" Visor back down, I'm asking Scottie and Butch, and they tell me that as far as they know, the laptop hasn't been touched. "What about the officer who was first on the scene?" I have to make sure.

"Not Scope either," Butch says, and I shrug, having no idea who that is. "Hampton officer Clay Gibbons, he's new. People call him Scope, like the mouthwash. Don't ask me why. A decent cop and cool guy but can't smell anything anymore, as you've gathered. Chicks find him *dreamy.*" Snidely, and it's rather obvious no matter what Butch might say, beneath it all he doesn't like this officer nicknamed Scope.

"Who calls us *chicks* anymore? And you said it. He's *cool* and *dreamy,*" Scottie's voice and gushing sigh. "As in cool and dreamy like fresh mint and getting ready for the prom . . . Maybe explaining the nickname," as she retrieves a fingerprint-dusting kit from the field case.

"Or he can't smell his own bad breath, which is the more likely story," Butch retorts, going at each other again, bickering, fogging up the face shields on their helmets.

Barely listening, I focus on the fireplace, approaching the mantel. Eyeing the computer, recognizing the brand, the profile, a 15 incher, and I'm betting a 4.8 GHz 6-core processor with at least one terabyte of storage. Plus, Thunderbolt ports. Possibly 8th generation depending on how new. Could be fingerprint instead of password protected, which will be a challenge considering what's in the other room.

Under normal circumstances, if push came to shove, I could press the dead woman's finger to the scanner and unlock her computer, her phone and possibly other devices. But she's covered with a caustic chemical, and I can't say with certainty what shape her ridge detail might be in if her skin is bleached, burned and blistered.

And then there's the not-so-small problem of cross-contamination if the *decedent,* possibly a murder victim, starts *touching* things at the scene with *dead* fingers. So to speak. A crazy thought, and imagine that playing out in court. Welcome to the modern world, where the old ways of doing things are irrelevant and all bets are off.

". . . Seriously, he has polyps or something, said he'd been meaning to get the problem looked into," Butch is saying to

Scottie about the officer they call Scope, and I cautiously approach the laptop as if it's a wild animal I might scare off.

Unsure what to make of it because I can't fathom why someone would prop it up on edge, leaning it against the back of the mantel. Say the laptop weighs 2.04 kilograms (4.5 pounds) and falls 1.52 meters (5 feet), the energy at impact will be 30.39 joules (22.4 foot-pounds), I do the math. Not enough to break a bone, but it could crack the display and cause other serious damage.

"Been meaning to, will get around to it, and check's in the mail. You dudes are all alike when it comes to the doctor." Scottie clucks like a chicken over the respirator's intercom, unscrewing the top from a jar of black magnetic powder.

"How do you know what you *can't* smell?" Butch carries on with the verbal tennis match. "How do you know what *isn't*? Or what's *not*? How do you realize how bad something's gotten if you aren't actually *aware*?"

"I don't know, Socrates. To be or not to be stupid is what Scope should start worrying about, plain and simple." Twirling the dusting brush, knocking excess powder into the open jar. "It's called 'go to the damn doctor.' "

"Who are we to talk? We hate the doctor." Butch's gloved hand offers her a roll of lifting tape as he films.

"Don't speak for the both of us, because I *love* my doctor. And my nose works just fine. As does yours, especially when you put it where it doesn't belong."

Standing in front of the fireplace, looking at the computer eye level on the mantel, and I'm really bothered. Words like *staged* and *a gift* float up from my subconscious. And *Come look at me.* That's what I'm sensing. Someone screwing with me. Not just with first responders but specifically with *me.*

"Look, when we first walked in here, the odor practically knocked us over." Scottie dusts an edge of the coffee table, looking for latent prints that might not be Vera Young's. "It's really dangerous if you can't smell anything. What if there's an electrical burning stink and you don't notice? Or carbon monoxide, because that for sure will get you fast. Or smoke? Or a gas leak? Like cyanide gas, God forbid . . . ?"

I don't add to or edit their carping. But if I did, I'd remind them that carbon monoxide is colorless, tasteless, odorless, that's why it's called the invisible killer. And the majority of people, possibly including Scottie, Butch and Fran, can't smell hydrogen cyanide, HCN, which is sufficiently swift and deadly to be used in capital punishment. A terrible way to die, asphyxiating while feeling like you're having a heart attack, as I've heard it described.

It would be helpful to smell such a horror coming should you walk into a place where HCN is leaking or has been left as a trap. But less than 40 percent of the population is genetically capable of smelling what truly is reminiscent of bitter almonds, and I should know. I carry the gene, can smell cyanide, but weirdly my twin sister doesn't and can't.

So much for being identical, but at least I feel confident that HCN isn't what I detected when I first got here and put on my gear. I didn't smell almonds. I'm pretty sure what I smelled was household chlorine bleach.

". . . 'To be or not to be' is Prince Hamlet. Not Socrates." Butch likes to remind us he has a master's degree in English literature.

"Hate to break this up," I interrupt. "But what did this Officer Gibbons — Scope as you call him — actually say to one or both of you directly? What did he actually observe when he tried the front door, found it conveniently unlocked and walked into the apartment?"

"He said he wasn't aware of an odor, for reasons already discussed. He noticed his eyes and lungs felt irritated, but he's also allergic to dust." Butch looks at me through scratched plastic, his own eyes watery blue on the way to bloodshot. "He made it as far as the bedroom doorway, and when he saw the body, that was it. He got on his radio and was out of here."

"The computer was on the mantel when you arrived, just like it is right now?" I ask that next, and I'm assured the answer is affirmative. "What about Scope? Any reason to think he might have touched it?" As I pick up the laptop in my double-gloved hands.

"From what I understand, he didn't touch anything." Scottie centers a section of tape over a white paper card.

From where I stand, I can see the blackened ridge detail. The inverted tent and whorl of a latent print she's lifted from the coffee table.

"I mean, I asked him point blank exactly what he did when he was in here," she adds.

"He said he got as far as the bedroom

door and called for assistance," Butch confirms.

"Was the door open or shut when he got here?" I inquire.

"Partially open, pretty much the way it looks now."

After that Scope waited in his cruiser, keeping the scene, the perimeter secure until backup arrived, I'm told over my helmet's intercom. In other words, until *we* got here. NASA special agents taking care of their own, in this instance, an outside contractor who reported her badge stolen yesterday and now is suspiciously dead.

"He said he didn't see anything weird and nobody in the area," Scottie labels the card, sealing it inside a clear plastic bag, then labeling that too.

"I'm going to need butcher paper, something to place under the computer so I can take a quick look before we package it to bring in," as I stand in the kitchen, holding the laptop, having no safe place to set it down without risk of contamination.

"Coming up." Scottie walks to the open scene case on the floor, out of traffic, in a corner. "I have a feeling the suicide note is on the laptop," her voice in my head.

"Why would you think that?"

"Because it's printed, and she has a

printer in the bedroom," she explains while Butch changes the batteries in one of his cameras. "Printed on plain white paper in 14 pitch. Arial font. Bold and in all caps."

"I guess someone wanted our attention. And they've got it," I decide, and I can see Joan passing by the bedroom doorway again, covered up in a chemical suit and full-face respirator helmet like the rest of us.

But she's not in body armor, doesn't wear a gun, a Taser, not even pepper spray or a radio, and I'm reminded of the vulnerability of death investigators and other frontline responders. At a crime scene, most people would assume Joan's a cop like the rest of us, yet she has no means of defending herself or anyone else. She couldn't even get on the air and call in a mayday.

"Gloves clean?" I ask Scottie as she covers the counter with a swath of white paper.

"New pair." She holds up her hands to show me.

"Excellent." I set down the laptop, and Butch is ready with the video camera.

They watch me lift up the computer's silvery metal cover, witnessing in real time the look on my face and almost profanity that rushes out of my mouth.

"Holy sh . . . !" Stunned by what was

closed inside, out of sight, sandwiched between the small display and keyboard.

20

"Whoa!" and "No way!" are what Scottie and Butch have to say about the NASA Langley ID smartcard and its Pandora Space Systems lanyard.

"Vera Young's badge that she called us about yesterday," I explain, and I almost can't believe it. "Obviously, not stolen or even lost, it would seem. And this very minute I might be just as baffled as you are."

"Unless she wanted us to find it," Scottie offers, the three of us talking over the intercom. "Maybe she was trying to tell us something."

"Or someone is," I reply darkly, getting more unsettled the more we find.

"If so, what? That she was mentally ill?" Butch doesn't say it unkindly. "Because that's the first thing that comes to mind."

"I wouldn't have thought so after talking to her," I point out. "When I questioned her yesterday about her badge, she seemed

265

agitated, frustrated, slightly defensive, et cetera. But not unstable, and when you consider the work she was involved in, I doubt Pandora would have sent her here if there was a question about her mental health."

"Well, there's something irrational about all this," Butch maintains.

"I suppose that depends on your definition of *irrational*," I reply as I think of the unlocked SUV with the key inside, the unlocked front door that allowed an officer to enter, and now the laptop with no password or fingerprint required. "Maybe to somebody what we're finding makes sense."

"Not to me so far." Butch has out another camera, begins taking photographs in situ of the badge and lanyard on top of clean white paper.

Probably the best thing is to process for prints and DNA back at our headquarters, I suggest. But the bigger question I raise is whether the smartcard might have been used anywhere it shouldn't have been, especially while it was supposedly inactive.

"Yeah, don't ask me what happened there," Scottie says. "I promise I inactivated it the minute she called us yesterday late afternoon to report it stolen. But I've searched the security database, and the ID number originally assigned to her hasn't come up anywhere since last night."

"When she used it to return to Langley, to Building 1110," I presume, and she confirms as I think about what else she just said:

"... *The ID number originally assigned to her hasn't come up anywhere since last night.*"

The word *assigned* jumps out. It's all too easy to forget that passwords, identification codes and numbers, and even radio frequency bands are assigned by humans who decide, for example, that 154.4075 should be for local police, fire and rescue. If the frequency band is for a radio station, the Federal Communications Commission (FCC) decides the call sign, such as the Howard Stern show.

It has two home frequencies on Sirius XM Radio, Howard 100 and Howard 101. Even the stars and planets have names and numbers that we decide. Kepler-186f, Gliese 581g, HD 40307g, Tau Ceti e, to name a few exoplanets light-years from here that might be earthlike, possibly habitable, and I'm reminded there are creative ways someone might try to outsmart NASA's security system.

"I'm going to take a look at the metadata when I get a chance," I let everyone know, and I have a hunch that I don't want to explore out loud at the moment.

That if someone knew what he or she was doing and could hack into our security system, this person could have changed Vera Young's ID number to something else that wouldn't come back to Vera had her card been used unlawfully. Especially if it's a number that's almost identical. One digit off, and the search will come back empty handed.

"From what I can gather from the system," Scottie is explaining, "Vera Young's card was swiped at 9:05 yesterday morning when she entered Building 1110 for work, and it would seem that was the last time it was used anywhere on campus. Which is consistent with what she said, I believe? That when she tried to reenter the guard gate much later in the day, she realized her badge was gone. Forcing her to get a temporary one."

"Haven't seen a temporary one anywhere, by the way," Butch says.

"But other than early last night, it would seem she didn't use it at all." Peering at me through her helmet's visor, Scottie's face is bright red, sweat beaded on her forehead. "At least that should give you some peace of mind, right?"

It doesn't. I'm not about to trust anything

and know there are other ways to outsmart the system. Just as there are ways to have signals and frequencies that are almost identical to those around them, making it harder to find an intruder. If I had peace of mind to begin with, I don't now, and it feels that I never will again.

"I hate to sound naive, but is it possible she simply misplaced her badge?" Butch is helping label latent fingerprint cards, the Sharpie awkward in his layers of gloves.

"Not if she used her laptop to print a suicide note," Scottie makes a good point. "It would seem she might have known by then that her badge hadn't really been stolen or lost. That it wasn't gone, after all."

"Unless her complaint was a bald lie off the bat." Fran is off the phone and back on the intercom, making her way toward us as I tap-tap the laptop's return key, the display blinking out of sleep mode.

"And to quote *Alice in Wonderland,* things are only getting curiouser and curiouser," I let everyone know. "Her computer isn't password protected."

"Oh wow," Butch and Scottie in unison, and the joke is if both of them were women, they'd have their periods at the same time.

"Seriously? What NASA contractor wouldn't password protect his or her every device, most of all a laptop?" I add.

"None," Fran pipes up as she reaches us. "They might lose their car in the parking lot or not know their own phone number. Or leave the SIPRNet room door wide open. But not to password protect their own computer? That I'd never expect."

"It looks like the exact same note that was printed and left in the bedroom." Scottie bends close, studying the file open on the display, Vera Young's alleged last words right there:

To Whom It Should Concern

It was quite the great ride until I was placed on a wall and no matter which way I went, I was going to fall.

Nothing can put me back together again. Soon enough you'll understand how it is that someone can reach the existential place of no way in or out. And do the unthinkable. And be sorry and not.

Please tell my sister that I won't miss her, and she's been right about me all along. Sisters always know best, and mine would be the first to say that I've earned what I'm about to get.

I wish I felt regret but it would seem that code isn't in my software anymore.

■ ■ ■ ■

It ends with *"Goodbye for now,"* yet another peculiar thing to say in a so-called suicide note.

As if we'll hear more from its author — or someone — at a later date, which makes little or no sense if that person was about to hang herself. It will be helpful to check the time stamp to see when the file was created and last saved. But I'm not going to know that at a glance without changing the metadata by making keystrokes. Or worse, causing a problem with the evidence itself.

The file name at the top of the screen is "Document 2," which is generic and typically generated by the software if the user hasn't saved the file and named it yet. It occurs to me with a spike of alarm that the note might not have been saved, and that would be unfortunate if it wasn't, to say the least. Good luck explaining that in court.

"Rather cryptic and sort of ominous," Scottie says as we look at the laptop's display, at the note open on it while Butch films as if making a documentary.

"Not *rather* or *sort of*," I reply. "It sounds threatening. 'Soon enough you'll understand how someone can reach this point,' " I

271

paraphrase. "That sounds like something bad is on the way."

"Something bad *was* on the way, that's for sure." Fran hovers by the front door with her cigarettes out, thinking about another hit or two. "Something bad enough that she had to douse herself with bleach and take her own life, if a suicide is what we're dealing with. I'm taking a quick 10-27." Helmet off, she steps outside, and I don't blame her, as hot and bleary eyed as I'm getting.

"Truth be told, how do we know the dead lady wrote this as opposed to someone else doing it to cover up a homicide?" Scottie says to Butch and me, the three of us in the kitchen.

"At the moment, we don't know that at all," I agree, tearing off strips of red evidence tape.

"Especially since it would seem a password wasn't needed to access the computer, which was in plain view on the mantel." Scottie helps me seal the top of the trash bag before transporting it to our evidence room.

The laptop needs to be packaged, but first I've got to make sure the note was saved, and I find out in short order that it was when it was created at 3:38 p.m. today. The exact time the motion detector was tripped in the Yellow Submarine airlock, and I go still inside, listening to myself breathe as sweat drips into my eyes.

Contemplating the bizarre thought that at the very instant someone clicked on "Save," an airlock detector in 1111-A interrupted my briefing at Langley headquarters by sending an alert to my phone.

Just one more oddity in a pileup of them, and I swap out my gloves and shoe covers, dropping the used ones in a red biohazard bag I've placed on the counter. Making sure I don't cross-contaminate by tracking anything from the living area into the bedroom.

Making sure my respirator is defogged and seated properly, the filter working fine. Determined not to make a mistake right about now, and it would be all too easy, my underlying mood having gone from unsettled to wide-open paranoid.

Focus. Focus. Focus.

Rubbing my finger and my thumb. Small circles, rubbing and rubbing, as if I can feel the scar through my layers of gloves.

"Why would you leave Carme?" Mom crying hysterically. "Why would you do such a thing?"

Demanding an answer and I don't know the question.

"She told me to, Mama." Terror stricken with

no idea what's wrong.

"But why would you leave without her!"

"She told me to get a ride with the people we know from church. The Powells."

"Why?"

"I don't know! But that's what I did." While the Hampton uniformed officer watches, waiting by his car, waiting to haul me away.

"Then where have you been all this time?"

I try to make her understand it wasn't my fault. The Powells took their boat to the pool today. Tying up at the marina at the Officer's Club. Giving me a ride back, the water as flat as glass, they said. Racing around. Dropping me at our dock after dark and late for supper. It wasn't my fault, I keep saying, as frightened and dismayed as I've ever been.

"You left your sister, so it is your fault!"

"She told me to. She didn't want me there!"

"That's no excuse!"

I stop in the doorway. Waiting. Not moving a muscle at first. Not to jot a note or sketch what's strung up on the closet door like a life-size Halloween doll, eyes bugging, tongue sticking out as if trying to scare us.

I'm suffocating hot in my chemical suit, full-face respirator, ballistic vest and tactical holster that includes extra ammunition magazines, handcuffs and Mace. Also, my radio, the volume turned off, only Fran taking calls while we're in here with everything slaved to the Bluetooth intercom sounding over tiny speakers inside our helmets. Probably about 20 extra pounds of gear, and for the second time today, even my scalp is sweating as I do my best to shut out Fran several feet behind me in the living room.

She's going back and forth with dispatch and the hazmat team, her big voice inside everybody's heads each time she transmits.

". . . While we're dealing with the 10-15, that's going to be best," she's saying cryptically, using the code for *chemical leak* instead of *suspicious death,* never sure who's listening.

"10-4, Alpha 3. 10-23 until you clear." Dispatch lets her know that the team is ready and on standby.

"Copy that."

Not so much as an allusion to the 10-14, the 10-31 or 10-32, all unique to NASA. As their enforcement agents we have the same problems other departments do, but all sorts of unusual risks too. Including police calls relating to *contractor personnel* (the dead woman), an *unlocked door* (her SUV) and *unsecured classified information* (her unprotected laptop).

Just to mention a few of our 10 codes, but

anybody monitoring us isn't going to pick up much beyond our 10-16 at this 10-20, our *special building check* at this *location.* Nothing comes across as urgent or sensational, Fran an old pro at keeping critical information off the air, her voice as cool and smooth as polished steel.

"All right, without a 10-27 I'd estimate 2200 hours, maybe a little longer." She's letting dispatch, the hazmat team know when we expect to wrap up the scene and remove the body.

Without saying there's a body, of course. Without divulging anything important, and I detect her moving closer to me, feel her aggressive energy, can almost hear the swishing of her chemical suit, the slippery whisper of her Tyvek shoe covers over hardwood. Then she's next to me in the doorway, and we're shoulder to shoulder like Jedi wannabes in our gunpowder-gray tactical chem suits, helmets and weapons.

"Guess who's on the way?" her voice sounds breathily over the intercom, talking to me while Scottie, Butch and Joan listen.

"Uh-oh," I reply. "I've got a feeling it's not Santa Claus making the rounds three weeks early."

"I have it on good authority that some TV news crew is headed here," Fran says, both

276

of us watching Joan as she sorts through her field case in the bedroom's north corner. "Therefore, when we leave and have to decon, we'll be sitting ducks because it's not like we can jump in our cars and haul ass out of here."

"Wonder how anybody found out," Scottie's voice from the living room.

"Let's hope it's not Mason Dixon," I say as he pops into my mind.

"Nope, it's not Calendar Boy. Some local affiliate, and I don't want to see any of us on the 11 o'clock news," Fran's about to have a fit. "But we've got to shower in the trailer first. Every last one of us has to, and nothing's to stop some local news crew from running their cameras and trying to get into our business. Or making us look stupid, and most of all don't let anyone piss you off."

"Best thing is to ignore them," Joan's response as she removes the wrapper from a pair of disposable plastic tweezers.

21

In her late 50s, her face weathered by her love of the sun, she has shoulder-length honey-blonde hair I almost never see as it's up under a cap or tied back when death calls.

Joan will tell you she's a battle-scarred warhorse who's seen it all, including (I might add) her share of men she's married, divorced, dated, lived with and everything in between. But despite her easygoing disposition, I can tell she's unhappy with this case, what she'd call a lose-lose. One of those where nothing you do will turn out right. Because it's feeling like that even to me.

It's feeling weird. It's feeling wrong. Everywhere I look, I'm getting conflicting information.

"As soon as Scottie and Butch are done in there wrapping up the laptop and every-thing, I think they should head out so we don't have a queue at the trailer," Fran's voice in my helmet. "Imagine getting that on film, all of us standing outside in these Gumby suits while we wait to shower."

"Sounds like a plan," I agree. "We can help Joan with whatever's needed in here and keep out of the television crosshairs."

"What I want to know is how the hell did what we're doing get out?" Fran is none too subtle when she smells a rat.

That's how she puts it when deciding someone has loose lips or is an out-and-out snitch. Someone who leaked that we're crawling over a death scene at Fort Monroe, possibly a homicide, at least this is what she's implying, and if an aerospace contractor working at NASA was murdered, it will be huge news. That's for sure, and I continue doing a high recon of the bedroom. Not moving from the doorway, looking at the closet in the far wall, at Vera Young hanging against the shut door.

Her bare feet brush the pine floor, wide board and old, stripped of its yellowish color where a corrosive liquid has splashed, trickled and pooled. When the air stirs or Joan walks past, the body moves slightly, creepily, grotesquely, and it doesn't take a cyber ninja or forensic pathologist to determine that a computer cable was the weapon of choice. Vera's or someone else's, the engineering eerily recognizable to me.

Or maybe it would be better to say that the way the thin white cord has been wrapped around her neck and run over the top and bottom of the shut closet door is a configuration that fires curiosity shaded by an uneasy familiarity. Bringing to mind bent-pipe telemetry, where a signal sent from the ground and up to a satellite is then bounced back down to another location somewhere on the planet.

Similar to what we'll do here at Langley when we link to Ames before a bad storm hits. And as I look at the deadly rigging, I'm not seeing how she could have done this to herself. I'm not sure she or anyone physically could or would, and once again, where's the container that held the chemical?

"Not here it would seem," I confirm with Joan as I move away from the doorway. "And at a glance it appears that the cord around her neck goes with the laptop from the fireplace mantel. I'm not seeing a charger anywhere else."

"Seems she could have found a simpler way to hang herself, assuming she did it." Joan opens another field case, this one packed with forensic crime lights. "Why so elaborate?"

I don't offer an answer, and as is often true in tragic cases, we may never discover the why. But what I do know unequivocally is that the mechanism of Vera Young's death is just plain sloppy. Way too sloppy for someone who knows how to garrote, to dispatch a target instantly, silently, the way we're taught in special ops. There should be only one furrow around the neck, made by a ligature that's approximately .375 centimeters, or less than .15 inches in diameter.

Or something slightly thinner than heavy twine or a clothesline, leaving a non-angled furrow in front and on the sides, with sparing or no damage at the back of the neck. There should be no petechiae, none of the pinpoint hemorrhages caused by the cord being tightened and released as the victim struggles. What I'm seeing is typically associated with manual strangulation. And that's certainly not what this is either.

As if two totally different assailants are involved.

One precise enough to rig up the cable on the door. And another who's violent and vengeful, because that's what I'm feeling as I stand here. I'm picking up the emotion of the scene, which is both clinical and enraged. Both precise and out of control. Both coldly calculated and hateful, nothing computing the way it should. And I strongly sense that what I'm seeing is what I'm meant to, but why and who? What am I being told?

I watch Joan return to the closet, flicking on what looks like a small black flashlight with a purple lens. She begins painting ultraviolet light over the body and the area around it, looking for subtle evidence. Particles and fibers that fluoresce in different intensities when the phosphors in them are excited by UV radiation.

"You thinking the bleach was poured on her after she was strung up?" Joan's voice in my helmet as she glances at me. "Because that's what I'm thinking."

"Agreed," I answer her over the voice-activated intercom. "I've got no reason to think it was poured in some other area of the house. No visible drips or splashes of bleach or anything similar between the closet in here and whatever trash receptacle she might have used."

"And had she been moving around, she would have been dripping."

"She would have left a trail," I reply. "And I'm not seeing anything like that."

"I think it was done right here," Joan returns to her field case, out of the way on top of a folded disposable sheet in the corner. "And you're right, it's not like bleach or some other caustic chemical was rained down from the heavens on top of her head. So, where's the container it was in? I have to say, I don't like where this is headed."

"Me either." An understatement as I crouch by the bed, turning on my flashlight. "On that note, how are we doing for false positives? We should be okay with chlorine bleach unless luminol is involved, and we won't be using that."

"No reason to," Joan agrees as I shine my flashlight under the bed. "I'm not seeing any injuries that make me think we're looking for blood someone might have tried to clean up. No problem with false positives, not all that much lighting up. And for what it's worth, she dyed her hair. When you get up close, you can see dull areas of graying from the chemical, probably bleach messing up the cuticles and removing the dye."

"A couple banker's boxes and a lot of dust bunnies," I let Joan know what's under the bed, getting off my knees, standing up. "And there was no gray in her hair when I interviewed her yesterday."

I wander toward the dresser, on top of it the printer and a mobile phone. Noting the wastepaper basket nearby, no bleach bottle in it, while Joan deliberates over how to collect fibers lighting up on the dead woman's sweatpants. Getting closer, I study the computer cable looped twice around her badly bruised neck, and from there running tautly straight up and down, from the bottom to the top of the door, disappearing on the other side.

I calculate the white cord would have to be at least 20 feet long. It's probably tied to the inner doorknob. Or maybe the clothes rod. Perhaps a coat hook screwed into the wall. Something sturdy enough to bear more than 100 pounds. Not your typical leather belt or one from a bathrobe, but a mechanically efficient way to relieve suffering or solve a problem. Except I don't believe for a minute she did this to herself.

Impossible to figure how this petite 54-year-old woman could set up such a horrific contraption before shutting the closet door on her own existence. I try to imagine her on fire with a toxic chemical like bleach while feeling the roaring pressure of the cord around her neck compressing the major blood vessels. What I'm seeing doesn't at all jibe with that. In fact, I'm fast concluding she was dead when she was strung up like a spider in its own web.

Had she been alive when that closet door was shut on her life, I would expect evidence of freneticism, of panic. I would bet on her thrashing and struggling like mad, digging her own fingernails into her neck, desperate to free herself. I see signs of no such thing, but what I do get loud and clear is an intentionality that's mocking and loathing. Not her energy but someone else's directed at her, I can't help but think as I take in the brownish ribbons and splotches, the burn pattern showing the position she was in when the chemical was poured over her head.

Running down her arms and torso. Soaking her sweatpants and sports bra, bleaching them pink in swaths. Splashing on her feet and the floor around the closet door.

The whites of her eyes are blood-red from pinpoint hemorrhages caused by the pressure of the thin cord digging into her flesh and partially occluding the carotid and jugular.

"Is it just me, or does she have an unusual amount of bruising?" I reiterate to Joan, because I want to be sure I'm right. "It's been my experience in working suicidal hangings that the ligature mark is single and angled up toward the ears. With little or no contusion."

"Whereas in a garroting," Joan adds, nodding, "there's little or no angle because the killer's standing behind the victim, pulling hard from a more level position."

"Right. Leaving a rather horizontal dry furrow but not all this black-and-blue contusion," I add. "And typically, there's little or no hemorrhage in the eyes. It's more like she was manually strangled. Or garroted really, really sloppily as she tried to pull and squirm away, causing the cord to slip several times, possibly explaining why she looks like that."

"I'm thinking the same thing, except I'm not seeing any signs of a struggle," Joan's voice comes back. "No scratches on her hands and arms, no other obvious injuries. I wouldn't expect the petechiae if she's a suicide, but I guess it depends on what happened once she had the cord ready to go, and boom! She pulls the closet door shut, triggering whatever contraption she or someone cooked up that lifted her partially off the floor."

"Reminds me of what we call a bent pipe. And I'll just keep saying it, Joan. No way she did this to herself."

"*Bent pipe.* Ummmm . . . ? That's a snowboarding term maybe . . . ?"

"Telemetry. Pulleys and levers, things slingshotting up and down, bouncing off satellites and back to earth. Engineering, in other words," I summarize.

"Okay, over my head, but even if she could have done this to herself, would it cause the bruising we're seeing?" Joan leans so close to the body she could kiss it.

"No way," I repeat.

Not in the usual suicidal hanging for the simple reason that having a blood pressure is necessary for blood to leak out of damaged vessels into surrounding tissue, causing the site of injury to bruise. That requires the heart to continue pumping, meaning you have to be alive. And the longer the heart beats and blood circulates, the more dramatic the swelling and discoloration.

"She shouldn't look like this if for no other reason than she shouldn't have survived very long. Not that I'm the end-all when it comes to experts," I explain to Joan as we discuss and debate over our helmets' Bluetooth intercoms.

Not looking at each other necessarily or seeing our mouths move, as we play out the mechanism of death. In a normal garroting or hanging, once the ligature completely compresses major blood vessels in the neck, the victim would become hypoxic within seconds. As the oxygen continues to be cut off from the brain, he or she will pass out and within minutes be dead. But such a scenario wouldn't account for the furrows and dramatic dark discoloration, Vera Young's neck Prussian blue and black in places like a thunderhead.

"If she were alive when a caustic chemical was poured over her, I can only imagine her panic and pain," I explain. "She should have flailed and fought like crazy and screamed bloody murder."

"I don't know," Joan's voice in my head, "it's more likely she was already dead by then, and for her sake I hope so."

"That's what I think too," and I again bring up the missing bleach bottle or container.

It should be near the body, and there has to be a logical answer why that's not the case. For that matter, there has to be a sensible explanation for why her SUV was unlocked with the key inside. What about her alleged stolen badge turning up with an alleged suicide note concealed by a laptop that's not password protected? Why was her apartment unlocked? Did she intend to make it easy for her body to be found? Or did someone else intend it?

Who?

Such questions click against my awareness like freezing rain, like bugs batting against the screen on a Virginia spring evening. Noisily distracting and nonstop as I move about with my handheld analyzer, breathing through the charcoal filter, nothing making much sense. But it never does when someone you meet is alive one day, dead the next, and not peacefully or prettily.

Her eyes stare blindly from a purplish-suffused face, tongue protruding as if she's angry and spiteful. Hardly recognizable as I compare her to the woman I talked to yesterday. Words like *small* and *fragile* come to mind, and also *haunted*. During the 45-some minutes I was with her, she ranged from upset and spooked, to haughty and irritated, to entitled and humble, laced with defensiveness and apologies. And finally, bored, her aura a vibrant hot mess of unsettledness, paranoia, resentment and wounded pride.

I found her defiant and obstinate, but charming when she wanted to be. I knew the instant I sat down with her that she was scheming, genuinely arrogant. And quite vain, not a trace of gray in her short dark hair, wearing pricey designer glasses that I don't see anywhere. Her pantsuit was dark blue with a red-striped blouse, the heels of her black leather Prada boots impractical for test bed and hot-bench work in a lab.

Unlike her younger team members in jeans and wrinkled shirts, she seemed more their unwilling and precious superior than a peer. In summary, I wouldn't call the woman I met yesterday pretty but rather attractive in a cold smug way. Not the sort to kill herself while dressed in nothing more than gray sweatpants and a sports bra, the dye bleached out of her graying hair.

An unexpected indignity if you're going to take your own life publicly, gruesomely, it flashes in my thoughts like a beacon nonstop.

Not what happened.

I suppose we're to accept this was part of a suicidal ritual.

Not what happened.

To degrade and punish herself.

Somebody else did the punishing.

It wouldn't have required much if you're reasonably strong and have the advantage of surprise. Especially if the victim had no reason to doubt the person and see anything so hideous coming.

Someone she knew very well.

All she'd have to do is turn her back on the person for a minute, and I imagine someone attacking her from behind, pulling the ligature tight, instantly compressing the major blood vessels in her neck. I estimate Vera to be about 5 foot 3, weighing at most 120 pounds, petite with very little musculature, not necessarily much of a physical match for whoever might want to overpower her.

Including another female.

But that doesn't mean that her assailant didn't lose control of her. Doesn't mean Vera didn't try to free herself even if we see no signs of it yet. And I point out that she has moderately long fingernails, and were she attacked, it's possible the assailant has scratches.

"I'll get the usual fingernail scrapings and clippings during the autopsy," Joan replies. "And that's going to come around way too early with the way this night is going. I'll probably just crash at the office. I'm going to be up and busy dealing with her. It's even possible they might decide to take care of her tonight."

"To make sure the bleach doesn't continue to do its damage," I assume.

"Yeah, I don't want her in the cooler all night with that stuff all over her. But I can't wash her unless I have permission from the chief, who's out of the country at the moment, and I doubt she'd agree to it. If one of the forensic paths doesn't whip out the hose and do the rinsing, it will be used against us in court. Which is plain stupid. All because I don't have *doctor* in front of my name?"

"Well I do, and I hate being called Dr. Chase. It just means strangers on elevators, planes and trains, or Uber drivers and waiters volunteer their health problems and complaints to me."

"You're also not an MD. And MDs *make sure* you know it, right?" Joan's voice edged in snarkiness, sounding inside my helmet. "So, imagine if you also don't have a PhD."

"I'd rather you work hard and always ask why," I tell her as I step back into the living room.

Not seeing anyone as I swap out soiled exam gloves for new ones while Joan checks the bedroom's ambient temperature again. Just the two of us in here now, Butch and Scottie having left for the hazmat trailer, and Fran has ducked outside again, to do what I don't know.

Possibly to smoke and talk as she's gotten increasingly agitated, and I can tell she's had enough. Constantly on her phone and radio, exam gloves off and on, face visor up and down as she storms around. And whatever is going on, it has her attention in a

292

chokehold and her knickers in a knot.

"Just so you know," Joan holds up the thermometer, squinting at it, "when I first got here, the temp in this room was 70 degrees. Suggesting that's what it was until we started opening the front door. She should be cooling down a little more rapidly but not much."

"And what's the temp in here now?"

"About 67, her core body temp was 86 a few minutes ago, which we'll factor into the equation. Slender and barely dressed, she's going to cool more rapidly. I think we can make a pretty good estimate based on heat loss."

"About 12 degrees . . . ," and I begin to calculate. "Hmmmm. That's more than I would have guessed if she died late this afternoon. In other words, soon after the alleged suicide note was saved at 3:38 p.m."

"Do you think she wrote it?" Joan's wary eyes behind her plastic visor. "Because if she didn't . . . ?"

"I know. Who did?" I agree. "Who the heck are we dealing with?"

"Not someone I'd want to mess with," her uneasy voice in my head. "That's for sure."

22

The rule of thumb is a dead body will cool approximately 1.5 degrees Fahrenheit per hour, stabilizing when it reaches the same temperature as its surroundings. But this isn't an exact science, and many factors can cause misleading variations and anomalies if one is uninitiated and not exceedingly careful.

"Whatever originally happened here, somebody's rearranged things, mucked it up. That's my opinion and I'm sticking to it," Joan decides as I move my spectrum analyzer's antenna around, watching the display. "In the first place, I'm all but certain she's been dead longer than we're supposed to think . . ."

"Supposed to think?" Fran is suddenly in the doorway as if beamed in, face visor down and gloves back on, bringing to mind an ill-tempered Klingon. "Now we're talking about somebody who's *trying* to make

us *think* stuff? We've gone from a suicide to Jack the Ripper? From 'goodbye cruel world' to 'catch me if you can'?"

"The file on the laptop was created at 3:38 p.m.," I remind her, but it doesn't seem to sink in.

"And?"

"And that's the exact same time the alert sounded on my phone while we were doing the briefing at headquarters this afternoon . . ."

"Oh crap, I did *not* make that connection." Her eyes are glassy, her upper face slick with sweat behind plastic. "Okay, I admit that's screwed up."

"Therefore, if the note was saved almost 4 hours ago," I continue as it's getting close to 8:00 p.m., "then that may conflict with the time of death based on her postmortem artifacts. Am I in the ballpark, Joan? Does she look like she's been dead less than 4 hours?"

"Well, admittedly it's hard to say because of the bleach and everything else," she answers. "But if I had to guess, I'd say she's been dead at least 6 hours. And if so, then she couldn't have written the suicide note. Unless she was undead for a moment. Or the time stamp on the file has been altered somehow."

I continue sweeping the bedroom with my divining rod, my magic wand, sniffing out electromagnetic energy, looking for band-widths occupied by signals that could have crept in from anywhere. Perhaps rogues uninvited but unintentional. Or deliberately invasive and unwelcome. Mostly what I'm detecting is what I'd expect when hunting down electromagnetic energy streaking through time and space at the speed of light.

It's all around us, except normally we can't see it. Or hear a sound. Not without a technical way to snag such signals, and if my sniffer is my fly rod, then the fish are biting like mad. Hand over fist I'm catching the amplitudes and frequencies of x-rays and optical light, in addition to micro-, radio and gamma waves. *How many angels can dance on the head of a pin?* My NASA educator mom's favorite medieval quote about having faith in the unseen.

Just because it's not right in front of you doesn't mean it isn't. Just because it isn't there doesn't mean it's not. She would say such things during science homework ses-sions, assigning exhausting hypotheticals to my sister and me. If a housefly is buzzing about 4.3 kilometers per hour (2.7 mph) inside a jet moving at 515 knots (592 mph), how fast is the fly flying? Is the fly flying the speed of the jet? What about the passengers who are seated? Is the fly moving at a different speed from any of them?

Brain scramblers like that since the time I was out of diapers. For as far back as I can go, our parents have explained to Carme and me that to be in touch with the spectral world is not so different from viewing the visible one through a microscope. It's not for everyone. Not even for most. Take germs for example. Or bacteria. Would you really want to see everything that's on your person, food, pillows, toothbrush, the hand you just shook, the hot date's tongue in your mouth?

Would we choose to visualize everything around and in us, and the answer is no. I daresay that most people today aren't so different from those in the 17th century when scientific virtuoso Robert Hooke wrote his runaway bestseller on the microscope, *Micrographia.* Including foldout illustrations of such horrors as a flea, which prior to this had been felt more than seen in the straw and bed linens, on livestock and family pets.

The Bubonic-causing devil wasn't something everybody cared to meet face to face. Only those socially and personally unbothered who couldn't put down Hooke's book, sitting up at night enjoying a good fright that in modern times would have been turned into a franchise of horror films, no doubt. It's a shame nothing like that would be popular anymore. Hooke wouldn't top the bestseller lists today, would be considered quite the bore.

Moving around, and I really might look like a Ghostbusting freak right about now, a ghoulish one. Prodding and probing in my dark-gray chemical suit and respirator helmet. Hovering near the body with my handheld sniffer, poking my antenna at energy fields, rousing them like flying nanodragons I call by name. Starting with the cellular bandwidth of 800 megahertz (MHz), indicating a wave configuration that repeats itself 800 million times per second, moving at the speed of light.

Also, the familiar noise of mobile phones and Wi-Fi routers, those of neighbors and inside this apartment, plus clocks, exhaust fans, refrigerators, washing machines, TVs. I can point out the ubiquitous microwave oven signal at 2.4 MHz, and it could be coming from just about anywhere, especially if a door seal leaks. I'm almost always going to pick up police, fire and rescue radio bandwidths, meaningless ones to the rank and file, 26.965 MHz, 156.05 MHz.

Or how about 462.5625 MHz for a frequency that might not slip off the tongue all that easily. Just ask any cop or EMT, it's much more practical referring to channels 1, 2, 3. In my world, I think of signals as fingerprints unique to each device, and the trick is to hunt down and recognize what might be lurking between and beneath all those squiggly waves of electromagnetic spaghetti streaming in bright colors across my small screen.

The frequency of 75 MHz is probably the nearby lighthouse. While 1,025 MHz may be the runway marker beacons for the Instrument Landing Systems (ILS) at Langley Air Force Base. But what's grabbed my attention like the big fish that mustn't get away is the noise floor, the weak waves and peaks that intensify each time Fran keys her radio, talking to dispatch and members of the hazmat team.

The signals are coming from somewhere near the body, getting stronger as I get closer, holding up the antenna like the Statue of Liberty. Turning in slow circles, scanning.

I keep my eyes on the display, making my gentle pirouettes as the software I created constantly does the math.

Nothing all that complicated, a simple fusion algorithm that subtracts out expected signals from unknown ones saved in files the analyzer has been recording since I arrived at the scene. The way I typically explain it is to imagine hiding in plain view inside a crowded living room.

Then gradually remove everything around you one item at a time. The other people, pets, couch, lamp, potted plant, wallpaper, draperies and so on, all of it disappearing. And guess what? Eventually, you're not hiding anymore. You're sticking out like a sore thumb, which is what the software is doing inside this bedroom in real time, scaring out whatever might stealthily be tucked out of sight.

Sensors of some kind.

That's what continues to strobe brightly in my mind, especially since the dead woman's expertise was in sensors and robotics. Who's to say what sort of research she might have been conducting on her own, including on her own self here inside her own apartment? There could be tiny transmitting devices inside her clothing, her belongings or perhaps implanted in her body. I know what I'm like, given my curiosity and relentlessness.

It's not unheard of for researchers like me

to take projects home reasonably and with permission. Not rockets and moon habitats, but small drones and their pieces and parts, or even a broken crash dummy or two needing special TLC and technical attention, if justified. Could be anything, but the frequent flyers that typically end up on loan at Chase Place are antennas and plug-in tools, sensors and software, 3-D printers and media, plus analyzers, tactical gear and ammunition I'm expected to try.

In other words, nothing terribly exotic, and all of it recorded in a handwritten log that I keep locked inside my gun safe in Building 1195C.

"I'm not exactly sure how to move her out of here without getting bleach all over everything," Joan's tense voice inside my respirator helmet, and trained by the best, even she's stumped by this one. "But I think we're going to double pouch her, put her straight in the van, and then straight into the decomp room. And you thought there was nothing new under the sun."

"I learned a long time ago not to think that." Surveying the double bed, neatly made with oversize black pillows and a black duvet.

On the other side of the room are the closet and the body. Flanking them are two small windows with the shades drawn, and as is true in the rest of the house, there's no apparent sign of a struggle, nothing amiss except for the obvious. I note the cell phone, the stack of copying paper and computer printer on top of the dresser. In a chair is the black nylon Prada shoulder bag from yesterday, when I questioned Vera about a badge that she probably knew darn well hadn't been stolen.

What was she up to? What was the plan, and was it hers alone? I don't believe for a minute she actually thought her badge was missing or had been pinched. It would seem that she staged the entire drama, including her migraine. Why? And who was she helping, if anyone? What was her real motivation for calling the NASA Protective Services emergency number from the main gate yesterday when her badge wasn't in the glove box?

The most logical explanation for the stunt she pulled was to create an alibi for letting someone else borrow her smartcard. Or making it appear someone else did, and in either case, that would be extremely serious. Not only would such a thing have gotten her kicked out of NASA, but depending on who used her ID and for what purpose, she could have been charged with violating

U.S. Code §794.

She could have been busted for spying, punishable by a $500,000 fine and 15 years in prison. Treason lite as I call it, the very thing that will land you on posters displayed in every NASA center lobby.

"I can't think of any other reason for it." Fran leans against the doorframe, talking about the bleach and DNA. "You know, to mess up biological evidence, which really won't matter if Vera Young killed herself . . ."

"She didn't," it's what I believe, and I'm sticking to it.

"Except someone will make it a problem . . ."

"They will anyway," because they always do, and civil lawsuits and life insurance battles aren't ours to win or lose.

But if somebody else is to blame for her being strung up from her closet door, Fran goes on and on, then the bleach is a problem. It will be turned into one, that's for sure, defense attorneys casting doubt and confusion in the minds of jurors, if nothing else.

"What other point would there be except to screw up the DNA?" she wants to know, and unlike her freaked-out demeanor in the tunnel, she's acting in charge and in control, not particularly bothered by a dead body doused in a dangerous chemical beyond the challenges it presents.

But the case has her attention in a way it didn't before, and I can feel her warming up to the seriousness. It's like watching gauges in the cockpit creep from green to yellow to red as I explain that bleach contaminates evidence, and is problematic for DNA but doesn't necessarily destroy it.

"Chlorine bleach won't, at least not completely," I reply. "Oxygen bleach will absolutely. But that's not what we're dealing with, by the way."

"Definitely chlorine. That's what I smell whenever I take this thing off." Fran taps the carbon filter built into her helmeted respirator. "I'm voting for everyday household bleach."

"And you would bother with that in a suicide?" I ask what by now should be a rhetorical question.

"Dammit. I know. Why would you? I mean, this is frickin' screwed up. I mean, what the hell?" Fran's voice blurting over the intercom.

"Yeah. That about sums it up." Joan is crouched by the body, lifting trace evidence one fiber and fleck at a time in the glow of UV. "Why would you care about your DNA or any other evidence if you're about to *off* yourself?"

"Not unless it's some mental illness thing," Fran suggests.

"Nope, that's not what we're dealing with," I reply. "As I've said, she certainly didn't strike me as mentally ill when I talked to her yesterday." Moving the antenna around her dead body, watching the signals on my display as I scan her extremities.

Her hands. Wrists. Ankles. Bare feet.

"She definitely struck me as deceptive," I add. "And I'm pretty sure she's lying to us even as we speak."

"I know, it's like what we're seeing isn't right," Fran stares at the body. "Has she been dead 4 hours? Six hours? Eight? One thing tells us one thing. Something else tells us another."

Someone was in here after the fact.

"What about livor, rigor?" I ask Joan about postmortem artifacts, changes to the body after death that might give us important information.

Such as, when did Vera die, and was her body moved at any point afterward? Once again, it's plain and simple science. Not something as esoteric as a Mars rover, spacewalking or spectrum analysis, but the mundane question of what happens when you die and your circulation stops.

Just ask Robert Hooke's competitive colleague Isaac Newton what occurs when an apple is released from its tree. Freed from the tether of its branch, not floating but falling.

23

Gravity.

And blood, like everything else, settles according to the laws of it, resulting in a deep reddish discoloration known as livor mortis that indicates the position the body was in the hours immediately following death. Rigor mortis, or the rock-hard rigidity of muscles after they're no longer producing adenosine triphosphate (ATP), has similar intel to offer.

Not all of it polite. Most of what death tattles is primitive and quite rude as long as you know how to interpret the unseemly language. If you die on the toilet (for example and truth be told) and your loved ones lie to preserve your dignity? Well, sorry to tell you, but livor mortis will rat you out with redness and seat-shaped blanching on your dead derriere.

Same thing should you suffer a fatal event in bed and your lover decides to spare both of you embarrassment hours after the fact. Well, here's another news flash. Once you're as stiff as an ironing board, if some well-meaning person dresses your cold stubborn body in pajamas and leans it against a chair? It won't convince the medical examiner that you took death sitting down with your clothes on.

"Rigor's still forming and almost set," Joan reports. "Same with livor, not completely fixed but getting there."

"That's interesting." Fran watches from the doorway as I move the antenna close to the body, around the face and hair. "It's sure sounding like she's been dead longer than that file on her laptop would have you believe."

"Typically, rigor and livor take about 8 hours to be fixed," I add.

"We'll know more when we examine her at the office." Joan walks back to her scene cases. "But I concur."

Not looking at us as she moves about suited up. Only the top part of our faces showing, and I continue to have the eerie sensation that we're in a parallel universe communicating through thoughts.

"Although the bleach-like stuff is going to make it tricky, not to beat a dead horse. And that's not a good cliché right about now." Joan's voice. "How do you conduct an external exam without rinsing her first? None of the medical examiners will want to work in a chemical suit, and I'm not sure what they'll do in a situation like this. Like I said, the chief's not around to ask, and she's probably the only one who would know . . ."

"Because they can't rinse off the body first without running the risk of losing evidence," Fran interrupts. "Is that what you're telling me? Because that can't be good."

"There's only so much I can do in here and when I get her to the morgue." Joan returns the UV crime light to its proper slot, closing the heavy-duty plastic cover in loud snaps if I could hear them.

"The inconvenience and increased difficulty caused probably tell us something about motive," I point out. "Which may not be to eradicate evidence, which bleach isn't going to do anyway. But it certainly interferes, causing major obstacles in working the scene, transporting the body, doing the autopsy."

"Okay. So, maybe that was someone's intention," Fran considers.

"*Someone's*. I agree, because I sincerely doubt it was hers," I decide. "Otherwise, where's the darn bleach bottle or container?"

"Obviously, somebody took it," Fran says.

"Why? If the point is to disguise a crime scene?" Joan asks.

"Unless the point was to *undisguise* it," I offer what I've about decided, knowing it sounds a little crazy. "Removing the bleach container instantly signals that this sure as shooting isn't a suicide."

"Why would anybody do something like that?" Joan puzzles. "Why not leave the bottle right here on the floor where one would expect to find it?"

Sabotage.

"Maybe what we're dealing with here is more than one person," I ease them closer to what I'm calculating and intuiting. "Maybe we're talking about two individuals who weren't necessarily in the same place at the same time. Not physically. The first person came here, murdered Vera Young and covered it up. Then after the killer was gone, a second person appeared and sort of undid it all. And the result is, we're asking questions. We're not buying suicide. Couldn't be further from it."

"Huh?" Fran booms in my helmet, hurting my ears.

"And we need to ask who might have

made the sandwich and gotten into the beer," I go on. "The killer or someone else. Another person who showed up later. It will take a while for the DNA to tell us anything, including who bled in the steam tunnel. Joan," I direct my next comment to her, "you're gonna need to light quite the fire under the labs. We don't have months to waste, not if you ask me. Because this is bad."

"I'm good at lighting fires."

"I think the fumes must be getting to you . . ." Fran crabbing at me, and I can't stop thinking about the note Vera Young supposedly wrote:

. . . Please tell my sister that I won't miss her, and she's been right about me all along. Sisters always know best, and mine would be the first to say that I've earned what I'm about to get . . .

She's telling us or someone that she deserved to die like this? Nope, and no way. Not the woman I met. Not in a million years, and I wonder what her sister might have been *right* about. Neva — that rhymes with Eva, I recall Vera telling me — and I move my sniffer's antenna with my double-gloved hands. Aware of the sounds of my own breathing, sweat drenching the clothing beneath my chemical suit.

311

"Hmmm . . ." *That's interesting.*

Eyeing the display and what's happening to certain peaks and waves whenever Fran radios anyone. And I ask her to radio me.

"What for?" her voice a tad annoyed.

"Just do it," I reply.

Gloves off, she keys her handheld, "Alpha 3 to Alpha 5. Test, test."

Loud and clear, the low-level signals ringing like a bell, as we say. Although not literally making a sound I can hear but getting stronger each time the radio transmits at harmonic frequencies. Reminding me of tin can telephone, the silly game Carme and I played when we were little kids. Pretending we were spies with secret comms, connecting two Big Gulp cups by a string.

And it's as if the dead woman and Fran's radio are playing the same game. Tethered by an electromagnetic wave. What lights up one, lighting up the other.

"Resonant sensors, not digital ones," I confirm. "Possibly invasive multi-array biochips for directly measuring biomedical parameters."

"And that means what?" Joan rolls the stretcher toward the closet.

"It means I wish this lady had decided to die somewhere else!" Fran retorts with a frustrated blast of air and expletives that almost takes out my ears over the intercom.

"I'm thinking she has sensors on her skin or implanted in her body and likely both, considering who and what she was," I reply. "That would explain what I'm seeing."

"What kind of sensors and what for?" Joan begins collecting red biohazard bags next, picking up after ourselves.

"I think it's a safe bet they're related to robotics. And one of the greatest challenges when we create anything in our own image is how to perfect fine muscle movement. What we natural-born humans take for granted in our feet, wrists, hands, fingers," I explain, setting my analyzer on top of a scene case.

I change out my gloves, looking at Joan, and we nod at each other. It's time.

"Shall we open the door to see how this death trap was set up?" I ask, and the answer is Joan moves next to me, our chemical suits touching.

"Let me be a spotter in case she decides to fall on top of you," she says.

"Thanks. That would not be my idea of a good time," gripping the antique fluted glass knob, I ease open the closet door, and Vera Young's body moves heavily against wood bleached of its cherry color in spots and drips.

Held fast by her tether, the computer cord wrapped and knotted over the knob, not much else inside. Coats, a pair of galoshes, an umbrella, and the same alarm is spiking in my mind:

Homicide. Homicide. Homicide.

In the first place, how did she manage to shut the door when the cord was tight around her neck, her feet barely touching the floor? And then there's that blasted missing receptacle for the caustic chemical. It's obvious someone else helped, and neither Joan nor I say a word, both of us thinking our murderous thoughts. Already we know this isn't your garden-variety case, and it will be a circus when it goes to court.

"Oh boy," my voice carried on a sigh. "We've got to be super careful here."

"Yep." Joan has her hands on her hips, staring at what's fast turning into her most difficult patient in recent memory.

"Not that there's a playbook, protocol or documented procedure for how to handle something like this," I add.

"Nope," Joan says. "If there is and you want to look it up, it will be listed under *Shit Show.* One thing I'm clear on is we don't want to cut through any knots. Not unless you want my chief shipping me off to Leavenworth."

"Can't afford to lose a perfectly good drinking buddy," is my retort.

Neither of us looking at each other as we talk, and good thing I know my way around tools. The obvious solution is not to cut through the computer cable at all, and I recommend instead that we lift the body off the door and onto the floor, which we first cover with a disposable sheet. Instead of cutting the cable, I'll remove the doorknobs, leaving the entire rigging intact.

That's exactly what we do while one of Fran's crime scene officers captures it on video since Scottie and Butch have left the scene. We double pouch the body, cool and rigid when we lift it up, Joan gripping it under the arms while I get the ankles. Strapping it onto the stretcher. Draping the morbid cocoon with a burgundy cot cover.

We roll out our grim cargo while the local NBC news crew surrounds us with cameras that dart and turn like orbs of blinding light in the frigid blustery night. We don't answer shouted questions, pushing onward to the back of the black medical examiner's van. Opening the tailgate. Collapsing the aluminum legs of the stretcher. Lifting it.

We slide Vera Young inside for the last ride she'll take while her organs are still in place.

And I hope like crazy we won't have to remove her fingers.

"Don't worry." Dick keeps saying that at the sink, standing close behind me, tearing off tape with his teeth, bandaging my hand.

As I ponder the likelihood of my losing the pad of my right index finger. Should that happen, what about the fingernail? If I lose that, then what?

The first interphalangeal joint is next. Very bad when right-hand dominant.

". . . You're gonna be good as new . . ." His fingers stained dark orange from Betadine, not wanting to consider what may be inevitable, and he won't say it.

Partial amputation. I could manage the cyclic, hold a pencil, a pipette, shoot a gun. Not ambidextrous, a competent southpaw. Not optimal. Could medically disqualify me from going to space. From wearing a 280-pound Extravehicular Mobility Unit, and cumbersome gloves that don't fit so great. Using delicate instruments, tools. Riding the robotic arm like a rodeo star.

"You don't know what you can't do until you can't do it anymore," Dad's always saying.

Viewed as unskilled. Reckless. Not to be trusted. Clipping more than a finger. Clipping my wings.

". . . Captain Chase? How are we holding up . . . ?"

Impatient, distracted when I know better, the evidence there near our feet on the blood-spattered tile. The airman and his mop detouring around the wooden-handled carving knife as if it's a murder weapon, apologizing every other minute. Cleaning up with his bucket of hot tap water and chlorine bleach.

"Sorry, sir. Excuse me, sir," he says repeatedly but not to me, the sharp fumes like a nail in my head.

Woozy, fading in and out like a signal I can't catch, jolted each time Dick repeats my name. Loudly. And often. Captain Chase this, and Captain Chase that, making me feel like a reprimanded child. Or somebody old and confused. As if he doesn't know me anymore. Because of what I did.

"Oh shhhh . . . Oh shhhh . . . Oh shhhh . . . !" under my breath.

". . . You're doing great. You still with us, Captain Chase? You're doing great. Let's get you to the medical clinic."

"Oh shhhh . . . !" Trying not to sob.

Dick turning off the water in the sink, my right hand wrapped in layers of gauze.

"Are you up for a ride in the car? Captain Chase? Do you think you could manage that?" Moving away from the countertop, his arm around me, holding me steady. "There we go. All's good."

Yes, better, much better, I can walk. The shock of the injury beginning to pass even as I fear being maimed. Fear it and my future with every cell of my being.

It's after 10:00 p.m. I'm headed to the barn, and I don't mean it figuratively.

These days I live in one, start with that. Wasn't born in one but when Carme and I turned 12, our parents engaged in construction and woodworking wizardry, converting the old barn's upstairs haylofts and grain bins into living and work areas. That's where my sister and I hung our hats until college, and now I'm back and have been since Colorado.

Sleeping in the same bed, utilizing the same spaces, surrounded by the expected memorabilia one accumulates. Reminding me of the Faulkner quote about the past not being gone. It isn't even past, and he had that right, just like Einstein did in his theory of special relativity. Certainly, there are days like this when it feels everything really might be happening at once, and maybe I'm just tired, but I've lost any concept of time.

It could be the actual hour on my phone

or much later or earlier, maybe not this day or year. All I know is that it's windy and dark with hardly anybody out, and it would take nothing for me not to know where I am. For everything to look unfamiliar in the stark frigid blackness as I head home after the day I've had, pretty sure it's far from over as I fret about the EVA and rocket launch, as I fret even more about Dick and what to tell my parents about Carme.

What will I say to Fran? Most of all, where is my sister, and is she safe? That will be the first thing asked, and I have no good answer or feeling about it. I haven't heard from her. I'm afraid I won't and more afraid I will. Feeling sick with a volatile mix of pain and outrage, stunned fury, grief and high-voltage fear.

What have you done!

I've got to keep it contained. Keep my mess to myself, concentrating hard while driving carefully in the overcast dark, the angry cloud ceiling lower and the humidity up. The weather is changing more rapidly than predicted, and I've not checked on the storm's progress in hours.

Focus. Focus. Focus.

Twenty minutes out from home, driving on not much more than a country lane, I'm constantly on the alert for deer, watching

319

my mirrors, unable to shake the sensation that what's being watched most of all is me. I've been feeling it ever since I got that alert on my phone, and Fran and I checked the Yellow Submarine tunnel. I'm feeling it out here in the middle of nowhere, not another car in sight.

Streetlights are few and bleary in the fog, and intermittently I'm driving past clusters of lighted homes dressed up for the holidays, then woods and fields as dark as a black hole. Shapes and reflections play their tricks on my eyes, and I can't wait to get out of this gear and my disgusting wet clothes. A shower and food are first on the list, and by midnight I'll be back at Langley, ready to assist Rush Delgato in Mission Control.

Still no word from him, and I'm feeling overexposed and all alone, low on fuel and in need of a hard restart that will reset my processors and line up my pistons. There will be no sleep tonight, with plenty to follow up on. I may have to dash to the morgue at the crack of dawn, depending on how it goes when they check Vera Young's body for sensors or other implanted devices.

That has to be done before everything else, scanning with computed tomography, CT, and possibly magnetic resonance imaging, MRI, if Tidewater's 1.5-Tesla magnet is up and running. I also told Joan to try a handheld scanner, the kind the TSA uses in airports to help zero in on the location of any chip-type transmitting devices detected. Every last one of them will have to be recovered, hopefully with a biopsy needle to keep the mutilation to a minimum.

But I'm contemplating all sorts of scenarios about how to manage such unfortunate but necessary extractions from the body. Trust me when I say they'll be problematic for about every reason imaginable, and that gruesome thought ricochets me back to next of kin. Who's supposed to be taking care of that? I could kick myself for not thinking about it prior to clearing the scene, and I try Fran again.

"Where are you?" I ask over my truck's engine, a beast of a V-8 that rumbles and snarls.

"At home and about to get cleaned up," she says, the background quiet because unlike me, she got a head start and is no longer driving in wet stinking clothing that makes me think of jungle rot.

"Don't rush," I say with just the faintest jab. "As you can tell, I'm still in my truck." Sticking her harder.

"What's up?"

"Next of kin. Any thoughts about contacting someone? Or how we might go about it?" What I'm really asking is if Fran intends to do it herself because darn it, she should.

24

"Got no idea, but Vera Young should have an emergency contact on her personnel form," Fran doesn't *really* answer what I *really* asked, and I already know where this is going.

She's not going to make the call. She's going to make me do it.

Crap!

"Scottie's back at HQ dealing with evidence, and I can get her to pull the file, send you an electronic copy ASAP," Fran goes on to suggest what I didn't have in mind. "I suspect the sister she alluded to is who we're talking about, someone who also works at Pandora but maybe at a higher level."

"Neva."

"Huh?"

"That's her name, apparently. N-E-V-A. As in Nevada except it's pronounced with a long *e* like Eva," I reply. "Why is the default that I'm the one reaching out? Why can't you pick up the phone and tell this poor woman her poor sister is dead, and not in a natural way? And we're sorry for her loss but could use a little information and so on?"

"Because you're so much better with people than I am," Fran's voice fills my truck, and when she's suddenly sincere, reasonable and oh so earnest, I see right through it. "You're the cyber person, the NASA scientist who understands psychology and what goes on in 1110," she says.

"Uh-huh, keep talking. But you're not selling it." Making me do her dirty work as usual, Major Chicken shirking anything requiring a bedside manner.

"More to the point, you're the special agent who interviewed her yesterday," Fran tells me how qualified I am only when she doesn't want the job. "Therefore, hands down you should talk to the sister, Neva, Nevada or whatever. I assume her last name isn't the same as the dead lady's."

"I don't know," but I doubt it. "Vera said she was divorced with grown kids, so presumably Young may not be her family name."

"Well, I'm sure there aren't too many people at Pandora with the first name of

Neva, and I'd start with upper management to narrow down the search," Fran's know-it-all voice inside my truck. "In fact, I'm googling it as we speak. Doesn't take a rocket scientist, and bingo! Her last name is Rong without the *w*. As in R-O-N-G. Recently hired as the CEO of Pandora Space Systems. Nothing like going straight to the top, and I have no doubt you'll know more once the two of you talk."

"Maybe text me a phone number," willing myself not to drive too fast. "But I'm not calling right now."

"Let her think you're just trying to be helpful, let her know what's happened but within reason," Fran says as if she's not hearing me, and I don't know how to act. "And also, see what else we can learn about Vera's mental health and the people she was working with, okay?"

"The question is when such a call should be made," I reply. "I don't want to release any information until we confirm identity. In fact, I won't."

"Seriously, Aggie? Can there be any doubt who the frick she is? I mean, you sat down and talked to her yesterday!"

"I know this is hard to believe, but she looks a little different right now. Or at least she did when we were unhanging her from the closet door, her skin slipping, coming off in places where she's burned. Her face reminiscent of a frog with its tongue out. As decomposition sets in with a vengeance."

I see Vera as I say all this, looking exponentially worse the longer we were with her. I wouldn't call her recognizable, and even if she were, it's astonishing the mistakes in identity that are made.

"We can confirm who she is when she's fingerprinted in the morgue," I lay out a plan to Fran. "We're just talking about waiting until morning, not even 12 hours from now. In the meantime, let's make sure Joan has the copy of Vera's prints that we have on file. After that and the autopsy, then we reach out to next of kin. That would be the safest thing to do."

"You're right. But it's hard to imagine Vera Young's team members haven't already notified people at Pandora including the CEO sister," Fran makes a good point. "Which will make things somewhat easier, I guess. You know, if the bad news has been broken to them already."

We agree to hold off calling next of kin until morning, and Fran says she'll see me back at Langley. Will look for me at Mission Control.

"So much for that beer you owe me

because it's all but certain the government's shutting down," she adds. "I'll be heading back to work shortly."

"I'll see you there, but not for a few hours. Unlike some people I'm still in wet, stinky everything," rubbing that in again, and I end the call.

On Beach Road now, and up ahead is the WELCOME TO FOX HILL sign with a seaside theme, including a lighthouse, mounted on what looks like fishing pier pilings on the roadside. If it's possible to relax, I do. Relieved as fatigue sets in unmercifully now that I'm not gushing adrenaline with home in sight. Not literally in sight, but I feel its magnetic pull, our east Hampton neighborhood tracing back to the early 1800s, quaint and unspoiled, some things not changing much.

I always feel a sense of reassuring calm as I drive the narrow tree-lined streets past the modest homes of people who don't have a lot except self-respect and a strong work ethic. It seems nothing can be that bad if I'm on my way to the cove where I grew up and still live with the in- and outlaws, as Mom likes to say.

Except everything *is* that bad, and the quote from the alleged suicide note sticks in my mind like a ghost image burned into a

TV screen:

"Please tell my sister that I won't miss her, and she's been right about me all along . . ."

I don't want to think about it but have no choice, knowing why I'm so bothered by those words. Desperate to banish them from my mind, hating the reminder of what Dick said about my own powerful twin. Truth is I'm rattled. Rattled in a way I've not been in years, and I've got to stand my professional ground.

Focus. Focus. Focus.

No matter what comes my way, even if it's about my sister, and I can't get it out of my head that Dick didn't seem to know where she is. He went so far as to wonder if she might be here in Hampton, and what's to say she isn't? If he doesn't know and I don't? Then I can't imagine who might, and the fact is, my special ops fighter-pilot twin could be anywhere she likes.

A bigger question is what my parents might know, especially Dad, and I recheck the time as I unlock my phone, curious if either of them have a heads-up that I'm about to blow through the door. I've not had a chance to fill them in on anything. Maybe Fran has.

"It's me," I say when my mother answers the landline at home, our number the same as when I was growing up.

"Hi, hon. How funny you called," she says.

"Why's that?" Talking to her hands-free as I drive through our neighborhood.

"Because I was just about to call you, literally was reaching for the phone," and this happens a lot, both of us simultaneously thinking the other one's thought.

"I'm on my way," I let her know. "Almost at the Methodist church," and it's dark, not a car in the parking lot.

But the Nativity scene is up and illuminated when it wasn't this morning. The three kings have been blown over, a shepherd has lost his crook, and one of the lambs has been upended, its plastic legs sticking straight up in the blustery air. Fortunately, Mary and Joseph are no worse for the wear, baby Jesus resting peacefully, no straw left in the manger.

"Is it just me, or are the decorations up earlier?" I wonder out loud.

"You say the same thing every year at this exact time. And total transparency, the volunteer firefighters were out there before it got dark making apple cider doughnuts. Before everything closed because of the weather. I confess to making a quick stop."

"Please tell me you didn't."

"They were plucking them out of the deep

fryer," she says, and true to stereotype, the firefighters I know are fantastic in the kitchen. "These may be the best ever. Not that there was any room for improvement." She's eating doughnuts over speakerphone openly and without apology. "They literally melt in your mouth."

"And you're literally making mine water," I complain because empty calories have to be burned off if you're me, and I've not eaten since the Bojangle's steak-and-egg biscuits I wolfed down early this morning after the gym.

"I've put aside half a dozen doughnuts with your name on them."

"Get behind me, devil," as I do the math and my stomach rumbles like a thunderhead.

Six doughnuts x approximately 100 calories = my having to sprint or run hills for at least 30 minutes.

I can just make out the 7-Eleven through the fog, about the only place open I've seen so far. Driving like a snail so I don't overrun my headlights, and several times I've felt my tires slip on slicks of black ice.

The convenience store is lit up green and red some 3.2 kilometers (2 miles) up ahead, and it will always be Zooms to us. That was the name of the cozy white-brick market when Carme and I were coming along, our family ritual on Saturdays to have lunch where the fishermen hung out. Hot food like burgers, pizza, not much could be more welcoming after long hours out in their trawlers and crabbers, and when I envision my sister from those early years, I'm not surprised she faced future trouble that I didn't see coming.

Kids feel hurt but don't understand serious damage, and my parents didn't discuss in front of us what that ride home from the swimming pool might have done. I heard nothing about the delayed and long-term effects of trauma on someone supposedly identical to me. But then again, Carme never really was. Not identical in the true meaning of the word, and I guess it all boils down to the old cliché that you can't tell a book by its cover.

The two of us may look and sound the same but we couldn't be more opposite in the way we spin. Until last spring, I'd place her on the low end of the spectrum when it comes to subjectivity and emotionality, which probably is a good thing when flying helicopters tricked out with missiles and mini-Gatling guns. In Carme's world, there's no option for error. But in mine it's inevitable when the focus is aviation risk-threat analysis combined with the chaotic human factor.

It was no surprise our freshman year at Rice University that she latched on to information systems and algorithms, with segues into military science, game programming, cybercrime and other weapons necessary to fight fire with fire. While I set my heading bug on aerospace engineering and quantum mechanics, taking time out to explore the exoplanets of literature, music, religion, criminal justice and philosophy.

Along with extended stays in the computer security lab, where I steeped myself in the dirtiest data-tampering tricks of the trade and the people who try them. Gearing up to slingshot through the ether on a tether of extreme technology, like a nerdy Spider-Man or ninja, as my sister likes to say. Except I'm not her, not the superhero type.

But more a quiet fixer obsessed with how things work or fail, and who we are and what anything means. More EQ than IQ, I suppose. Shy. Unhappy in crowds. Uncool. Too much in my head. Possibly all of the above. Unlike Carme, who doesn't meet a stranger. Or feel all that sorry for much. Or take no for an answer. Or doubt herself. Or ever give up.

I know who my sister is. That added to what Dick told me, and I almost can connect the dots that might account for her recent behavior. The operative word being *almost.* As in not exactly and maybe not at all. It wasn't that long ago that Carme was in control. Doing fine, not unkind, cold blooded or violent. I have to ask how things could go so wrong so fast, and my unsettled mood is ringing like those harmonic signals lighting up when Fran keyed her radio.

". . . How are you doing besides stressed and exhausted?" Mom's soothing voice that I love so much as I remember heading out to Zooms at high noon, didn't matter the time of year or the weather.

Unless it's a nor'easter, the watermen go out and come in, and I can see Dad, Carme and me sitting on those wooden benches as hard as church pews, eating submarine sandwiches and talking to all the Bubbas, as we called everyone, including ourselves. Carme especially would go to town. *That Bubba did this, and the other Bubba did that while the Bubbas over there did the other thing,* and she never did know when to quit.

She'd go on and on until I was laughing so hard I'd spit out my drink, and my belly would ache. Once I almost choked, thought I was going to need the Heimlich maneuver.

Especially when we'd get to "tawkin' reeel south'rn," and I've never denied being a little bit redneck. Maybe more than a little bit.

". . . You must be starving," Mom worries about me as if I'm 10. "And I won't ask what the case is beyond what's in the news."

A stock line in my house from my years of interning with the police. My parents never pried for what they didn't need to know. Only Carme would. Always having to find out everything, her business or not, and if the information isn't offered, that's never stopped her. Whether it's unearthing personal details about someone or figuring out a password.

". . . A suicide, it seems," Mom's voice, "and not that it's ever a good time, but this close to the holidays, my Lord . . . I just hate that bad things ever happen . . ." A slow, quiet sigh fills the cab of my truck, and she sounds weighed down, weary. "I just hate things being sad," she adds, and I detect pain in her tone like a distant beacon.

It was this time of year when she was diagnosed and I resigned from the air force, left Dick and my post in Colorado, returning home to help her die or live, either one. For a while it was touch and go. She would pull through and she absolutely wouldn't in a true quantum conundrum. Both things true at the same time. Until they're not.

"I'm fine, and yes, it's a sad case, but suffice it to say that things aren't always as they appear," and I envision Vera Young's decomposing body hanging from her closet door like a work of monstrous art. "But lest there was any doubt, just because you work for NASA doesn't mean you're not a redneck."

"Well hon, I could have told you that."

"Here I am driving a tricked-out pickup truck with run-flat tires, and wearing a pistol on my hip that I just had on in the shower," trying to make my mom lighten up. "And if wearing a gun in the shower doesn't make me a redneck, I'm not sure what does."

"I'm not sure what it makes you or why you'd do that." She can handle a gun like nobody's business but isn't what I'd call a fan.

She's also not laughing, not so much as a smile in her voice, and I don't believe it's because of the so-called suicide she really doesn't want to hear about. My mother is a sensitive, fearless force of nature. We rarely discuss police work, cybercrimes, politics or much that's negative and depressing, and whatever's bothering her at the moment has nothing to do with any of that. I can tell.

Reminding me of what she often says. That the most powerful word is the one left unsaid, and there's something she's not saying. I know this for a fact because I know her. Maybe better than anyone.

"I guess wearing a gun in the shower makes sense if it's a *Psycho* thing and you're worried someone might murder you while you're minding your own business naked, trying to clean up . . . ? What shower are we talking about?" Mom sounds completely distracted, trying to figure it out.

"I wasn't naked, and it wasn't that kind of shower. Think of cold water blasting down like Niagara Falls while I was in the chemical suit I still have on. We had to rinse off inside the hazmat trailer before leaving the scene."

"Sounds like a good way to get pneumonia in weather like this."

"It's really just the clothes I have on underneath that are soaked, and that's mostly from sweating. No pneumonia but I feel like I've been slimed. Anyway, it's been a night, and I'm sorry I'm getting in so late and may not have time to drop by the house before I've got to head back to Langley. No matter what, the EVA will happen as scheduled, and I have to head to Mission Control in a couple hours."

"Chase Place is always open with the lights on, and I'm warming up supper anyway. And I understand Dick is in town," she adds with no warning.

25

I've not said a word to my parents about him being here.

I didn't know anything about Dick's unscheduled visit to Langley until last night, and my instructions were very clear that I wasn't to discuss the matter with anyone. That includes family. Sensitive and classified information isn't the business of best friends or next of kin, and I'm accustomed to sitting at the dinner table with a head full of information, not a word of it spoken.

"Where did you hear anything about him?" I inquire cagily as I roar along slowly in my truck, watching for ice, not addressing what Mom said about Dick one way or another.

I won't inform her of anything about his visit here. I'm not going to mention that I briefed him. Or gave him a ride to the air force base while he divulged distressing information about Carme. It won't help matters for Mom to be told, and she might just lose it if she knew what I do.

"The Mason Dixon Line," her voice inside my loud truck telling me the source of her intel about the commander of Space Force, my former boss, who I thought was a friend.

And I almost swear again, "Darn that pushy piece of sh . . . !"

I don't mean Dick. I mean Mason and his show, *The Mason Dixon Lyin'* as the joke goes. I know my mother listens to it, watching him on streaming video, and when I say she watches *him,* I mean precisely that. It's embarrassing the way she drools over some local celebrity who's the same age as her unmarried twin daughters.

"What did he say?" I'm working hard to sound calm, creeping along, the 7-Eleven glowing like a lighthouse half a mile ahead.

"That it's a *mystery.* Mason must have used that word 10 times if he used it once. The rumor on the street is that the commander of Space Force made a surprise visit to Langley. He went on and on, speculating about what Dick's doing at NASA."

"Seriously?" Tucking in my alarm so it doesn't show. "Where the hell-o did Mason get any of this to begin with? Not from me. Not from anyone who would know. We've kept Dick's visit confidential and didn't even know about it until the last minute."

"Interesting. I assumed Mason heard it from you," Mom ponders through the speakers in the dash. "I assumed you talked to him directly. I was going to ask you what he's like in person, not stuck on himself, I hope . . ."

"He left me a voice mail. I've not called him back. And don't forget who his uncle is. I guess it's possible the governor might have known Dick was coming here. Beyond that, I don't know," I reply before changing the subject. "What's Dad up to?"

"Well, he's actually not home," she stops me in my mental tracks because it's simply not like him to be out at night, certainly not at this hour.

"He's still at work?" as my tires find a patch of ice, fishtailing a little.

"Came home and then went back out again."

Dad's not agoraphobic, and it would be easy to confuse his introversion for misanthropy. But it's complicated. He's complicated, and even as this is running in a subroutine beneath my thoughts, I'm reminded of how similar to Fran he's become. Or better stated, she's gotten more like him ever since her own phobias kicked in her doors and stormed her castle.

"Oh boy," under my breath and not meant to be heard.

"What is it, Calli?"

"Never mind. I was just thinking."

"You always are."

"Sometimes I get ambushed by insight," I reply. "You know, having clarity about why people get under your skin, and who they remind you of or what. And Fran's been quite the pill today, making me insane, starting when we had to check out a motion sensor alarm in a steam tunnel."

"Oh dear, oh dear. Fran and tunnels. And how did she do?"

"Exactly how you'd expect. Anyway, sometimes I can be slow picking up on things," and what I'm really saying is that Fran's phobias are all the harder for me because they remind me of what I've lived with at home.

My unassuming, painfully shy Dad. Who I haven't always forgiven for not showing up. For getting others to take care of what he can't. Others like Dick Melville, who was in the Air Force Academy with my father when he resigned for the same reason I did. A family emergency. His father was killed in a car accident, and there was no one to take care of his mother.

Like me, he came home to the cove and

341

went to work for NASA. But I don't let people down the way he has.

"Where did Dad go?" I get back to that, and the 7-Eleven is just ahead, a bearded man emerging from the glass front door.

"All I know is something came up, don't ask me what."

"Because of the shutdown?" I ask dubiously.

My father may be as eccentric as they come, but he's not the sort to hide out in his office trying to button up various research projects before he's locked out of his building.

"I suppose everything's related to everything," Mom's voice inside my truck as I keep my eye on the bearded man.

Big and bulky, someone who is far more fit and powerful than he looks in his baggy clothes. Carrying his steaming coffee to the 7-Eleven gas pumps, where his black Ford F-150 is parked, a woman with long hair in the passenger's seat. A cross between a lumberjack and ZZ Top with no other customers in sight, and the bearded man has snagged my attention for a reason.

"Is he planning on staying out all night or did he say?" I ask Mom about Dad as I take in the antennas on the Ford pickup, the covered bed, the signal jammer dome, and the backpack the bearded man has slung over his shoulder.

The way he's dressed sends my flag up a notch. His coat unzipped, no gloves, nothing binding in this deep freeze, and it doesn't escape my notice that he handles the knapsack carefully. Seems mindful of jostling it, and I have to ask why it's with him to begin with.

Paying for gas didn't require a dark-green backpack carried inside the 7-Eleven, a backpack that easily could be tactical, by the way. Why not just carry cash or your wallet? And if nothing unusual is inside this backpack, why not leave it in the truck with his wife or girlfriend, whoever the woman is?

But I know the answer. I'm all but sure I do, almost willing to place a large bet on what he's hauling around. Magic wands and sticks to poke things with, and no doubt he has additional transmitters, receivers and weapons on his person. Accoutrements, shall we say, that people like us don't let out of our sight or safekeeping.

"I don't know what the plan is," Mom says while the bearded man stares at my NASA truck going past, stares hard in a way that holds my interest.

I can't begin to figure out what the Secret

Service is doing undercover out here in the middle of an Arctic blast that's feeling as empty and forbidding as outer space about now. But if I'm right and this is the second time I've spotted agents and their tricked-out stealth wagons in the past few hours, then I have to wonder why. And believe me, it goes light-years beyond mere curiosity.

I'm not assuming it's a fact that the bearded man showing up in my neck of the woods is related to Dick's visit to Hampton. But I can't help but feel pretty convinced there's a connection. What exactly I don't know, and each time I replay what I was told about Carme, I feel upset again.

I can think of a lot of things I don't want right about now, and being tailed is one of them.

I watch the black pickup truck in my mirrors until I can't see it anymore, troubled by the bearded man walking out of the 7-Eleven at just the right moment, rendezvousing with me like a robotic arm grabbing a cargo capsule hurling past. It's not hard to notice or figure out how such an intersection of orbits might occur. It's just math. Simple geometry, using points, distance to triangulate. He saw me coming or more likely his divining rod, his fish finder, did. Imagining his green backpack and what he might have in it, possibly equipment similar to mine, cruising the empty frozen night, fishing. Following what's biting.

I don't consider him or his truck random because I don't think anything is, and I'm about to decide I'm not the one running into the Secret Service agents. But rather they're running into me. Deliberately. Because trust me when I say if they don't want me to know they're around, I won't.

Not under any circumstances, certainly not considering who and what they're up against, meaning I'm not naive and they aren't either. I'm on their Electronic Crimes Task Force and not exactly an unknown quantity, which is why I was invited to work with the Secret Service to begin with. As a cyber investigator, I'm well versed in a lot of their same stuff.

Therefore, if I'm being monitored for some reason, agents in such a detail will have been briefed that I'm a birdwatcher when it comes to antennas, jammers and similar devices. I don't believe there's one I haven't met. So, a bearded dude with a backpack strolling to the gas pumps didn't fool me, and I have no doubt he didn't try. Quite the opposite as I recall the way he stared at my police truck.

But what's palpable to me this very moment, as I drive in my wretched state of hot wet messiness, is my mundane and self-indulgent appetites. I crave his big coffee with thick white steam billowing up. I sure could use one of those and a pit stop for about every reason imaginable. Hungry, tired, on the way to dehydrated with a fierce thirst, and I've had no access to a toilet since I barreled out of headquarters to pick up Dick many hours earlier.

There's no bathroom in the hazmat trailer, and it's not my idea of a good time to have a full bladder while deconning in a cold shower that feels like a fire hose, scrubbing myself from head to toe with dishwashing detergent and a stiff-bristled brush. Especially with everything on . . . street clothes, chemical suit, ballistic vest, weapon belt with its holstered Glock, loaded, a round ready in the chamber . . .

Especially when other cops are watching, sniping and sparring . . .

Especially with a TV news crew capturing all of it . . .

"Since when does Dad decide to dash back to work at this hour, government shutdown or not?" I have to ask, because what Mom's telling me seems close to preposterous. "When I talked to him earlier today, I got the impression that everything was status quo. It's not like we haven't been furloughed before more times than I can count. Is everything all right?"

"We were in the kitchen when his cell phone rang," Mom's quiet voice, and I turn up the volume, listening for nuances that might hint what's going on. "He wouldn't say what the problem was, but he had to leave. Didn't finish dinner, grabbed a few things and his coat. And was picked up."

"*Picked up?* And you definitely got the impression there was a, quote, 'problem.' As in something urgent, something that's gone wrong."

"I sensed his concern, yes," with hesitation in her tone. "And such short notice. To be honest, he didn't look happy. Not that I'd expect him to be happy about being called out in the middle of the night in subzero temperatures, not knowing when he's coming back."

"If there's something urgent going on, I can't imagine I wouldn't know about it. Do you have any idea who called him?" And I can't get Dick out of my head, reminding me of that silly tin can telephone game again.

The two of us connected by a string, only this one isn't visible and what's going on isn't child's play. At least, that's how it's felt ever since I was sitting inside this very truck with him. It's as if we're still together. But we're not. Yet I sense him, can't break the connection, as if his energy has me locked in a tractor beam.

What have you done, Carme? What have you done!

"I don't know what's happened," Mom replies, and I don't trust the way she says it.

"What's happened." As if something has.

"But I got the sense they were headed to Langley first, seems I overheard a mention of the hangar. Then maybe Wallops, at least I overheard it mentioned," her voice drifting from speakers in the dash. "I'm figuring because of what's in the works for the launch? In addition to the Earth-observation instrument that was sent up from Cape Canaveral just the other week."

"LEAR. I know you've been busy with lesson plans that show kids how to build such a thing. I know how proud you are." As guilt kicks in.

My NASA educator mother has no idea that LEAR is a ruse.

"So proud I could pop. Built by students in rural Iowa of all places," she can't resist adding. "Winning the NASA national science competition, as you may recall, and it's all the more amazing because it just so happens that Mount Ayr Community School is where Peggy Whitson graduated. The first female commander of the International Space Station, and she also holds the record for the number of days a woman has lived in space. Almost two years total."

"Qualifying her to take over the bridge of the Starship Enterprise and be issued the first astro-passport, as far as I'm concerned," feeling worse by the moment.

"Imagine how those Iowa schoolkids are going to feel hanging out at Mission Control in Wallops, watching her in real time install the LEAR in outer space."

"I can't imagine," meaning it in more ways than one.

"I'm so excited, you know, since my lesson plans are involved. I can't wait to see how thrilled those kids will be when they watch their instrument being installed by our astronauts."

They wouldn't be thrilled if they knew the truth, I can't help but think. Their washing machine–size box will make it to a research platform eventually, just not on this launch. The students, the teachers, the public will be none the wiser, and it's not my favorite thing to fool anyone, including children and my mom. Even if by no choice of my own, I do it constantly.

Not that Mom wouldn't understand the sleight of hand required if we're to keep certain information under wraps and away from the scrutiny of those nations and entities that would be much too interested. My NASA mother would understand. But she can't be told that the Low Earth Atmospheric Reader wasn't actually launched two weeks ago. Something else was that isn't simply another scientific instrument for measuring ozone or global warming, or deflecting space debris moving 10 times faster than a speeding bullet.

I'm quite confident Mom has no clue about what's actually being installed in about three hours during a complicated and dangerous EVA. She'd have to be in bed with the intelligence community to be aware that her prizewinning Earth-observing instrument from the cornfields of Iowa is actually a quantum machine, a node. And that in a difficult and dangerous feat of engineering, the two US astronauts currently on the Station will bolt it to the steel structure, where it will live in the near-absolute-zero vacuum conditions that are quantum computing's natural habitat.

Cold and quiet in the black box of space. Surrounded by the Station's 16 habitable modules hosting astronauts and cosmonauts from nations competitive with us even as we try to get along, leaving our politics and differences on the ground where they belong. Mom wouldn't know and maybe my father doesn't either that once the node is installed, NASA will have established the beginning of a quantum network.

Moving us closer to creating a quantum internet, and to whoever is the fastest and the smartest go the spoils. Whoever harnesses quantum first rules this planet and beyond.

". . . It's just astonishing what young people can do this day and age, and that they care enough about spaceship Earth to worry about global warming, to want to save our farmland, forests, seacoasts and polar bears," my educator mom goes on about LEAR.

"It really is extraordinary," as I feel bad about leading her down the same faux primrose path as everyone else.

"Imagine your teacher challenging you to build an ozone detector among other things. And abracadabra! You do it, and it's going into space," she says, and *among other things* might be the understatement of the century.

26

"Exactly," I answer, not letting on how worried I am about the spacewalk, and the rocket launch from Wallops, and everything. "Yes, we've got a resupply headed up to the Station, in addition to the EVA, and if you imagine the telemetry involved . . . ? I can only assume Dad was called in for all that."

And that's not true either. I'm not assuming any such thing. More likely, Dick is directing what's going on, and I'm suspicious about who picked up my father. Or who he's meeting and if any of this is connected to my MIA sister. How can I not think it is after what Dick told me?

To listen to him, Carme is out of whack and off grid. The very conditions that he said are the most dangerous to any vehicle. Loss of control. Loss of signal. Added to that, one Pandora person has vanished, and another is suspiciously dead. If my sister is truly involved somehow, then what's happened to her, what really? It's as if she's been horribly reprogrammed, and what do they think she might do next?

"But Jeez," I'm saying sincerely to my mom, "I hate to think of Dad at Wallops in this weather. And it's a terrible drive after dark with that one-lane road in and out. I sure hope he's not headed there."

"Same-ol', same-ol'," is what she has to say about the way any of us live. "As you well know, my dear, when the going gets tough, that's when some of us get going while the rest of the world runs home and locks the door. And *Jeez* is right, poor George. I'm just glad he's not driving."

"Who picked him up?"

"He didn't say, and I didn't ask," she replies, and I'm not sure I believe her.

"Maybe you noticed what kind of vehicle might have pulled up to get him?"

"An SUV, big, caught a glimpse when he went out the door, but I couldn't tell who was driving. You know how dark it is even with all my lights everywhere. Anyway, I didn't go outside and don't know more than that."

"I guess he'll stay in the dorm at the old navy base," I suppose, and I've spent my share of nights at Wallops in the World War II bunker-like building, sleeping in a single bed, not much else including food or a bathroom to yourself.

"The dorm is pretty stark but the safest thing if we're clobbered," Mom's disembodied voice. "But last I heard it's hopeful that we won't get a direct hit, that the worst is going to miss us."

"As usual, no one knows what the weather's going to do until it does it," I reply. "But it sure would be good if the launch went as planned, and I suspect it will as close as we're getting. Just a few hours out."

"I believe the cargo going up includes Christmas goodies for the astronauts, not just ours but all of them. A shame if they get the Grinch this year instead," Mom worries.

"Dad didn't give you any indication what's expected? Why he was called instead of some other flight dynamicist? I mean, not that anyone can hold a candle to him. But why Dad? Depending what's going on, why not someone else?"

She says she wondered the same thing but doesn't know. Nor does she have an answer as to why he wouldn't have gone earlier today. What's so urgent? If something is screwy, why haven't I been told, and is whatever happening something Fran knows? I don't trust much what Mom is saying, and every other second, she asks me where I am. It's as if I can't get home soon enough, and I tell her I'm passing the old cemetery.

Now closing in on Francis Asbury Elementary School, where Carme and I attended until the 5th grade. Except to be accurate, we skipped the 1st and 5th grades, meaning we were there all of three years before skipping other grades in Eaton Middle School and Phoebus High, finishing up by the age of 15. Our precollege education was public and accelerated, and I feel sweetly sad, passing the single-story brick elementary school with its circular drive, the old hardwood trees strung with holiday lights.

The locals start their decorations early, in some instances at Halloween (my mom) or the day after Thanksgiving (most everybody else). Mailboxes, chimneys, porches and rooftops are wrapped, festooned and dripping with glittering strands of electric colors. Illuminated plastic Santas shake in the wind as if Old Saint Nick is laughing hard. And maybe he is. Although nothing is amusing or festive to me right now.

Not when one Pandora employee is missing and presumed murdered, while another one's alleged suicide most certainly was gruesomely staged. And then precisely and methodically *unstaged* for my benefit. Making sure I would know. Making sure I wouldn't let someone get away with murder. And also to be warned, which I am every time I think of the death trap rigging that resembled bent-pipe telemetry.

Or at least this is the beginning of the bizarre theory playing out in my mind nonstop. One that factors in my sister being connected to one or both events, and therefore presumed to be some kind of deranged murderer. To be out of touch and out of control like some autonomous aircraft outfitted with a warhead. When in fact I don't know that she's hurt anyone at all.

She wouldn't.

There's no real evidence so far. Not that I can see. But that doesn't mean my brazen other half hasn't incriminated herself somehow, and now is nowhere to be found. I believe that even Dick doesn't know where she is, and it would seem that in the past few short hours I've managed to cross into another dimension.

I find myself constantly checking my phone for an email, a text, and at the same time not wanting to hear from Carme because it's easier if I don't. Doesn't hurt as much. Isn't as scary. As if I'm supposed to change the way I feel about her with the

356

flip of a switch. Instantly. What doesn't Dick understand about loyalty?

He has no right asking me to choose. It's not up to anyone but me to decide how I'm going to handle things with her when it's time.

"Would you care to tell me what happened in there?" asking it hours later, and I can smell my shame as he pours us another drink.

"Thanks, but I shouldn't. I think I've been reckless enough for one day." Smelling bourbon and my damaged flesh as I sit at the kitchen table, my bandaged hand out of sight in my lap.

Detecting the iron odor of blood and adhesive.

"Don't be so hard on yourself!" Liz rustling up lunch. "It could have happened to anyone."

Staring at the TV mounted on the wall, ironically turned to her show, a taped episode of *Kitchen Combat.* Texas Rangers versus military cops duking it out during a Tex-Mex cook-off and margarita marathon. Watching Liz in two places at once. In the past on a recording while being with her in the flesh. Right now. Inside her kitchen.

Having drinks with Dick after almost losing my fingertip. Still might. Won't know for a while if the avulsed pad glued back is viable.

"The bagels weren't thawed all the way, and I pushed too hard with the knife." Just the thought makes my finger throb as I finally answer Dick's question. "Trying to slice them in half for toasting . . ."

"When I asked what happened, that's not what I meant." Looking at me with a glint in his eye like a pixel gone bad.

Or a gravitational grin or vague reflected light from an invisible distant planet. A pull of disapproval that's new. Indicating disappointment. A change of heart. Finally finding out I don't measure up.

"I meant why is everything always your fault, Calli?" Getting up as his bombshell TV star wife walks over with her famous bean burritos smothered in green chili.

"That's a pretty tough thing to say." Liz setting down our food, always taking my side, doesn't matter if I don't deserve it. "Be nice, Dick."

"He's right, and I'm sorry." I can't look at him. "I take full responsibility."

"And that's the sort of BS I don't want to hear again." Taking a bite of burrito, using his fork. "If you're going to be helpful to me ultimately . . . ? I mean, do you want that, Calli?" Dick pinning me like a butterfly to a board.

"Yes, sir."

"Then you need to be more like your sister," he says, and the way that feels, there are no words.

"I'll never be as good at certain things . . ."

"I mean dammit, Calli? You need to quit caring so much. You've got to care but not care. At times, you can't care, period."

"Don't always say you're sorry." Liz is quick to remind me I've got nothing to apologize about.

And yet the very reason Carme stopped caring about anything very much is because of what I did to her. I wasn't my sister's keeper, and something bad got milled into her chip that wasn't there before.

Unable to stomach the notion of snitching on her, of reporting back to him or anyone, I'm tied in knots. Does he really expect me to pick him over my identical twin?

Maybe I'll take orders, I think hotly. Maybe I won't, getting more offended by the moment. Not sure what I'll do, and as we say in quantum computing, it all depends. Before tonight, throwing my sister under the bus or not wasn't a coin to flip. A choice to make.

"*. . . I need to talk to her . . . ,*" hearing Dick as he sat in my truck, staring at the back of Dodd Hall.

Until now I've had no reason to question her behavior. Never before has there been a suggestion of criminal activity. I know she's done a lot of things, including taking out bad guys. But in the line of duty. Justifiably.

". . . She's capable . . ."

But in the line of duty. Justifiably, and I can't believe I'm even having these thoughts, and screw that, screw it all. I'm not going to promise anything to anyone, and I ease up on the gas, slowing my police truck at the entrance of our mile-long unpaved shared driveway. Black-velvet dark, leading to the cove where my dad grew up like his father and grandfather before him. Going back to when Lincoln was assassinated, the Chases have been rooted here. Free to be who and what we are, believing people are more alike than different.

Except I found out in short order not everyone feels the same way. The tree-lined lane I'm driving slowly along may look peaceful enough, but once upon a time it was the scene of a feud worthy of the Hatfields and McCoys. This was in early days when Carme and I hadn't entered Earth's atmosphere yet, not quite born, and therefore we didn't witness the invasion firsthand.

But we've certainly gotten the lowdown about the clan of unpleasant nonrelatives who immigrated to Hampton from the land of Yankees. Not that I've got anything against the North, only against uncouth and ignorant aggressors from anywhere. Flat-earthers, Neanderthals, I have plenty of sobriquets for the tribe that managed to infiltrate the Chase's tiny hamlet on Back River and start a land dispute among other squabbles that on occasion turned near violent.

Resulting in my shotgun-toting paternal grandmother (may Judi rest in peace) taking matters into her own hands as the women in my family do. Going out in the dark of night to plant pink and white dogwood trees down the middle of the driveway, her not-so-subtle message simple. *Pink* for the women who will blow you away if you mess with us. And *white* for, well, those trashy neighbors who used their side of the driveway to come and go while our folks went about their business on the other.

Over the years, the bad would move on and more good came to settle, and thankfully those less gentle days are over. Nobody skirmishing. No civil wars of uncouth aggression. Just people coming and going. Busy being busy. Too consumed by social media and binge-watching whatever's streaming to notice things going on right in front of them. I don't know all the neighbors anymore, and many don't stay on the water during what they consider the off-season.

For some, this is but a fair-weather home, and the rest of the time they live elsewhere in bigger cities like Richmond or Williamsburg that don't have the breathtaking views and daily dramas of coastal living in a part of the world that includes NASA, the navy, the air force. Around here it's nothing to see attack and surveillance aircraft, Unmanned Combat Aerial Vehicles (armed drones), aircraft carriers and nuclear subs cruising by.

I can't imagine living anywhere I'd love more. But it all depends on what floats your boat, and a lot of people don't notice much. At least they're polite and friendly when we pass each other on what my dad christened Penny Lane after he and Mom got married.

That's the name of our side of the driveway, painted neatly on a sign that my headlights flick past as I turn in, small rocks pinging against the truck's undercarriage.

The other side of the driveway has no sign anymore. But when it did, it was called Them Lane, a name Mom came up with, and I remember in the old days her sitting on the front porch, rocking Carme and me back and forth in the slider, shaking her head, making that clucking sound with her tongue like she does when there's "a heap of meanness" in the news, as she puts it.

There isn't much she hates more than bigotry and the petty ugliness that goes with it, and like a lot of people, we've put up with our share. The feuding neighbors didn't have to live here anymore for others to join into their nasty games. Egging our cars, hurling rolls of toilet paper into Mom's lighted trees, driving over the shrubbery, thinking it great fun to sabotage Dad's garden with weed killer, poisoning the ducks and geese Carme and I had named and fed, sinking the bass boat, leaving a snake in the bird feeder.

To mention a few of their unamusing shenanigans, and we couldn't prove a thing. Not that we doubted the identity of the offenders, and as I like to say, you don't have to live on Them Lane or anywhere special to be a bigoted a-hole. The only requirements for membership are an overwhelming need to judge others for how they look, walk, talk, and whether or where they go to church. And what they own and who they love or don't.

The cruel dues paid ensure a privileged position in a primitive pecking order, and the higher the rank, the lower one sinks into a hell of his or her own making. That's what Mom says. Stupid and wasteful. What a destructive way to live when we come from the same stardust, every last one of us. She wrote it up in her most popular NASA lesson plan, number 112, from many years ago, the title "Live Among the Stars." Her bestselling one to date for her science, technology, education and math, STEM, outreach, with more than 100,000 downloads last year alone.

Which must be some kind of record, and as I round a bend in the driveway that follows the curve of the river, Mom's presence begins to glow sapphire blue. Eerily, like an interstellar nebula. Like Cherenkov radiation from an underwater nuclear reactor. Her blue light pollution lifts the foggy gloom as I get closer to home, listening to her over speakerphone.

". . . After a shutdown? I don't know, hon, I can't seem to get back on track like I used to," complaining about the furlough. "Who can when you never know if your funding's about to be cut? Again. Or when you'll be locked out of your building and computer. Again."

Truth is, Mom's not felt on track since an ultrasound showed a mass on her spleen. When she was diagnosed with non-

Hodgkin's lymphoma, there was no question who would take care of her. She's always called me her familiar.

"At least you can work from home," I hear myself saying to her as I bump slowly along, driving closer to the blue glow.

Thinking of my sister's silly joke. *Don't move toward the blue light, or you'll wake up dead on Pluto!*

"Well, as you of all people know, we're not supposed to do any work at all . . ." Mom's dubious voice, forever a school-teacher at heart.

And no matter how resourceful, she believes in doing what's right, including following instructions and rules. Or you go to the principal. Within reason, that is. Maybe. And it all depends.

"Overall, you're saying her behavior has seemed more extreme . . . ," thinking of what Dick said about Carme.

"I know, I know," I reassure Mom, "but all those kids out there are waiting on pins and needles for your lesson plans . . . You're like the ice cream truck coming, jingle, jingle. You make people want to help themselves."

"Ha-ha-ha. If only that were true."

"Actually, it is," and I'm not making it up. "The kids can't get enough. Not to mention the teachers relying on you. Look," I lower my voice as if we're conspiring, "as long as you don't use a NASA computer, who's going to know what you do in your own home at your own kitchen table while nobody's paying you to work?" I feel my ire rising again and try to put a lid on it.

"Listen to you," Mom's surprised voice. "Since when are you such the rule breaker?"

"Only when they're stupid and harmful."

"Goodness, aren't you full of it tonight? What on earth's gotten into you?"

"Maybe everything," as I enter what looks like Orbit City meets Christmas World.

"Lights, lights everywhere, and not a one can think," to quote my sister's nerdy rhyme that she used to singsong all the time, poking good-natured fun at our mother, who isn't a mindless hoarder with an obsession. But close when it comes to her strands of miniblues that start with the twin stone columns I'm passing through, built of native granite by my great-grandfather. His pièce de résistance the copper plate etched with *Chase Place,* patinated green and pitted from unfriendly BB guns.

My run-flats roll slowly over loose stones, nearing our rambling white frame house, gracious and inviting in a nimbus that glows like Saint Elmo's fire over silvery metal roofs, huge live oaks and magnolias. Mom's minilights flicker excitedly, wrapped with engineering precision around trees, and illuminating an astonishing topiary she sculpts and trims with hedge clippers, transforming boxwoods, arborvitae and other perennials into cosmic wonders.

I drive through Jetson-style buildings on columns, rockets and flying saucers, crew capsules, planet-scapes inhabited by whimsical extraterrestrials in hues of blue, twinkling and shimmering a brilliant welcome. The rampant dragon breathes cobalt fire as I pass by, and the inflatable Santa astronaut is having a turbulent time but is ho-ho-happy. And I could swear there weren't this many lights when I left for work in the pitch dark this morning.

Mom must have been industrious after she got home, the trees and boxwoods around the barn winking like galaxies of blue-eyed aliens. Never a good place to park around here. Nothing near the door, and I pull off the driveway onto the balding grassy area near the dock where I always leave my truck. Noticing Fran's house on the other side of the garden, the windows glowing, a TV flickering through the draperies in the den.

Easton is up way past his bedtime in case

the government shuts down and Fran heads back to Langley, dropping him at Mom's on the way. Sometimes carrying him in conked out, and he wakes in the morning across the way as if teleported. Not ideal or beyond criticism, I suspect.

But when you grow up with furloughs and rockets, you don't keep the same schedule as most folks you know. At least, we never have.

27

My boots squish wetly as I hurry through the biting cold, and a powerful weather system is headed here for sure.

My sensing it isn't easily explained, maybe similar to animals knowing an earthquake, tsunami, volcanic eruption, stampede or other disaster is on the way. The silly family lore is that nerdy me came out of the box equipped with my own seismograph, temperature and pressure sensors, static ports, pitot tube, and ability to understand what clouds have to say.

All of which are letting me know what's coming, and no matter how inconvenienced or distracted I might be, storms are magical to me. For a moment I fantasize that everything will stop as it did eons ago when squalls raged in and we'd batten down the hatches, everyone together. Watching thunderheads go to war over the river, taking umbrage darkly, hurling lightning bolts and booming like cannons.

Leading to the usual Chase contemplations about energy and mass, that everything is about the laws of physics and chemistry, including the big bang, and the way biological creatures act. Most of all people. Learning my mom's homespun wisdom of letting momentous events play themselves out, like when lightning split the old tree with the tire swing by the dock.

Once we got past the loss of our woody childhood playmate, the joke was that the live oak became a dead one. Eventually we took it down, using the lumber to help build the loft that Carme and I would occupy on the barn's second floor. Fortunately, not every natural drama is hazardous, and I love going to sleep to the loud hammering of a hard rain on the corrugated tin roof. Or best of all, waking up to a foot of snow piled on tree branches, pine boughs, the bird feeders, big flakes drifting down like in a paperweight.

I always knew the instant my eyes blinked open in the early dawn, could feel the damp chill, the silence as complete as when I'm surrounded by acoustic foam in the anechoic chamber. As insulated from outside interference as when in the HIRF lab. I'd sit up in bed, pushing the curtain aside, feeling the window's ice-cold glass, the porch light illuminating black tree trunks and dark-green tightly furled leaves against pure white.

Darting around in a limbic hunt for coats, mittens, boots, wherever Carme and I stashed them last because Hampton is surrounded by water that warms the air just enough to be a spoiler. On the wrong side of the snow line, often we're slammed with only the miserable stuff. Sleet and rain, ice and downed power lines, the grocery stores sold out of milk and bread, total pandemonium during life and work as usual.

But a showstopping snow (didn't take much) was a rare gift that meant no school, and nonessential government employees like Mom and Dad not going in. It meant hot chocolate and staying up to watch TV, and building fires and igloos, snowball fights and sledding. And Carme and I lying on our backs in deep powder, making angel wings, and trudging new paths, leaving our footprints for all to see, if only temporarily.

Everything fresh and clean until it wasn't anymore, and my face is numb. I can't feel my feet as I haul my gear through the volatile night. Blasts of frigid air grab at my chemical suit, my gear and hair, and I'm struck once again by the spell nature casts, all creatures great and small hunkered down, huddling to keep warm, the air heavy and stone still. Just the sounds of the wind kicking in angrily, rocking trees and shaking shrubbery like frantic pompoms, sending dead leaves fleeing and swirling.

Walking fast, head bowed, nearing the family timber-framed barn. Need to get inside and out of these wet things fast before they flash freeze on me, the windchill somewhere in the neighborhood of −23 Celsius (−10 Fahrenheit), if I had to guess. Headed to my private habitat, for all practical purposes a monster garage that in an earlier era was appointed with stalls and haylofts for donkeys and cows.

Kept warm and well fed by all accounts, and in more recent memory my sister and I fostered a number of rescues. A potbellied pig, a gaggle of ornamental chickens, rabbits and my pet fainting goat, who easily collapsed in a panic. I named him Boo after my favorite character in *To Kill a Mockingbird,* prompting Carme and others to blurt out the poor goat's name loudly and when least expected, causing him to topple.

No furry or feathery friends at Chase Place now, not since the family bulldog, Ruger, went on to glory last spring, and gosh darn it's cold. Scary cold, like you'd die in no time if stranded outside, and I'm shivering badly, my keys jingling as I stiffly find the right one with my frozen fingers. Hurrying past the shut bay door, big enough to drive a tractor or small airplane through, and mind you I said *small*.

Dad may be an inventive genius, but he's not always practical, can be more than a little forgetful, what we kindly refer to as being the absentminded professor, except he couldn't possibly teach the brilliant madness brewing inside that brain of his. But I'm here to tell you it's the little crap that will get you, which is why I always work out problems on paper first. Although there's no need to bother when it's a question of a 10.6-meter wingspan (35 feet) fitting through a 9.1-meter-wide (30 feet) bay door.

A minus B, simple subtraction tells you the result won't be optimal. Did no good to tell him either, and moving the fuselage of the '54 Piper Super Cub inside the barn was fine. Towing it out after he'd put the wings back on was another story when it was time for a test flight on the grass strip that used to run along the river a couple decades ago.

That plane eventually got traded up for the '65 Beechcraft Baron he keeps in a hangar at the Newport News airport, the plane Carme and I learned to fly. We were too young for lessons when it was the misfit of a Piper, although I have fragmented memories of being in Mom's lap, looking out the side window, our plane powered by what sounded like a huge lawn mower. Feeling the cool wind rushing in. Looking down at our house and barn getting smaller.

As we soared over the river, I could see the runways at Langley Air Force Base. And NASA's A-frame gantry, looming on the horizon like a colossal swing set, as if built by giants. I remember wondering why anyone would be earthbound if the choice was that or traveling through the air, the ether, and heading to the side door I always use, I wonder why the porch light is out.

Because it was working fine this morning when I left for Langley in the pitch dark. Looking around, I listen to the wind howl and moan around the eaves, blowing through trees in an agitated stage whisper. The hair prickles on the back of my neck as I feel a presence again, that same strange sensation of being watched, aware of it like the insidious pull of a magnet or electrical vibration.

The lock clicks softly as I turn the key not twice but once to the left. It's also not right that the dead bolt wasn't set, and I walk in, the security alarm beeping instantly. That's good, at least. Shutting the heavy oak door behind me, I'm enveloped by warm darkness, deep and dense like velvet, mindful of the familiar odors of old wood, paints, solvents and possibly something else.

A whiff of a fragrance so fragile it might be imagined, and there it is again. And just as quickly gone. As if I'll turn around and find Carme close enough to touch. Smelling faintly of White Musk. Seated at a worktable, looking like a hologram of me. Armed with pencils and a binder full of graph paper. Working out problems and predictions in the language of everything, math.

I enter the code on the alarm system's keypad, and the beeping stops, silence abruptly returning as the air vaguely stirs near my head. I feel it again as faint as a breath, and it's not the heat pumps kicking in. It's not fans blowing or a draft, and if it's what I think it is, then that's not normal, either. Especially when Dad isn't home.

Someone's been in here and maybe still is.

Quietly, with no sudden moves, I lower my gear bags to the floor. My right hand releases the gun from its tactical thumb-drive holster, index finger straight out above the trigger, weapon drawn and ready.

Listening, motionless like a hulking iceberg in my frostbitten ballistic and chemical gear. Trying to stop shivering inside, to slow down my breathing. Whatever stirred overhead like a hummingbird seems to have vanished in thin air. I know it's not a barn owl, flying squirrel or other nocturnal critter flitting about. Nothing alive by the usual definition, and I'm on red alert.

Too many things aren't right, and I streak down the list. Extra strands of lights around the barn as if welcoming me home. The porch light out. The dead bolt unlatched. The motion-sensitive lantern-sconces not coming on when I walked into the entryway just now. More disturbing is what stirred overhead in the dark, stealthy quiet, creating but a whiff of rotor wash. I throw on the dead bolt and reset the alarm.

"Anybody home?" And what a dumb thing to shout out loud, one might suppose.

Except not by my calculation. Mom's an acre away inside the house, and I know that because I was just on the phone with her. Fran's home with Easton. Dad's possibly at Langley and could be on his way to Wallops Island. In any case, he wouldn't sneak around in here with the lights out, spying and not answering.

So, unless an unknown intruder managed to unlock the door, bypass the alarm system, and wears my sister's signature White Musk scent? I'm not coming up with candidates for who might be in the barn besides me. Unless it's *her.* Otherwise I'd be a lot more aggressive than I am right now. In kill mode, if necessary.

"Carme? Are you in here?"

I'm not afraid of her. Even if I should be, and I don't want to shoot my sister. That can't happen, and we also don't need to be shooting each other. Thoughts like this scream through my head as I feel along the wall near the door for the light switch. Flipping it up and down, up and down.

Click-click-click-click.

Not working, and I need to dial it back, take deep breaths, take it easy. If I've learned nothing else, it's to get in sync and pay attention. Not to freak out. Doing what I was trained. Laser focus. Nothing personal because birth and death aren't. Only everything else.

I'm aware of my thawing hands burning and full of pins. Of my trigger finger and the residual numbness in the scar. Not as bad as it was, but I don't have the same sense of touch, and if she wanted me dead,

I would be.

"Carme, if you're in here, say something!" Setting my truck key, my ID badge and lanyard on the small table.

Easing away from the door, mindful of the doormat and boot scraper, the coatrack, the small table. More worried about bumping into something than being attacked, which is stupid. Never doing anything with her perfection and calculated finesse. As if she's artificial intelligence and I'm "try, try again." *If at first you don't succeed. I think I can, I think I can,* and finding the master switch, I flood the main workshop with incandescent light.

Blinking hard in the glare, ready with my gun, scanning from where I am. No immediate signs of a break-in, and I don't see anything flying or perched, including in the rafters. At a glance, everything seems as I left it last, the workbenches, test beds, the 4-post car lift, the 1950s beige Formica countertops and cabinet facings. The familiar shopworn drill presses, saws, sanders, lathes, grinders and other machines. The tool cases and hardware organizers. The paint-spattered white sink that I've scrubbed with Ajax until I can feel the grittiness in my sleep.

Plastering the walls are vintage war and

aviation posters. Plus, the calendars Dad won't take down because they mean something to him. 1986, the year he and Mom were married. 1991, when his twin daughters were born, and 1964, when he was. Hands down his favorite is the classic cars calendar for 1968, the year the astronauts on Apollo 8 took the first selfie of Earth, filming the "blue marble" on their way to orbit the moon.

When he happened upon a '68 Camaro in need of an overhaul and therefore affordable, it was meant to be. A signal, a sign from above. The muscle car of his youthful dreams is now parked off to the side, covered like a dead giant in a gray pouch, shamed and brought down by the Lilliputians of entropy and chaos, a dash of antimatter thrown in for bad measure.

Not gone but over. Not going anywhere anymore. Dad cranks it up regularly, and moves it to make sure the battery doesn't die and the tires don't rot. But not much beyond that. I can't remember the last time he took off for a joyride in his chariot of fire engine red with a front black stripe. I'm not sure when Carme and I last sat in the black leather bucket seats, not since we graduated from college. But in the earlier days, we did what was cool and expected, tootling about in the hottest ride in town.

For techno-nerds and motor heads, we weren't into it, didn't reminisce about where the car came from or what it meant to anyone. We didn't care about the high-performance V-8 engine or how we sounded when we percussed through the middle of town, our hot-rodding overcast by a past we didn't discuss. Didn't relive what went on those months the Camaro was on the lift, taken apart and put back together again. Didn't talk about the summer our guileless father and his flamboyant traveling stunt-pilot friend rebuilt the engine, completely overhauling every inch, restoring the car with original parts.

In mint condition, as good as new, and if only the same were true of Carme. But not everything can be fixed, and the '68 Camaro is one of those things in life you can't get rid of or keep, either one, which is why it stays under wraps year round. I don't want to look at it, and rarely do anymore unless I happen to be here when Dad fires it up.

"Rats . . . !" Under my breath, crouching to struggle with my bootlaces, the frozen double bows, while keeping up my scan, Glock in hand.

I have no desire to take the cover off that

car, go for a spin, fueled by bad memories and hauntings that I'll never stop analyzing. Better if we'd never owned it. Better if our father's flyboy friend hadn't helped himself to it. To the barn. Our house. Our hearts. Paying attention the way he did.

"Jiminy Cricket!" Frustrated out of my mind, trying to make my thawing fingers work, and if Carme wanted to take me out right now, I'd be so wasted.

Boots off, next my sopping-wet socks, leaving them, my gear bags to deal with later. I remove my tactical vest and gun belt. Unzipping the chemical suit, peeling it off in rustling plastic sounds that bring to mind a deflated wading pool. Leaving a heap on the floor, everything else I've got on soaked through and through, including my vintage leather jacket.

But considering that it survived a world war only to be handed down and eventually dishonorably discharged to a vintage lingerie boutique. Where it was flaunted by a sexy female Rambo mannequin in the window. Misunderstood and undervalued. Which was where Dick and Liz rescued the jacket for me (no questions asked). And after all it's been through, I suppose it will dry just fine. And I'm not stripping down further. Not until I get upstairs. Pistol pointed down, my heart thudding hard, I begin to move about, searching, making sure I'm alone while certain I'm not.

Sensing something around me, aware of it as vividly as humidity or prickly heat. But I don't feel scared.

"Carme?" And of course, no answer, her name hanging in the air.

Heading to the far side of the room, I survey tables arranged with tools, with components for all sorts of autonomous creations that might be creepy crawling, buzzing or zipping around. Wandering past workbenches scattered with spare arms and rotor blades. Controllers, camera mounts and carbon fiber . . .

She's somewhere near.

. . . Damping plates. USB and ribbon cables. Power modules and handheld lasers. Distribution boards and taillights . . .

Feeling her attention like gravity.

. . . Robot switches, servos, wheels, couplers, cogs, gears and boards . . .

"Carme? Are you here . . . ?" And I almost yell, *Come out, come out wherever you are . . . !*

28

Lifting the car cover enough to see through the driver's window. Knowing she's in there.

Sitting in the dark with the door locked. Doing what, I never can figure out. Spending hours without anybody knowing. Unless she makes sure we do when her rude mood strikes.

"Come out, come out wherever you are!" Holding up the gray cover.

On to her shtick of slipping under it, worming through the barely open driver's door, pulling it shut so no one can tell she's inside. Unless she honks the horn or starts the engine.

"Carme? I see you." Peering through the window at her shaking her head. "Unlock it, this is stupid."

Making faces, gesturing for me to leave her the heck alone, calling me a tagalong, but I'm not going anywhere ever again. Doesn't matter what she might do or say. Holding my ground, rapping on the door.

"Open the door, Carme!"

"Go away!" Smushing her face against the glass, and boy will Dad be unhappy with that.

You don't need to touch the glass, he's always saying. Carme doesn't care, opening the door, finally letting me in. Both of us in the bucket seats, in complete darkness, smelling the old leather. And looking at her is like looking at me.

Flipping on the lights in a small space that once upon a time was a cow stall, I notice the workbench and what's on it.

The carbon fiber spheres weigh anywhere from 100 to 800 grams (0.2 to 1.8 pounds), ranging from volley- to medicine ball size, 11 round frames resting on 11 beanbags. Missing number 12 is our flashiest invention to date, a cantaloupe-size mirror ball that Dad, Carme and I were noodling with when she was home last.

None of this is supposed to be out in plain view, for crummy sake. It wasn't when I headed to Langley this morning. Certainly, I would have noticed. I have to walk right through this area on my way out the door. I know I didn't leave all this exposed and neglected, and if Dad was working in here today, when might that have been?

He came home from Langley late afternoon only to turn around and go out again. But even if he did manage to slip inside the barn for an hour or two, for sure he would have locked Mom's holiday gift back in its storage cabinets or at least covered the workbench with a tarp. Dad isn't careless, and he may be forgetful, but not when it comes to her.

Had she wandered into the barn, her big holiday surprise was blown. She would have walked right into a gaggle of Personal Orbs Not Grounded (PONGs) that eventually will live on a Perch Recharger (PRCH) she can remotely access with an app on her phone. There's no end to the fun she'll have, and I can imagine her festively floating her autonomous little friends around, picking styles and colors, figuring out the coolest PRCH, which can be almost anything you want and not limited to just one. From a boring charging station to a hat rack, light fixture, ceiling planet mobile, a living plant, a tree, whatever you come up with, limited only by creativity.

All that's required are sensors and a power source, which is what I've added to the Norfolk star pine in my office upstairs. An idea my sister had last month after our interviews in Houston when she was home for a week. And we spent a lot of time at this very workbench, coming up with all sorts of ideas, including the mirrored disco ball that's more than just glitzy.

Its reflective open-air frame can go stealth by blending with the surrounds like a squid. Imagine a skeleton orb hiding in foliage, mirroring the leaves and flowers around it. But such a thing can also be used for bouncing light off objects and taking measurements. Or answering questions, making reservations and running cyber errands, googling and interrogating databases. The orb may be able to do a lot of things by the time all is said and done.

But for now, I imagine it spinning over the property with others of different sizes and colors, smooth or sparkling like Fabergé eggs, their open frames caging rotor blades that vanish when spinning fast. PONGs just have to be round, and in our workshop all of them start life a luminescent sapphire blue in honor of Mom.

That doesn't mean they can't change hues, have special moves and skills, each orb with its own unique personality, a pocket drone assistant and spy, a red balloon following you around Paris, so to speak. Who knows what else because the sky's the limit, the roly-poly pals equipped with intelligent onboard systems, antennas, sensors, mini-cameras, all sorts of things with room to grow. But even PONGs need to rest, and each is tethered by a Signaled Transient Mechanism, STM (my dad and his acronyms), basically a gentle electromagnetic charge that attaches to the PRCH like an invisible ornament hook.

On deployment the signal is dropped, the charge releases and as the orb undocks, the internal multistack rotor system fires up, each blade moving independently. The lively balls can quick-stop and turn like a Formula 1 Ferrari, and of late Dad and I have been adding LEDs that change from red to green. They can shine in a steady beacon or strobe like mini-UFOs, whatever's your pleasure.

Tinkering, plotting and planning for months, the goal is 12 orbs for the 12 days of Christmas, hovering, orbiting and dancing through the night sky over our cove with its blue-blazing lights. But all fun and games aside, our autonomous orbs one day will be put to good use as assistants of sorts, grabbing objects in grippers to help out around the office or house, especially if someone is older or infirm.

Making deliveries, tracking weather and people. Perhaps being sent as advance teams to check out a route or crowd size, flying over while live-streaming video and a full report. Or how about cruising around to help you find a parking spot? Or if you work at NASA, the bicycle or car you lost. Or buzzing about to see what and who else might be in the area, perhaps hackers snooping on what law enforcement and the government are up to.

The capabilities are endless. Including a day (sooner than later) when much larger orbs will pick up and deliver passengers. And I'd be the first to say that it's hard to imagine what sort of world we'll be living in when people are floating around like the Good Witch of the North in her bubble.

"If anybody's in here, you'd better let me know," I say out loud, gun in hand. "Carme? Is that you . . . ?"

She could be on the property. She could be inside the barn this very moment, and I'm not afraid. Carme won't hurt me.

Don't be stupid.

I keep telling myself blood isn't thicker than madness, desperation or whatever seems to be fueling her. Cain killed Abel, after all, and knowing such things makes little difference when it's the identical twin I love like my own self. I'm not naive, but I'm not listening. Right now, I don't care what Dick said about the missing Pandora aerospace engineer. I don't care that there's a Pandora employee dead. I care only about Carme.

If she's behind such atrocities or in any way responsible, then I remind myself she's not the sister I know, certainly not identical to me or anyone in the Chase family. Not anymore, and it would be nothing for her to get into anything on the farm where she was born and raised.

She wouldn't unjustly kill anyone.

My twin sister could help herself to what she wants and take out anybody in her way, considering the caliber of military operative and intellect we're talking about. I can't imagine tracking her, not that I've ever tried. But I'm not sure I could, not even with one of my magic wands. Not if she's gone irretrievably AWOL. Turned. Lost her way. Those early bent underpinnings finally giving way.

No.

One thing I do know for a fact. Carme isn't to be trifled with or underestimated. Trained to confuse and conceal, she could mirror electromagnetic intruders I routinely sniff out, and I might not notice her. All she has to do is pick devices that transmit in frequencies close to what I typically track and expect, peaks overlapping other peaks.

As if she's wearing an electronic ghillie suit that causes her to vanish into the background. Sort of hide-and-seek with a quantum twist, the easiest way to disappear is to be in two places at once and duck behind your duplicate. A neat quantum trick best illustrated when Mom had worn-out bedsheets to repurpose, and Carme and I ended up ghosts one Halloween. Talk about being impossible to tell us apart, and that gave me the idea of setting two full-length mirrors across from each other.

My twin and I stood between them back to back, the same size, draped exactly alike in our flowing dingy white linens with eyeholes cut out, each staring at her own reflection in her own mirror. Presto! I couldn't see Carme anymore. All I could see was my own ghostly self, and all she could see was her own ghostly self. Even though we were so close we could feel the other's heat.

In separate places and together at the same time. Present but absent. Like Schrödinger's cat, a quantum conundrum, *This End Up* when the arrows point in opposite directions. The stuff that keeps me awake and happy at night, my bread and butter, my passion, and Carme could be at my back even as I'm thinking this. Not literally, but she might be looking at me, watching every move I make.

I won't find her unless she decides, and that's pretty much been our lives. She pilots, and I go along for the ride. Or sit something out. Whatever she says. Like the summers we played intramural basketball on Langley's championship team, the Water Bears. She and Rush were cocaptains and most valuable players while I was the manager, which suited me fine. Turns out I have quite the knack for keeping score, engineering drills, designing logos, bolstering team spirit, counseling psyched-out overachieving NASA jocks.

I worry Carme has me sufficiently distracted that I'm not thinking clearly. Causing me to question myself, to second-guess, to be extra careful about checking off every box. Especially if I don't really want to know the answer, and padding barefoot back to the main room, my heart pounds in my neck as I lift the cover from the Camaro, just to make sure. And there it is when it can't be, the cheek-shaped smudge on the inside of the driver's window. Obviously not left over from when Carme was a disturbed little girl.

"Jeez," under my breath, hollowed out by

the sudden flashes of images, the memories . . .

Focus. Focus. Focus!

The car may be a lot of things, but it's not a time capsule that's been left as is for the past 22 years. It's accessed regularly, kept up and cleaned, and I peer through the glass at the familiar black leather interior. The ashtray open as usual with the key inside. The shifter for the 4-speed manual transmission. The radio with its big silver knobs, and the 8-track player. In the glove box should be Three Dog Night, the Grass Roots, Elton John.

Cassette tapes from our parents' era that my sister and I would listen to when driving around. Or while sitting inside the car, parked and covered like it is right now, with her behind the wheel, deliberately leaving smudges on her window to punish everyone. Me in the passenger seat, together hiding from the world, and I try the door. Opening it a little, and there's the scent again, White Musk, and I'm always saying that Carme ought to buy stock in the Body Shop.

What am I supposed to think? Nothing other than the obvious. She's been here, might still be inside the barn, and door shut, cover straightened, I walk away. It may sound strange to say but not to me that at times I sense her presence palpably, even if I know for a fact she's hundreds or thousands of miles away. I can feel her thoughts like vibrations along a thread, the matrix of our shared reality a delicate web where every impulse and motion are experienced, the good with the bad into infinity.

We've never needed convincing about Einstein's spooky actions at a distance. It rather much sums up what goes on with us, can't nudge one without nudging the other, everything double fun or double trouble. And turning off the light, I backtrack past Mom's Christmas PONGs. Headed to my quarters, and while it's not intentional, the way my loaner crash dummy, Otto, is parked near the stairs, one might wonder if he's guarding the second floor, where I live.

Not saying a guard dummy couldn't be a new thing, but he's not one. Just out of the way of traffic. Head cocked a little, slouched in his wheelchair all by his lonesome, the metal lifting ring protruding from the top of his hairless pate reminding me of a short-wave loop antenna.

"Don't be frightened." And yes, I talk to him.

My silent helper has no reaction to my being armed, dangerous and looking like death on a cracker, to borrow one of Carme's expressions. Staring at me sideways, a little quizzical, a little miffed, as if wondering why he's naked as the day he was made, wearing nothing but his tan synthetic skin. His chest unzipped and wide open, a few cables hanging out, his rubbery hands holding a set of keys like Saint Peter.

Except these are hex keys that I misplaced the other day while trying out sensors that aren't off the shelf but are ones of my own divining. Because information is dangerous when it's untruthful, whether we're talking about an airlock in a tunnel or the steel-ribbed chest cavity of a NASA anthropomorphic test device. Accurate answers to life-and-death questions are the only way we're going to know whether an environment is safe to work in.

Or what will happen when astronauts splash down in a certain type of crew capsule.

Will they suffer neck or spine injuries? What happens to the pelvis? What about the head? How disastrous if the data collected by accelerometers or load and motion sensors aren't to be trusted. Because I know all too well that humans aren't so hot about stating the facts, all too quick to buck up, keep the good ole stiff upper lip, take it on the chin and similar BS.

None of which is helpful, and I remind Otto and his fellow dummies that they mustn't be macho and lie about how many g-forces they can take in vertical drop tests with and without parachutes. They aren't being good test pilots if they make me think it didn't hurt when they're slammed around, shaken and stirred more exponentially un-gently than the last time they took a spin in a prototype flying taxi.

They don't have to cry and moan in pain, but don't call it a nice time or pretend you survived if neither would be true if a living dummy tried the same. I can't imagine anything much worse than being responsible for a vehicle design that results in bodily harm or death, and I pick up the hex keys that Otto seems to be holding for me. Very helpful of him. But I know he didn't find them where I might have left them last.

"Hmmmm."

It's as if he's reminding me to take off his arms, and replace his lumbar block with a newer one that twists in 6 directions. I'm not losing my mind. I know the hex keys weren't here the other day, couldn't find them anywhere, was sure I absently set them somewhere illogical. That they'd turn up eventually. And they did, boy howdy, in an insanely off-nominal way, pretty much like everything else this day.

I try to remember if Otto was holding them this morning when I hurried past. I don't think so. But I also wasn't looking, and standing perfectly still, I listen. I scan the rafters and all around, hardly breathing before climbing the stairs to the loft, where Carme and I still keep our separate quarters, even though she's hardly ever home. As much as our father loves the air force, it's not surprising that the remodeled upstairs is reminiscent of Dodd Hall.

More so now compared to when my sister and I lived up here before heading off to Rice University at the age of barely 15. Once I moved back home after Colorado Springs, I had to do a little refiguring. Putting in a kitchenette, for example, because I can't possibly make it to the house for every meal. No matter how much I crave my mom's cooking.

29

At the top of the stairs, I take a right, padding quietly over the wooden floor. Sticky and gross in my sweaty street clothes, and I feel the noise around me. Or imagine I do.

What I think of as dirty air, an atmosphere saturated by invisible electromagnetic energy I pick up as if I'm an antenna. Or maybe I'm overly sensitive and imaginative. But at times like this I halfway wonder if I'm a two-legged array, walking slowly along the dark hallway. Identifying different pitches and chords of the wind. B-flat. C-minor.

Recognizing shapes and odors. The plumb cut of the rafter that isn't perfectly vertical. The varying degrees of musty dampness as I follow the hallway to the northeast corner. Glock in hand, down by my side, intuition going wild, amygdala firing, picking up an energy field that moves as I do. Following me like a host of orbs I can't see, and I feel strangely safe, yet warned and wary as I step into my suite.

The blackout shades are down in both windows as they always are after dark, otherwise I'd see Mom's miniblues flickering like thousands of tiny flames in trees along the river and the dock. Flipping on the lights, I'm greeted by my computers and spectrum analyzers set up on the desk and worktables. I wander over to check, tapping the displays out of sleep mode, recognizing the usual peaks and waves streaming by in different colors, the expected noise floor.

I stop by the window nearest the bathroom, where my star pine tree, Glinda, is looking a bit woebegone and parched in her copper pot. Gentle, fernlike with delicate feathered branches that turn a vibrant spring green when touched by affection and the sun, my pet tree hasn't had so much as a ray of attention all day.

"I'm sorry," as I pick up the spray bottle of filtered water. "I know you're thirsty and had no sunlight. Not that any of us did, as overcast as it's been." Giving her a quick spritzing, and I don't need Darwin to tell me that plants are living and sensing.

Registering pleasure and distress, their electrical pulses are easily translated into music or math. And in the case of my little pine, she's a photosynthesis machine producing power through delicate flexible polymer "wires" and "circuits" made from organic materials that are wicked up through the xylem, the tubelike channels that transport water.

In other words, Glinda, as I've named her, is a PRCH. A living charging station. A place for orbs to hang out, snooze, and wake up refreshed, making me wonder if hundreds of years from now we'll be able to tell a drone perch from a pelican nest. Birds and PONGs might be one and the same. Maybe not even hundreds of years. Maybe decades from now at the rate technology is proliferating, and I've got to get out of these clothes.

Starting with my wet leather flight jacket, spreading it flat on a towel on the bathroom floor as I call Mom on speakerphone.

"I'm down and secure," I say right off, pilot talk for *I've landed safely.*

I shut the door and lock it. There. Better. I set down my cell phone on the edge of the sink, next to my pistol, keeping both hands free.

"I was hoping that was your truck I heard on the driveway," her voice sounds subdued inside my bathroom.

"Just letting you know I'm about to get

into the shower." Yanking off my white cotton blouse, reminded not to wear it when there's a chance it might get wet, not unless something's over it.

"I've rustled up a little snack and thought I'd deliver it." Mom's voice doesn't sound the same as a while ago. "Boneless ribs, cheese grits . . ."

"I don't want you walking outside," I cut her off, because the last thing I need right now is my mother coming here.

With her PONGs out in plain view, and the possibility that Carme is on the property, possibly inside the barn. It's also not like our highly evolved southern mother to volunteer to *drop off* dinner as if she's Grubhub.

She doesn't want me at the house right now for some reason.

That's what I'm sensing, but it can't be right. I must be really strung out and tired. All the same, it's a strange thing for her to volunteer, especially when Dad's suddenly out for the night. It's completely out of character for her to suggest dropping anything by at this hour. It's not like I don't have a kitchenette with plenty to eat, if only I had time.

"Is everything okay?" I sit on the edge of the toilet lid to pull off my pants. "You sound a little preoccupied or something, and I really don't want you walking over here, okay? I don't want to worry you, Mom, but there's a lot of weird stuff going on. And I'm not just talking about the furlough and the evacuation. Or Dad being called out in the middle of the night."

"I hate that he had to go anywhere, and admit to feeling sort of spooked."

Then why don't you want me to come over?

"I know I shouldn't say it because I don't want to give energy to it," Mom's voice as I look at my train wreck self in the mirror over the sink. "But I'm worried something's not right, that something bad is going on. Maybe explaining why Dick suddenly showed up when we happen to have a big launch here in Virginia instead of Cape Canaveral."

"Why do you say that?"

"Well . . . Huh. I wasn't born yesterday."

"And for the record, Mom, I've not heard a word about any problem. Hard to imagine I wouldn't know if there's a potential security breach, for example. Or a potential of hacking. When something goes wrong, I'm the Maytag Man no one respects. I get called."

That's the way it's supposed to be, and what I can't fathom is why Dad would have been summoned instead of me. He's a flight dynamicist, an inventor and not the trained expert in cyber security that I am. If there's a worry about some bad actor having a nefarious plot afoot relating to the launch, then why him? Why not me?

"It's . . . well, I didn't just fall off the potato truck," one of mom's favorite clichés, "and it's not like it's normal for George to be picked up in, well I'm just going to say it. What looked suspiciously like a government SUV. A Suburban. Black. And there may have been more than one."

Finally, she comes clean. And if there *may* have been more than one, then there were, and the specter of the Secret Service is before me yet again. And she's right. Something's not normal, and I need to get a briefing from Rush. Or from someone.

"I confess to feeling a bit off balance, it all seemed so hush-hush and urgent. Anyway, maybe I'm a tad lonely too," Mom is saying.

"Do you want me to drop by for a few minutes before I head back to Langley?" Running my fingers through my short dark hair sticking up everywhere.

"No, no, I'll be fine. And what weird stuff?"

"Things at work. Not to mention, what

you just said about Dad. Have you heard from him?" I inquire.

"No. And I'm sure I'm worrying too much. It's been quite the day, and maybe I'm a little jumpy," her voice is wobbly. "The way the wind's howling and moaning. And the extreme cold makes things shift, creak and crackle. Sometimes I almost think someone's walking around."

"Believe me, I know the feeling." Hanging my pants on the back of the bathroom door to air-dry before I stuff them in a dry-cleaning bag. "And we're going to talk as soon as I'm cleaned up and human again . . . I need to ask you something, Mom."

"Go ahead, but I'm not sure I want to hear it if it's going to spook me worse."

"I know. But I'd be less than honest if I didn't say that I've heard a few things that make me worry about . . .''

And I'm about to say *Carme* when the power goes out, throwing me into complete blackness, the heat kicking off, everything dead quiet except for the wind strumming its creepy rhythms across the roof. Playing up a storm as if the metal corrugated ridges are strings on a sad guitar.

My computers and equipment upstairs and down are on backup power, but that doesn't mean I'm okay with what just happened. Doesn't mean I trust it's a weather-related glitch. Or that my mom's miniblues have knocked out the power grid. I don't think any such thing.

Carme.

"Mom? You there? What was that?" Moving closer to the sink, feeling for my gun in solid dark. "Is your power out? Because mine sure is. Everything completely dead over here."

"Goodness!" Her voice inside my blacked-out bathroom. "The entire driveway . . . All my lights . . . ! Oh dear, I sure hope I'm not to blame. Oh dear and oh no! I just this *very* second plugged in the tree, thinking it might be cozy to sit in the living room. Maybe that did it. Could I have thrown a breaker? That will be simply awful, talk about being a terrible neighbor . . ."

Mom's an educator and not an electrical engineer, and the answer is no. It's not a breaker, and we didn't blow a fuse or put a strain on the electrical grid. I assure her she's not to blame, but now she's in a spin, getting more upset.

"I mean, I'm ashamed to confess I may have miscounted and put up more decorations than I should have. We didn't have that big inflatable Santa in a spacesuit last year, for example," her dismayed voice over speakerphone in my black hole bathroom.

85 watts × 24 hours = 2.04 kilowatts × 31 days = roughly adding $8 per month per 12-foot inflatable.

"But when I found him at a yard sale, well, he's pretty perfect, you have to admit, and certainly needed a home," she's saying.

"Santa didn't do it," and there can be no doubt about that. "*You* didn't cause whatever this is, Mom."

"Now where's the flashlight? I know there was one near the toaster last I checked . . . Dear me, I can't see my hand in front of my face . . ."

My heart hammers hard as I'm aware of the locked door, making sure it stays that way. Almost expecting something to break it down any minute, to snatch me up and maul me in the dark, and I hit my internal reset button.

Stop it.

Rebooting my mood. No place for panic or emotional preoccupation. That's when bad things knock on the door.

She wouldn't hurt me.

"Unless the wind took down a power line, or I suppose someone could have plowed into a utility pole, taking out the transformer," Mom's voice continues as the lights blink back on, the heat kicking back in and blowing loudly. Just like that.

"Well, thank goodness!" her voice exclaims. "Wouldn't seem my miniblues are to blame. And that reminds me, we need to pick up more."

"I'm pretty sure we have plenty . . ." Thinking back to the day before last, walking into the kitchen at 4:44 p.m., according to the clock on the stove.

I was carrying groceries into the pantry when I noticed multiple unopened boxes of minilights in a bag, smoking gun evidence of my mother's latest compulsive purchase. I always know. There's not much I don't notice. I'm pretty hard to fool, and unfortunate for my mother and perhaps everyone are my snap calculations, subconscious and on the spot:

Twenty boxes, each containing two 20-foot green wire strands with 100 blue minilights per foot = 4,000 strung along 800 feet of wire, or enough to reach from our back porch, past the barn, to the river at the edge of the yard . . .

"You looked in the pantry . . . ?" I'm cautious how I point it out, not wanting to embarrass her if it's slipped her mind what she bought.

Whenever she forgets anything, her first thought is chemo brain. Try as I might, she doesn't believe what I say, and there's nothing wrong with my mother's cognition. With anything about her except she stared death in the face and walked away changed.

"Because it seems I saw plenty in there on Sunday," I add. "Close to a thousand feet of them in a Pottery Factory bag."

Carme.

"Actually, nowhere near that amount as it turns out," Mom's voice comes back. "I happened to notice when I was getting supper ready. I must have miscalculated while running errands the other week. I could have sworn I had more than what's left in that bag, and the way people are shopping like mad? Well, I don't want to run out weeks before Christmas . . ."

We won't run out, and she didn't miscalculate. I'm as clear as day on what I happened upon while putting away cans of beef stock, spring peas and other items needed for her famous potluck soup. I know what I saw in the pantry because in my head I still see it as if I'm standing there. It also hasn't escaped my notice that there seem to be more lights strung along the dock than were there last I looked.

Carme's been inside the house.

She could be there now, but she's not going to hurt our mother. If my sister spirited lights away and added them to the dock or anywhere else on the property, I don't know why she'd do that. What's she trying to say? Unless she's trying to show she cares, reassure me somehow.

"Seems like all is good," Mom decides with a heavy sigh. "Power's on, everything working."

"All good here too," I confirm even though I don't believe anything is good or ever will be again.

"I do worry that power glitch is only the start of what we're in for tonight and tomorrow, though," and she has no idea what she's saying. "Now, Calli, what were you starting to ask me before everything went dark?"

"Nothing important," not after the power conking out while I'm stripped buck naked, midsentence about Carme.

Maybe it really was a coincidence, one of those so-called flukes or happenstances. But my instincts tell me otherwise as I stand in the lighted bathroom, holding my gun in front of the full-length mirror on the back of the door, which is still locked. And I try it again in case it's not. But it is. I tell Mom we'll talk later when I'm cleaned up with clothes on, and I end the call, turning on the water in the shower.

Catching myself in the mirror as I move about, reminded that no matter how hard I work out, I'm never satisfied, never happy with my chassis. A quiet sigh as I scrutinize, wishing for more long leggedness, less of a chest, better sculpted everything else. Carme and I both bulk up easily when we do a lot of lifting. But she's always been more buff, more cut, not tending to curves and pudge the way I am.

Just one more thing to make me feel *lesser than* when it comes to her, and I'm not sure I knew before now that my feelings toward my twin aren't always charitable. I don't think *jealous* is the word I'd use, and I shove the shower curtain open, the plastic rings scraping over the metal rod as if chattering unhappily. But resentful at times, if I'm brutally honest, not always knowing where I begin and she ends or the other way around.

Testing the water, getting the temperature just right, and I step in to wash away the sweaty, violent day. Soothed by hot drumming spray as loud as a rainforest, the bright scent of my shampoo lifting my mood. Closing my eyes, I let the water massage my face, swishing out my mouth, scrubbing my teeth, the inside of my nostrils, my second decon of the night, only this time it's psychological.

As if somehow everything I know and fear is washing down the drain, and then I feel it again. Something nearby, tethering me with its attention. Turning off the shower, reaching around for the towel. Stepping over the side of the tub, and if it's possible to have a heart attack at my age when fit as a fiddle, then that might be what I'm experiencing.

A massive thud in my chest, the top of my head lifting off as something tap-taps at the bathroom door again.

30

"Sisto, it's me. Hello, hello?" Carme's voice. "Open up."

Tap-tap. Tap-tapping the other side of the locked door.

"How do I know it's really you?" I sound like a pluperfect doofus when I ask, because who else could it be?

Dripping everywhere, frantically drying off and startled out of my gourd.

"Who calls you Sisto?" The voice is Carme's, and the answer is she's the only one who calls me that.

Few are aware of her pet name for me that goes back to our childhood. So many things shared by just us. Silly secrets and aliases, spy names, passwords and invented codes.

"Open the door, Sisto. And you'll understand." Through heavy oak, wrapping a towel around me as best I can.

Tap-tap, something hard like metal or plastic knocking again, and Glock in hand,

411

I open the door . . .

"Holy shhhh . . . !"

Letting in my missing mirror ball, number 12.

"Carme?"

Hovering in front of my head.

"Holy shhhh . . . ! Is that you?" Too shocked to move as I watch the mirrored skeleton sphere help itself to the bathroom, to whatever it wants.

Circling appraisingly from different invasive altitudes. Brazenly giving my immodest state the once-over. Then spinning at eye level and holding. Before floating into the steaminess as if it lives here. Drifting along the shower rod, following it like railroad tracks in lazy pirouettes, hijacked by my sister.

Has to be my fighter-pilot twin at the controls with those facile hands of hers, watching with the built-in camera, talking through the tiny speaker. Taking a good long look just as she always does when we've not been together in a while. A preflight of sorts, her assessing what shape I'm in, as if sizing up whether I'm worth taking for a spin.

"I guess you're not going to tell me where you are." Toweling my hair as the wind buffets the tin roof in varying tones, and the orb says nothing. "Are you here in the barn?

Maybe give me a hint if you might be close enough to catch a cold from . . ."

Such a strange thing to say, don't know why that tumbled out of my mouth. What our mother used to lecture us about when we hit puberty, laying out the parameters if we were to spend time with certain "subjects of interest." In the pet cemetery at Fort Monroe, for example. At the picnic tables in the dark parking lot at Smitty's drive-in. Sitting in the very back at the movies, not caring what you'd come there to see.

Mom was fine with our crushes as long as we didn't get close enough to the objects of them to *catch* anything. Ruling out pretty much everything and everyone I was curious about.

"I guess you remember her saying that," I keep talking, and the orb doesn't answer.

Not audibly. Spinning clockwise.

"I guess that would be a yes?" toweling my hair.

Reluctant to use the blow dryer while a PONG hovers overhead, and I almost worry about scaring it. But that's just plain dumb.

"You remember Mom teaching us about the birds and the bees, as she called her idea of sex education? Lecturing us," I go on, "and I won't remind you who usually listened, by the way. And who did *not.*"

Toweling my hair vigorously. "The latter being *you.* And why the sudden silence?" Glancing up at the orb at 2 o'clock like a silvery full moon. "Why aren't you talking?"

Nothing.

"Are you safe?" and with that, it stops rotating.

Only to start again in the opposite direction. Counterclockwise. She's saying no. She's not safe.

"Did you do something bad."

The mirror ball stops again, reversing itself. Yes, she's done something bad.

"Did you kill anyone? Or more than one? May as well tell me," as I'm about to die inside. "I'll find out soon enough."

Reversing her spin again. No, she did not kill anyone, and my heart sings. But not loudly or much.

"But people think you have. But it's not you. Someone else is doing something . . . Crap!" Frustrated and scared. "Can I be any more vague? Darn it, Carme, tell me what's going on," as she spins the same way, yes, yes, yes to all.

She's implicated in something terrible and involved somehow. But she's not to blame, and I need her to talk to me. To explain. To give me every detail. But not an audible sound even as she spins while I tremble inside, about to cry.

"You're not going to talk to me anymore?" Clearing my throat, tears in my eyes. "Carme?"

Gently drifting down, nose to flashy nose, looking reflectively at me, lightly butting against my forehead as delicate rotor wash gives my cheek a breezy kiss. Bringing to mind Carme leaning her head against mine, holding it there, her breath stirring my hair. Recharging each other, she's been saying all our lives. A melding of the minds, and the way we know the other cares.

Please don't die.

The orb lifts up like a helium balloon, as if trying to make me understand that she's doing the only thing she can.

"It would be good if you'd say something again."

She won't.

"If we could talk like we always do."

Silence.

"All right then, let me see if I can guess your logic," and I find the situation strangely comforting, horrifying and unbearable all at once.

Trying to keep my voice from quavering. Trying not to sob. Because my sister didn't go to all this trouble to be the usual outrageous mischief-maker. She hasn't been sneaking around like Santa's elf turned delinquent, breaking and hacking in and out of places, tampering with projects and crime scenes, overtaking and reengineering them. And I hate to think what else as images drift up from earlier in the day.

The dried blood spatter on the steam pipe in the Yellow Submarine tunnel. The alarm not armed when I walked into police head-quarters, the TV set to the International Space Station live video feed when it never is. Even stranger, the two astronauts about to conduct the top secret spacewalk were on the TV screen as I walked in, as big as life, prepping for the installation of the faux LEAR. Not to mention the scene at Fort Monroe, the unlocked doors and missing badge turning up, the bizarre staged and unstaged scene, and what I picked up with my signal analyzer.

Then I get home to the porch light out, the dead bolt unlatched, and who's to say Carme isn't behind all of it. Including Vera Young's stolen badge turning up, and the bleach and its missing bottle. I don't need a forensic pathologist to tell me she's dead viciously and unwillingly, and that every-thing about the homicide has been tampered with by different people with what would seem to be antithetical agendas.

One wanting to disguise. While the other blows the whistle. And I sure would like to find out what's implanted in Vera Young's body. What sort of sensors, for what purpose, and most of all, I want to know what any of it might have to do with my sister.

What have you done? I almost ask the orb, but I won't.

Reminded I need to respect this and every PONG as a person with instincts, feelings and free will. Otherwise I'll underestimate the spirit behind it, making it defensive. Or desperate. Remembering the drone is tethered to my twin and at the same time assuming no such thing. What I do know for a fact is she's not ducking Dick or me or anyone as a prank, to be a jerk or punish.

Carme is hacking her way into whatever she needs because it's the only way the two of us can be together for some awful reason. And I'm scared I might never see her again.

Don't leave me.

"If you transmit remotely and your voice sounds through the PONG's speakers, the risk is someone else might overhear," I say logically, calmly, could win an Academy Award for my acting skills. "Plus, you use more energy. Plus, you don't want me or anyone to record you since you seem to be MIA at the moment." As if it makes perfect sense, and I don't think it strange. And might even do the same.

No response.

"Dick's looking for you, but then you must know that," and of course Carme would. "A lot of people are eager to find you right about now. I'm supposed to turn you in," and she probably knows that, too, probably knows everything.

The orb just spins like the exposed jewel movement of a skeleton watch. Moving clockwise. Nonplussed and in no hurry.

"And finally, if a simple yes or no is as much as I'm going to get from now on?" Talking up to the ceiling, talking to my sister, and I need to finish getting ready.

It's midnight, NASA centers are being furloughed as we speak, and despite it all, I have to get to Langley. But how am I supposed to do that when someone unexpected has dropped in, and I stare up at the glittery skeleton sphere silent in gauzy veils of steam, spinning positively.

"Then all I can say is at least it's consistent with your style." This time my comment prompts a zippy whirl as if Carme just stepped on the gas.

Yes, she agrees it's her personality to be what she calls verbally economical and I call terse. Staccato. Insensitive and rude at times. I think she'd talk in acronyms and numeric codes all the livelong day were it socially acceptable. Brave and bold, yet isolative, distrusting, forever on the commitment lam. Here then gone, walking off the job, lost in space, that's my sister, shying away from nothing except getting close.

Her fear of intimacy isn't to be confused with fooling around because she has no problem with that. I should know, having spent many an evening with her at Fort Monroe, witnessing her do plenty that should have given her chronic colds and a few other ailments. Carme has a fierce will and insatiable appetites she's never hesitated to explore and satisfy. Where she falls short, if not flunks, is in the emotional department.

She's never been as intuitive and psychologically driven as I tend to be, but any ability she had to connect probably shorted out that late fall day when we were 6. Sort of like what happened to Fran after I came home from Colorado Springs, hadn't been living in the barn two weeks when I got the call on Christmas Eve. That she and Easton were driving through a tunnel when a tire blew. And the wrong guys pulled over to offer roadside assistance.

Maybe some damage really is permanent, and I don't blame my sister for not wanting to be vulnerable again. Not after what happened when the stunt pilot gave her a ride home in that sexy '68 "Carmararo," as he often playfully called it.

Taking a detour along the way as it got dark, turning off Beach Road into the cemetery. Asking her how many dead people there were in there, his headlights shining on headstones. Until he flipped them off, just them sitting alone in the dark.

"I don't know," Carme later telling me what she said. "How many?"

"All of them," he laughed, taking her hand, asking if she was his special girl.

One day he would take her to the prom, and when boys take girls to the prom, they park in places just like this. Cemeteries at night, no eyes or ears when you steal your first sweet kiss.

Or so he said, as it was relayed to me after the fact. Not that I know much. Just that the stunt pilot vanished, our parents making sure we never spoke of him again.

In later years when I started interning with Fran during high school, I let my fingers do a lot of sneaky walking through old records.

Not just at Hampton PD, but also Langley, digging everywhere for documents that might tell me more about what happened all those years ago. But nothing. Including the identity of the lawyer my parents took me to see.

In Hampton's historic district near where a lot of the breweries are today. Some balding man with wire-frame glasses, in a dark suit and bow tie. Possibly a commonwealth's attorney. But no one I recognize, and to this day I can't figure it out.

31

Feeling very small in my favorite cowboy outfit, sitting between Mom and Dad on a black leather couch with brass tacks in the armrests. The lawyer asking me questions about Carme and the pool.

"Calli, tell me again why you left your sister all by herself," from the leather wing chair he's pulled too close.

"She ordered me to leave."

"Now let's back up and think carefully because this is very important. Did Carme order you to leave . . . ?"

"Yes, sir."

"Or did the stunt pilot?"

"She did."

"I see, but whose idea was it really . . . ?"

"Hers."

"And the two of you are how old?"

"Six."

"Just turned 6, didn't you?"

"Yes, sir."

"And when's your birthday?" Jotting notes on a yellow legal pad. "Let's see how good that photographic memory of yours really is."

"November 22, 1991, at 2:22 a.m. Except Carme was born 8 minutes before me at 2:14 a.m. eastern time. Or 7:14 and 7:22 Greenwich Mean Time. So, we're not exactly the same age."

"Now aren't you clever with all those fancy numbers and talk. Well, same age or not, 6 years old still strikes me as kinda young to be arranging carpooling," cutting his eyes at Mom and Dad, nobody smiling except him now and then.

"Try to answer his questions, Calli," Dad next to me on the couch. To the lawyer, "She's getting tired. It's been quite stressful . . ."

"Of course, of course, but just to be very clear, Calli, it was yours and Carme's birthdays when you went to the indoor pool, when your stunt-pilot friend drove the two of you in your daddy's Camaro. A special treat on a special day. A weekday, both Mom and Dad working, and he said he'd take the two of you swimming at the Officer's Club and have you home at 6:00 p.m. sharp."

"1800 hours is what we said."

"Yes, everybody and their military time around these parts. But what I hear you telling me is it was Carme's idea for you to catch that boat ride home with . . . what's their name?"

"The Powells," Mom reaching for my hand.

"That's right, they'd take their boat back and forth to the Officer's Club. And you're telling me it was Carme's idea for you to leave her at the pool. Leave her to fend for herself on her birthday alone with a man the same age as your daddy."

"I don't know."

"I'm just wondering if it might *not* have been her idea. That's what I keep getting at."

"I don't know."

"Clever as you may be, you won't under-stand this word, honey, but it's important to figure out if something is pre-med-i-tated." Making fun the way kids at school do if you know too much. "My point is, did your stunt-pilot friend plan to take Carme to the cemetery all along?"

"I don't know."

"Was it planned in advance, and maybe you were interfering?"

"I don't know."

"They didn't want you there, now did they?"

Looking at me, somehow knowing they always made me feel that way.

"I don't know."

"Who did he think he was taking for a ride in that fancy car that the stunt pilot helped your daddy rebuild?"

"Carme."

"And he could tell the two of you apart?"

"I don't know."

"Was this stuntman . . ."

"Stunt pilot," Dad keeps correcting him.

The lawyer flipping through a big yellow notepad.

"Now, Calli, was this stunt pilot ever a little too friendly with you?"

"I don't know."

"Maybe touching you in private places, saying things that made you feel . . ."

"Now, don't be giving her ideas," Mom swooping in.

"Well, we need the truth, Penny. No matter how hard it might be to hear, now isn't that right, Calli? Didn't your parents bring you up knowing the difference between the truth and a lie?"

"Yes, sir."

"You sure that stuntman . . . stunt pilot never got a little too friendly, maybe a little too touchy, maybe made you feel uncomfortable . . . ?"

"I don't know," while shaking my head no.

Because he didn't make me feel that way. Didn't like me as much as her, and couldn't be bothered. Always looking right through me like the air he flew through.

"The reason I'm asking is you and your sister look exactly alike, sound exactly alike, and people can't tell you apart, now isn't that so?"

"Yes, sir."

"Cut out with the same cookie cutter, you've probably heard that expression. And I hear you dress alike, do your hair alike, do everything alike."

"I don't know."

"Sometimes you play tricks on people. Now isn't that right? The two of you swapping places now and then. From what I hear, you've done it a few times at school, and even at church not so long ago. And you get away with it, now don't you?"

"I don't know . . ." Shaking inside, trying not to cry.

"But you've done it many times, now isn't that right. You tell people you're Carme. And she tells people she's you. And you trick people. You get away with it."

"Calli, answer his question." Dad puts his arm around me, pulling me close until my ribs hurt. "He's just trying to help."

"It's hard on all of us, George. I need her to fess up to the fact that she and Carme are so identical they can fool people till the cows come home if they put their minds to it." The lawyer peering over his glasses at me. "Isn't that right, Calli?"

"Yes, sir." About to choke on shame, the lawyer sizing me up, knowing I'm to blame.

"Did you ever play that trick on . . . ?"

"Stop!" Mom cutting him off. "He no longer has a name. Just call him the stunt pilot, please."

"Did you ever play your little trick on him, Calli?" The old cracked leather creaking, he's leaning so close I smell dirty cigarettes and garlic.

"No, sir!"

The lawyer was mistaken, although I never corrected him. Trading places wasn't the sort of stunt (no pun intended) that Carme and I would have played on the stunt pilot (even if it's what he deserved) for the simple reason that she was madly possessive of him.

She didn't want me within a nautical mile of the two of them, and he knew what he was doing. In that regard, the lawyer was exactly right. Our former family friend was a predatory opportunist, sick and unable to change his pedophilic ways, never to be forgiven or trusted, by all accounts. While one doesn't always know when a wolf might be in sheep's clothing, it doesn't matter at the end of the day.

Not to me because I shouldn't have allowed Carme to drive off into the sunset with him. No matter what sort of harangue she might have pitched, I should have refused to leave her. I don't care how much she screamed her head off, her pretty face about to explode with rage like an overfilled balloon. I know what a jury would say when faced with the question of whose fault it was. I'm willing to place a large bet on the verdict.

Nobody's going to blame me, a child. But that doesn't seem to make it any easier to live with the damage that was done. Just ask Rush if you can track him down. I'll never understand why he puts up with my sister's dysfunctional behavior. On and off. Pushing away, pulling close. Within reach, then a ghost. Loves him, loves him not, Carme good and bad, her rhythms as predictable and powerful as gravity and solar flares.

If I didn't know before, I'm sure of it now, my twin sister is in serious danger and trouble. I have an awful feeling that the information Dick passed along to me only begins to scrape the surface. Even as such thoughts are streaking by like comets, I have no impulse to contact my mentor and former boss. I'm not thinking of him as my commander or friend.

I feel no sense of conflicted obligation or

pressure, not like I did when we were together but a few hours ago. No temptation to do his bidding, and I'm not about to interrupt him during his so-called important dinner, whatever he's *actually* and in *truth* doing. I can't trust what he says when it doesn't add up, and I have a funny feeling he didn't spend his evening with the secretary of state.

Therefore, I also can't accept as gospel his spin on the missing Pandora employee from Houston, and I feel manipulated, handled. When I think of the Secret Service cruising around as if taunting me to notice, I don't feel charitable, not happy when left out of important conversations. Not happy when someone withholds from me, especially if it's critical data, leaving me to conclude my loyalty to General Richard Melville isn't reciprocal after all. And why would it be? Dick isn't my flesh and blood, and I'm not inclined to inform him that yes, I might have news about Carme.

Not a good idea to tell him that she's turned into a drone, so to speak, and currently is roaming the ceiling inside my bathroom, where I just got out of the shower. Talk about sounding loony, and guess what? Not happening and forget it. I'm not telling anyone. Not Dick. Not Mom or Dad. Not Fran.

Arguing and making declarations in silence all by myself if I don't count the PONG watching over me like an autonomous angel. Unlocking my phone, I check on the launch countdown again. The closer it gets, the more I can't take my eyes off it, my adrenaline pumping.

−1:47:03:6 . . .

Still on track, not even two hours to go, the live video feed showing the rocket on Launch Pad 0A (LP-0A) glowing brilliant white like an egret, an American flag on the side of the nose, snow swirling like confetti. Thick hazard-yellow fuel lines snake up the 39-meter (128-foot) body, encircled by glaring lights and the 58-meter (190-foot) lightning-protection masts, before a backdrop of the ocean, choppy and pewter gray in the dark.

I can just make out the edge of the water tower off to one side, the storage tank for the acoustical damping system that will activate seconds before the rocket's main engines and solid boosters ignite. I tell people to imagine setting off a firecracker in an oil drum as you deluge it with a firehose to diminish the blast effect, the noise and shock waves. Then envision a 300,000-gallon tsunami roaring from the water tower through two parallel 7-foot-diameter pipes, emptying onto the pad in a kick-butt 41 seconds. NASA at its finest, the ingenious system dreamed up decades earlier to prevent 7.5 million pounds of thrust from tearing up the Space Shuttle and its payload.

These days it's mostly rockets and what's in them that we don't want shaken to death, and as I study the video feed, checking for any alerts or messages, all looks fine. As long as I ignore Rush ignoring me. Other than that annoyance, I get no sense that anything is out of order. I detect no activities or messages that might imply a possible scrubbing of the launch. Nothing concerning on the home front at Langley, either.

Nothing beyond Rush being his irritatingly elusive self, completely incommunicado, and it's starting to bother me a little right about now. In truth, more than *bother,* and more than a *little,* since we're partners last I heard. Rush is the primary communications officer, the mission manager for the EVA that's scheduled to begin about the same time the rocket lifts off from Wallops Island.

I'm just the telerobotics nerd on standby for the faux LEAR installation, and he sure as shooting better still be planning to show up at Langley's Mission Control. He'd better not be leaving me by my lonesome to deal with our two astronauts out on a spacewalk with a top secret on a tether. That sure as hell-o wouldn't be a nice thing to do, and then not letting me know?

I wouldn't do that to him or anyone, always there to be helpful, accommodating. Hauling his darn birthday present around in my backpack for weeks. Not including the time spent customizing it after hours and at my own expense in the home workshop. Wrapping the gift in an outdated sectional flight chart, wishing him smooth flying in the years ahead. Even going to the trouble of saying in the card that it's been a pleasure working on special projects with him.

And he can't bother answering a simple text or email, leaving me in the lurch after the darn day I've had. Well, actually, that day's over, I realize as I unzip my toiletry bag with an impatient sigh. And this day's starting out worse.

Something's wrong.

Not giving me the courtesy of a heads-up so I don't get sucker punched when I walk into Mission Control shortly before 2:00 a.m. to find him not there. Well, that ain't happening.

−1:35:44:4 . . .

I try Rush's cell phone, and it goes straight to voice mail again, his mailbox full just like it always is.

"Jeez!" Standing at the sink brushing my teeth, the orb overhead in a corner as if staying out of my impatient way.

Just like Carme does when I get like this, what Mom says is me finally going off like a whale spouting. There she blows, and Carme's response is to head to shore, flee as fast as possible. If she's watching me on a live video feed, and I have no doubt of it, then she can see what's coming as I finish drying my hair while interrogating Langley's security system. Entering Rush's badge number in a search field.

No records found.

It would seem he's not been on the Langley campus since late yesterday afternoon when his smartcard was removed from his computer at 1738 hours inside Building 1220.

"Where the hell-o are you!" Yelling now.

−1:33:14:2 . . .

I need to find him, and there's a sure way to do it. But this close to launch isn't a good time to be bird-dogging Ken, the chief mission controller. Not at Langley or any of NASA's 10 centers nationwide, each staffed by a skeleton crew because of the government shutdown. Only essential NASA people need attend. Of course, in my mind, that's all of us.

Ken and I go way back, even went to the same high school, where I was quiet and he was a star wrestler and our senior class president. I'm not surprised he's in charge of Mission Control at Langley, easygoing, not a nerve in his body. But he's going to have his plate full, and I hope he won't kill me. Because I wouldn't bother him if it weren't important.

−1:33:00:0 . . .

What if something's happened to Rush? And no one is the wiser? I feel confident that not a single mission controller already at his or her station has given it a thought if he isn't. Maddeningly elusive and most definitely not the early-bird type, Dr. Delgato, as he's more formally called, is notorious for rolling in like an ambulance in the nick of time.

Never hours in advance of a launch, an EVA or anything else, Rush just shows up when required, and I'm not much better. Both of us hate sitting around, and it's not like we have much in the way of disposable time. I've not had a chance to eat in 14 hours, for example.

"Good morning, it's Captain Chase," I say to the woman who answers the phone in Mission Control. "Know you guys are crazy over there . . ."

"No more than usual. Just not as many of us to go crazy. We're actually kinda lonely. Kinda bored."

"Yeah, as lonely and bored as a cat in the middle of a freeway. Wondering if I could grab Ken for a quick minute."

"I see him across the room getting another muffin. Gonna put you on hold."

−1:32:14:0 . . . Rooting through the toiletry bag . . .

Nobody, including Ken, is going to sweat when it's only an hour and a half out and Rush isn't in his chair. No one's worried if both of us aren't in Mission Control this moment because they know what we're like. We're also not the only smart people in the room, and the astronauts probably could install the node just fine without our help.

−1:31:54:1 . . . Where are the eye drops . . . ?

As long as every jot or tittle goes as planned. As long as there's not the slightest question or concern that might come up during an EVA that's extremely dangerous and could last hours.

−1:31:33:0 . . . Opening the medicine

cabinet . . .

As long as nothing unanticipated happens during a task that hasn't been done before in outer space. Ever. Involving a device that can't be jettisoned. No matter what.

−1:31:22:1 . . . Rummaging for Visine . . .

Plus, the top secret part of the equation means no one is supposed to know about it, for better or worse.

−1:31:10:1 . . . Getting the red out . . .

But again, I'm a worrier, and maybe I'm the only one who wouldn't find it normal that Rush suddenly and with no warning is off grid, not on campus, and hasn't been all day. Something's wrong. I don't care what anybody says.

−1:30:54:1 . . . Looking up at the PONG, looking up at Carme . . .

Waiting on hold while Ken and his muffin find their way to the phone, staring up at the mirror ball slowly turning. Wondering if my sister would sneak home and not let Rush know. Especially since today is his birthday. A big one. As of 28 minutes ago he's 40 years old, and it's difficult for me to fathom that she would spirit herself back to Hampton and not be desperate to see him.

Until she isn't. That she wouldn't want to do something for his birthday. If she remembered it. That she wouldn't want to sleep

with him. Unless she's sleeping with someone else.

"Hey! Sorry I made you wait," Ken's voice
sounds from my cell phone, and I turn off
the water running in the sink.

"What kind of muffins?" I want to know
as my stomach grumbles loud enough to
hear from space.

32

"Blueberry. Got plenty of coffee and the usual fruit, pastries waiting for you," Ken says, and I can hear the low murmur of voices in the background.

"Look, I'm running a little behind but will be there just like always," I make sure he knows. "Sorry to bug you, but I'm trying to track down Rush and not getting any response . . ."

"He's at Wallops."

"What?" As my thoughts blank out. "He can't be," I blurt out stupidly. "He has to be at Langley talking to the astronauts during the EVA . . . ," and who am I to be telling the Mission Control chief anything? "And I sure as heck can't get to Wallops, certainly never in time, can't begin to figure out why nobody told me . . ."

"You can copilot from here," Ken says, and I don't like that word anymore.

Copilot. It sounds like second banana,

second string, second fiddle. Once again, the manager while Rush and Carme are the stars.

"I figured that's what you were going to do," and Ken must be back at his station, computer keys clicking.

−1:29:52:1 . . . Rubbing myself down with an intense moisturizer.

"Sure, I'll be there doing whatever is needed. But what's going on?" and I'm furious inside my steamy bathroom, naked as the day I was born as a Carme-possessed PONG drifts around.

Rush is my partner in a top secret project that we've been working on for many months, and why he wouldn't keep me informed is beyond strange. It's infuriating and humiliating, and I can't help but take it personally even as I wonder what's gotten into me. I feel selfish. Maybe the most selfish I've ever felt in my life. Clicking back to the app while on speakerphone, checking on messages and the countdown.

−1:29:34:1 . . .

". . . Change of plans," Ken is saying, "orders from on high. Suits in DC got involved, sniffing out a chance for publicity. Some big-deal film crew. And with the furlough? It's a good thing because NASA won't be filming anything, not for public consumption."

"Well, I wouldn't have voted for Wallops," is what I have to say about it. "Not with everything going on. Not that I was asked," stopping short of adding that I thought the idea was for Rush and me to tag-team.

That's why we're partners. I don't know why he wouldn't inform me that he'd been sent to Wallops. Unless there's something else going on that he's not able to discuss, and Dick enters my mind even as I'm keenly aware of my sister's presence in the mirror ball.

Someone's told Rush not to talk to you.

And all roads lead to Dick. He doesn't want Rush and me communicating for some reason, and while I have no proof of this, it's what I suspect strongly. As elusive as Rush is, he wouldn't be this unfair or unprofessional, and even as I'm thinking all this, I feel Carme in the faint vibration and wind of the device that channels her psyche.

". . . You know, all those kids from Iowa or whatever, a huge PR opportunity," Ken continues to explain, and I can hear him drinking something. "They'll get to see Rush talking to Peggy Whitson as she installs their prizewinning science project, LEAR, as you know better than anyone . . ."

−1:28:34:1 . . . Don't forget deodor-
ant . . .

". . . Too bad about the timing, glad at
least someone will capture it on film," Ken
says, and he hasn't a clue that what's about
to be installed up there is a quantum node.

Not even the chief mission controller
would know, only those of us directly
involved who have a top secret security
clearance.

Jeez, I can't believe this!

"Then Rush is at Wallops as we speak," I
make sure, calmly, nicely, despite what's
raging inside me.

"Affirmative. He's already established
contact with our astronaut on Space to
Ground 1," Ken says. "All according to
plan," he adds, and I thank him, telling him
we'll see each other shortly as we end the
call.

"If you know something," I say to the
PONG hovering near the ceiling and witness to it all, "now would be a good time to
weigh in."

But the orb remains silent, its internal rotor system invisibly spinning in the barest
whir, the blades a transparent composite as
delicate as gossamer. Dad and I designed
the stacked rotor system to mimic dragonfly
wings moving too fast to see, the downwash

redirected away from the target almost imperceptibly. Like the flutter of an angel wing. Or a sigh.

−1:27:44:1 . . . Returning my attention to the Wallops live feed as I brush my hair.

Everything is still a go with no signs of a problem or threat beyond what we always expect at a resupply launch headed to the International Space Station, typically every three months, and a much bigger spectacle than the routine sounding rockets flaring up to deploy CubeSats and other devices, some no bigger than a shoebox. I note the usual number of cars in the parking lot near the pad, key personnel only, none of them furloughed.

As best I can tell, at most 10 vehicles, and no emergency lights. Just red beacons flashing in a snow shower that by all accounts won't amount to much on the barrier islands. But we're going to get a good dusting here with blizzard conditions at times, predicted to start within the hour, and how unfortunate for anyone out in the elements.

Tapping three Advil into my palm, swallowing them with a handful of tap water, and I can't help but feel sorry for the masses showing up for the launch. I always feel bad for them, and at the same time am amazed by their passion and fortitude. The hour is awful, the weather often worse, and while the risk of bodily harm to spectators is minimal, there's always the chance of what my Secret Service friends label that *unwanted event.*

−1:27:00:4 . . . Rewrapping the towel around me . . .

It could be all sorts of things ranging from disastrous to embarrassing. An assassination or a pie in the face. Anthrax sent in the mail or someone jumping the White House fence. How about a rocket blowing up like a small atom bomb? Or worst of all, multiple bad things happening simultaneously, especially with students and families standing right there. A catastrophic malfunction resulting in an explosion while kids and dignitaries are watching is the stuff of my bad dreams.

−1:26:51:1 . . . Picking up my Glock . . .

But no one said space exploration and all that goes with it is for sissies. And considering the fishing community, the cheerful hearty stock who run the seaside inns, businesses and restaurants of Wallops and Chincoteague, it should come as no surprise that a little sleep deprivation and frostbite never hurt the locals on launch day. Nobody seems to mind pitching in, working around the clock to keep the droves of visitors fed with a roof overhead.

Even helping out with boats on occasion, because what goes up must come down. When research widgets and gadgets tethered to parachutes land in the ocean, someone has to pick them up. It could be a UFO for all the watermen know, and they don't ask, don't tell, don't care. No problem ferrying the researchers out, or if need be securing whatever it is on their behalf.

−1:26:15:2 . . . My fresh-scrubbed face staring back at me from the mirror as the mirror ball spins . . .

Easy as hoisting a crab pot out of the drink, everyone happy to help. Frigid winds, downpours, heat waves, drone-size mosquitoes, gridlock traffic — nothing is going to stop die-hard space fans. Most of them rough-and-tumble NASA-loving islanders, the sort to have mailboxes shaped like rockets, and homebuilt crew capsules as yard ornaments. Along with inflatable astronauts and Space Shuttles, and painted-tire flowerbeds spangled with moons and stars.

−1:26:00:2 . . . Opening the bathroom door . . .

Of course, American flags are as common as rooftop lightning rods in the Land of Rockets, and there are an awful lot of trucks. Tourists aren't quite as enthusiastic this time of year, but during warmer months they pour in from the mainland of Virginia and all around. Plus, our proud partners showing up, major aerospace behemoths, members of the military, the finest academic institutions in the land.

−1:25:40:0 . . . Walking into the bedroom as the orb follows . . .

But my favorite are those wide-eyed wonders from public schools like the one in Iowa whose students have been misled to believe that their Low Earth Atmospheric Reader will be installed during a space-walk that begins in less than an hour and a half.

For reasons of national security, LEAR will have to wait in silence and secret, its young wizards fortunately none the wiser as they and their beaming teachers gather in a special observation area at Mission Control to watch the EVA live feed.

−1:25:11:1 . . . Headed to the chest of drawers . . .

As we speak, enthusiasts are rolling up in herds, parking on the sides of the only road leading on and off the island. Gathering in the open-air VIP tent, or more miserably, standing outside in the field behind the visitor's center.

−1:25:01:1 . . . Digging in a drawer for cargo pants . . .

445

All ages, professions and persuasions, spectators congregating, waiting for blastoff, and as the countdown gets closer, the security perimeter widens, pushing everyone farther back from LP-0A.

−1:24:41:2 . . . Underwear and socks . . .

When it's an hour out, no one will be allowed within 1,524 meters (5,000 feet) of the rocket for obvious safety reasons and every other liability imaginable. All essential personnel will be at their stations if they're not already, in various bunker-like buildings and blockhouses. The unsung heroes behind the scenes are assembling, none of them furloughed, and the sort to find a way around it if they had to.

Driving up in 4-wheelers with cattle pushers, gun racks, tool chests. In hoodies, jeans, hunting boots, the true masters of space can pilot any dish antenna you've ever met. Doesn't matter if it's 1.8 meters (6 feet) in diameter or 10 times that.

Wallops Island fairly blooms with astral signal sniffers of varying sizes and shapes, most made of metal painted flat white.

Typically, these dishes are configured in arrays that bring to mind nosegays of monster morning glories, the petals being the parabolic reflector, the stamen the feed horn. Each flower, so to speak, is turned toward whatever it's tracking, except for those mushroomed straight up like a saint lifting open hands to the heavens, praising and imploring.

−1:24:20:0 . . . Sitting on the edge of the bed, putting on long underwear, keeping my eye on the countdown on my phone . . .

When the dishes are faceup as if waiting for a sign from above, it means they're parked, in sleep mode, off the clock. Or perhaps more apropos given the timing: furloughed. At any rate, they're taking a break from hunting down invisible objects and energies moving as fast as the speed of light. And like Santa's helpers and reindeer on their most important eve, there's no rest for any Wallops antenna right now.

−1:24:10:1 . . . Pulling on thick wool socks . . .

Each has its important role in the cosmic teamwork required to haul a 6-ton metal tube into the mesosphere and beyond. It takes a village to raise a barn or a rocket, and the National Oceanic and Atmospheric Administration (NOAA), and NASA's Near Earth Network (NEN), in addition to other ground stations locally and far flung, will be listening and looking constantly.

In fact, they already are and have been,

antennas linking, joining forces like people holding hands in a chain that stretches into infinity. Working for a safe bon voyage and a safer universe. Hooking up into arrays that transmit and receive, give and take, download and reciprocate, please and thank you, and together we're stronger. As all of us would be better off behaving, collaborating on what should and shouldn't be there. At least metaphorically.

−1:24:00:2 . . . Headed to the closet as the orb follows . . .

But specifically and in rocketry before and during liftoff, the telemetry will be coming in fast and furiously, the parabolic reflectors, feed horns and actuators trained on LP-0A like man's best friend listening to His Master's Voice.

−1:23:52:2 . . . Opening the closet door . . .

Scientists, engineers, flight controllers, our protective service forces and emergency first responders have been going down mind-jamming checklists for weeks and days on end. No page of NASA acronyms and jargon has been left unturned, ensuring all is optimal, everybody laser focused and on edge. Leading up to those first few electrifying seconds when the rocket pushes off in a massive explosion you can feel in your hollow organs for miles and see from the mainland.

Thundering up in billowing white clouds of steam, a pissed-off dragon propelled by orange plumes of plasmic fire. Shimmering, almost hovering as the air begins sizzling and crackling. Lifting, turning, streaking like a burning arrow in a northeast trajectory over the sea. Before receding into a ball of light like a fickle shooting star doing a flyby, headed back to outer space instead of to the ground.

−1:23:32:0 . . . Carrying a police polo shirt, tactical boots to the bed . . .

All told it takes less than 10 minutes from launch before the second stage separates, and the spacecraft (cargo capsule) begins slingshotting around the earth at 17,500 miles per hour. This can go on for days and weeks, the timing precisely calculated for when the Space Station's robotic arm is best poised to grab the capsule midflight at an altitude of some 400 kilometers (249 miles) straight up as . . . well, as a rocket flies.

−1:23:20:0 . . . Perched on the edge of the bed, pulling on my pants . . .

The azimuthal angle for rendezvous depends on how the world turns. As long as the spacecraft stays in bounds, orbiting above the atmosphere between 59 degrees

latitude north and south, it can be inter-
cepted while flying over anywhere and
anything. The Sahara, the Nile, mountains
in China, an Australian dry lake bed. It
could be over the Great Barrier Reef or an
algal bloom in the Indian Ocean when
Houston decides to snatch the spacecraft
from orbit like a wild flying beast.

—1:23:00:1 . . . Tying my bootlaces . . .

No greater show on Earth and beyond as
long as nothing goes off-nominal, and
almost anything you might think of can,
including the wrong sort of spectators showing up. While I have a lot to say about visitors in and out of Langley during public
events, I don't necessarily know who's going to wander in at Wallops. Their protective services division works closely with ours
but is separate.

I don't have any idea what important
people might be attending this morning's
launch and live-feed spacewalk, not a clue
about visitors on that wind-scoured island
100 miles from here. Probably not anybody
crazy famous, I wouldn't think. Difficult to
keep that from leaking. But one never
knows. There could be a celebrity, a promi-
nent politician or two allowed in the VIP
viewing room behind glass at Mission Control.

−1:22:51:1 . . . Pulling on my shirt . . .

I watch the countdown ticking by below the video feed. The seconds flicking past. Getting closer to liftoff, and I'm having serious trouble comprehending why my dad would be summoned out for any reason. Why him? And why would Dick and the Secret Service pick him up in those big SUVs, assuming I'm right about that? Is there a perceived threat, and why don't I know?

Are they at Langley or Wallops? Is it possible that the commander of Space Force is showing up at the launch with PR in mind, and for some oddball reason my dad is with him? Maybe Dick is supposed to be in that special room with all those kids watching a live feed of Commander Whitson tethering herself to the robotic arm and the node masquerading as an atmospheric reader. Bringing to mind a briefcase handcuffed to the wrist of a spy.

−1:22:01:1

Some 135 kilograms (298 pounds) of insanely sensitive payload must remain tethered to her at all times until she successfully installs the machine on the research platform. There can be no exceptions, including a loss of signal, in which event she's been briefed to pull a red tab and activate a beacon on her payload.

This will power up the quantum node, which has been in sleep mode on a backup battery supply since it was packed into the cargo bay at Cape Canaveral some two weeks ago. Up and running like a handheld radio in space, albeit an awkward one, and communication with the ground can be reestablished. Mission accomplished, disaster diverted. America's first quantum machine is installed in outer space. Even if almost nobody knows.

−1:21:52:2 . . . Gun belt going on . . .

What the plan doesn't take into account is that less than 1 percent statistical possibility of a catastrophic failure, with both the device and astronaut as casualties.

As usual I'm a worrier, always looking for the devil in the details. And there sure enough is one during a robotically assisted spacewalk while moving a secret payload from the launch pallet to the experimental platform at the end of the 100-yard truss.

I wouldn't want anything to happen during that approximate 30-minute continuous ride to and from the installation. That's when the less than 1 percent possibility factors in, especially when the arm is the greatest distance from the structure, 17 meters, or 56 feet.

That's an unmanageable reach when anchored by nothing more than a wire tether never designed for rappelling and sling loading people around.

33

Tethers are for short-distance mishaps, such as losing one's purchase on the handrails or taking a tumble off the Station. The wires come in 75-foot reels that can be clipped together, and aren't intended as a plan B should you get stranded. For that you might want to consider your Simplified Aid For EVA Rescue (SAFER) "jet pack."

−1:21:31:0 . . . Putting on a level III ballistic vest . . .

Problem is that might have saved you during virtual reality training at Johnson Space Center, but in the vacuum of weightless space the cold fact is there are only 30 seconds of the gaseous nitrogen propellant, which can't be resorted to without ditching payload. That would be pretty depressing after all is said and done.

Even in a typical mishap involving a reasonable distance, the SAFER is an unknown gamble. It *might* get you back to the nearest airlock. *Assuming* you manage the hand-control toggle switch *exactly* right. And line yourself up *exactly* right to hit your target while you and the Station are moving at Mach 23. One shot is about all you've got, and we can't be sure how it would go.

−1:21:00:0 . . . Finding a tactical jacket, gloves . . .

Fortunately and knock on wood, so far no astronaut has become untethered during a spacewalk, and I can't think of anything much worse. You'd be better off falling from a trapeze or high wire without a net. The latter you might survive badly, and hopefully there would be people around to help out and keep you company. But whether you live to tell the tale or not, most likely you wouldn't have the horror of knowing it was coming.

Not for long, maybe just a few seconds when you lost your footing or grip before a gasping audience under the circus tent.

But to be disconnected in outer space with no means of rescue would be an unimaginable fate. Floating and tumbling helplessly in nothingness, unable to stabilize or propel yourself in a vacuum with only enough oxygen in your Extravehicular Mobility Unit (spacesuit) to last at most 8 hours.

−1:19:41:1 . . . Walking out of the bedroom . . .

There's no Space Shuttle to send your way. It doesn't fly anymore. Nor will you be talking to anyone.

Ultrahigh frequency radios on and around the Space Station you just drifted away from are line of sight. You might be talking inside your helmet, but like the tree falling in the forest with no one around, you don't make a sound to anyone beyond yourself. Existentially alone with your thoughts, carbon dioxide making you increasingly sluggish.

Looking down on the blue-and-white planet that you now orbit, hurling around it faster than a missile while slowly poisoned by your own exhalations. Your body won't be recovered. Leaving it to orbit until it finally burns up in the atmosphere. Like Icarus getting too close to the sun. Like space debris. Or a dead satellite.

−1:19:33:0 . . . Gun drawn . . .

Watching the seconds tick past, wondering why I haven't heard from anyone about the Fort Monroe case. As important as rocket launches and spacewalks are, we also have a murdered Pandora employee who needs our attention, and I send Fran a text:

Heading to LaRC soon. Any new developments re: VY?

456

She'll know I'm referring to Vera Young. Was she autopsied tonight, or will that wait until morning? Do we know anything else? For example, and most importantly, what turned up on CT or MRI? Or has the body been scanned yet? Walking to the door that leads into my work area, gun ready just in case. But I know I couldn't shoot my sister, and if she's in the immediate vicinity, including on this property, then there's nothing I can do except make sure she's *physically* not in my presence that I know of.

And she isn't. Not directly, not in person, at any rate. The PONG she's commandeered is overhead, following me like my new best friend as I open the door, scanning my equipment, desk, the pine tree near the bathroom. Nothing out of place, and waking up a laptop display, I take a look at what a signal sniffer might have to say about my roly-poly friend spinning over my left shoulder.

"Well whad'ya know?" I announce, "Something chiming in around 2.4 gigahertz, imagine that."

I hold up the antenna and begin my strange little war dance, slowly turning in a circle. The peaks get stronger each time the drone is prompted to follow me, always some 45 centimeters (18 inches) away from my head. Both of us slowly spinning.

"Consistent with video transmission. An easy signal to hide behind when you're not the only video camera in town," I inform the orb pointedly, and it has no comment.

For all I know, Carme could be controlling the PONG from hundreds of yards away or even miles from here while the camera and other built-in sensors and devices download buckets of data to her even as I'm thinking this. In other words, my sister could control the drone from a car, from outside the barn, a hotel room, almost anywhere within the PONG's 9,000-meter range, about 6 miles if nothing interrupts the signal. But that doesn't mean she's not under this same roof, and if she is, good for her.

Brava! Because I'm not going to look. Not beyond what I've done. Not now that I'm clear on who and what I'm dealing with. Let's just hope I'm right.

Who else could it be?

I can keep asking myself that and come up with the same answer every time. But I'm not going to invade my sister's suite on the other side of the barn. I have no intention of so much as stepping foot in there. Carme has found me. I don't want to find her, and as long as she's not inside my quarters, that's all I can control. Technically. That's what I'm going to say to Dick if and when the day comes.

I don't want to think about how unhappy he'll be, can hear him now, chiding me for trusting my sister when I shouldn't. He would be right about that. Without any basis in provable fact, I trust her with my life at this moment. But that doesn't mean I want her within reach.

−01:18:12:0 . . .

"What now?" I ask my autonomous tag-along, realizing that unflattering label suits her a lot better than me right about now. "Because I've *really* got to go."

The PONG floats to the star pine tree, hovers over a branch, lining up the landing zone, electromagnetically attaching itself.

"No way! Oh no . . . !"

Hurrying past Otto in his wheelchair, and from across the room I can see that my truck key is where I left it on the table by the door. But my badge is gone.

"No, no, no, no, no . . . !" Stepping around my pile of wet gear on the floor.

Already late, and I'm not going to tear back upstairs to look because I know my badge and lanyard aren't there. I have a good idea where they might be. Or better yet, who has them.

Carme.

She could go anywhere at Langley and pass for me without the slightest question, and I grab my backpack, making sure to bring my wallet and police creds. A picture ID won't get me through a guard gate or open any doors, but it's better than nothing. I'd best have something with me. Armed and dangerous with no driver's license, and it wouldn't be good if I got pulled over by the state police.

Resetting the security system, heading out into a blowing snow that whips my hair and stings my face. At least the temperature is warmer, more like in the 20s instead of 0 and below. About two inches of accumulation so far, and I don't see footprints. Only mine. No tire tracks, either, the driveway and yard as smooth as vanilla icing on a cookie. If Carme took my badge and left the property, then it was before the snow began.

−00:40:22:0 . . .

I remotely unlock the truck and start it from a safe distance, another Secret Service trick I've picked up along the way. In case someone decides to leave an unpleasant surprise like a bomb, and if my sister has been here, how is she getting around? I can only figure she has access to a car, and as I drive past the house, I notice the Christmas tree lights glowing through the living room curtains.

Smoke drifts from the brick chimney, and my mom sitting in front of the fire strikes me as rather cozy considering all that's going on. Including the odd power hiccup earlier and Dad getting mysteriously called out. She might be lonely and jumpy. But not seriously worried that someone dangerous could be lurking about, and I think back to when I got here several hours ago. Wondering if Dad's white Prius was parked under the live oak tree near the back door.

Because now that I'm thinking about it, I don't remember seeing it. Pondering how Carme might have gotten into the barn to take my badge. How could she do that without my knowing? I would have heard the security system beeping if she disarmed and reset it as I just did. Unless she was already inside the house, and I remember sensing something overhead in the dark when I first entered the side door.

Possibly the mirror ball.

Who knows what Carme might have been up to all day with nobody home. But after I came in and reset the alarm, she must have changed the chime alert, turning it off. She would know how to do that from her phone, has her own personal code, piece of cake. She could have exited the barn without making a peep. Then covered up what she'd done by changing the setting back to chime again as it did when I reset the alarm a few minutes ago.

I call Mom to let her know what I'm doing, making sure she's okay, not feeling scared or too lonely.

"I can hear you driving past," she says, and now that I'm looking, I can see the empty snowy area where Dad parks his car.

Gone. And has been for hours. Probably leaving around the time Mom decided to call me about delivering supper to the barn. Cutting me off at the pass soon after I got home. Making sure I didn't head over there while my sister was in the area.

"Heading back to Langley and running behind," I let Mom know. "Is everything good with you?"

"Except you never ate anything." Her voice inside my truck as I drive through a Milky Way of tiny blue lights.

"I'm already late. Save me something for later. If I don't die of hunger first."

"I'm sitting in front of the Christmas tree, watching the NASA live feeds on my laptop," she says. "And it's quite the exciting double-header, students watching from all over . . ."

—00:38:11:0 . . .

"Especially those kids from Iowa," she adds. "Such an inspiring story . . ."

"Mom?"

"I'm watching Peggy Whitson as we speak in the airlock getting suited up with Jack Fischer . . ."

"Where is Dad's car?" I ask, and it's never a good sign when my mother acts like she doesn't hear me.

". . . They have to get her tethered to the arm *and* the LEAR on its pallet, which seems awfully dangerous if you ask me . . . ," chattering away about the EVA, and I already know the answer to my question.

"Mom? I just drove past the back of the house, and Dad's car wasn't there," I bring it up anyway, passing through her miniblue space-themed topiary. "I thought you said he was picked up."

Silence.

"Mom? Please stop ducking and dodging," rounding the bend in the driveway. "Where is Dad's car?" Even though I know. "I'm not getting off the phone until you tell me. Please. You know, I care about her too. Whatever it is, we're in this together. Just

463

like always . . ."

"I think it best we don't talk about this," my mom says, and Carme is around some-where, and nothing I've sensed about her has been imagined or made up.

If she's away from her deployment and acting like a fugitive, I have no doubt our parents know. There's probably nothing they wouldn't do for us, never been a doubt about whose side they'll take. Ours. Not so different from how I'm behaving right about now, giving my sister the benefit of the doubt until I can't anymore. Should that bad hour come.

It can't. It won't.

"Mom?" Taking a right at the end of the driveway, the headlights illuminating the sign Dad painted. PENNY LANE. "How lonely are you?"

My way of asking if Carme is with her, and by now I'm assuming our home phone has been tapped.

"Oh, I'll be fine," Mom's voice. "I believe you said you didn't see George's car in its usual spot? He probably moved it in ad-vance of the storm." Baloney, and her way of letting me know that Carme isn't there and has Dad's Toyota.

And I think of what MP Crockett said to me earlier:

"Playing musical cars, are we, ma'am?"

No doubt my twin sister has driven through the air force base's Durand Gate before. Perhaps regularly, but not with my ID. Because I would know if she borrowed it after hours. While I was dead asleep. Or off somewhere, leaving my badge safely at home, and I hold my phone in one hand, typing with my thumb as I keep my eyes on the road.

Entering my own personal ID number in a search field for NASA Langley's security system. Interrogating not just today but the past week, including the Durand Gate connecting us to the air force base. Hoping I'm wrong . . .

11 records found.

"Shhhh . . . ! Shhhh . . . ! Shhhh . . . !" Getting really close to cussing now.

Over the past three days, it would appear I've accessed the Durand Gate almost a dozen times at hours when I wasn't at work. Including less than 90 minutes ago. Or about the time the PONG began calling out my nickname, rapping on my bathroom door as I was getting out of the shower.

Holy crap. Right under my nose.

Imagining my sister confronted by MP Crockett, and knowing her, she gives as good as she takes from the jerk. Explaining

465

why he said what he did to me about musical cars, and perhaps why he's been ruder than usual of late.

—00:36:32:0 . . .

Tiny snowflakes click against the windshield, dancing and swarming in the headlights as I drive my truck back to work. Wherever Carme is now, I'm assuming she's in range to control the PONG remotely, but that could cover a lot of territory. We designed the drones to be controlled from miles away.

I imagine my sister parked somewhere, watching me on a video display earlier when I was getting ready in the barn. Talking to empty rooms, storming around with my gun drawn, doing my little twirls with the antenna. But if Carme's on the Langley campus now, I have no idea where.

My badge number doesn't come up again anywhere. Not in the buildings or facilities, and this could imply she's still somewhere on the air force side except for one thing. We grew up here, and if there's one thing we know, it's how easy it is to access NASA from the AFB if you simply follow Runway 8 to the taxiway that leads directly to our huge hangar.

From there you're home free, and I'm about to alert Fran that we have a security breach. And that I can't get through the guard gate, when my cell phone rings. I don't recognize the number. But the area code is 757, the exchange the same as NASA's flight facility at Wallops, and I can't believe it.

Who would try to videophone me from there, introvert that I am? Nobody I know. Certainly, none of the scientists and special agents I deal with routinely. Definitely none of the antenna cowboys. They would just get hold of me invisibly, the way nerdy folks like us prefer things, not having to care what you look like.

Touching the display, I accept the call.

"Captain Chase," and a face I've never seen before stares at me from my phone.

"Clearly, I've interrupted." The woman is handsome in a severe way.

Maybe mid- to late 50s, I estimate, with short white hair, looking at me from the small display with unwaveringly hazel eyes behind black-framed designer glasses that I've seen before. When I interviewed Vera Young yesterday.

You've got to be kidding me.

"Obviously, you're driving. I hope carefully in the weather you're having," the woman says from my phone.

"Excuse me, but who are you, and how

467

did you get this number?" and I already know she's extreme trouble.

The directness of her unblinking gaze, and how unperturbed she is by interrupting a perfect stranger at 1:32 in the morning. And of course, the glasses. If she's who I darn well think she is, I mean, is she freakin' taunting me?

"The weather has cleared nicely here at Wallops, not snowing anymore," she doesn't answer my question.

So, I repeat it, holding my phone in my left hand, clicking back and forth between her cold beauty and the countdown.

−00:28:00:0 . . .

As she's saying, "I'm looking at the data all around, and you've got a storm cell right over Hampton, must be snowing to beat the band . . ."

"If you don't tell me who you are and what you're calling about . . . ?" Careful not to overshoot my headlights, and the roads are getting slippery as I barely go the speed limit. "I'm going to hang up," and then she tells me her name, not that I'm the slightest bit surprised:

Neva (rhymes with Eva) Rong.

−00:27:56:1 . . .

As in the CEO of Pandora Space Systems, the sister of the woman whose body is cur-

468

rently at the Tidewater medical examiner's office. Not all that far from Wallops, and what is Neva Rong doing at our Mid-Atlantic Regional Spaceport, MARS? I try to think what might be going up in this morning's resupply or EVA that relates to Pandora, and can't come up with anything.

But I suppose in light of the company's cryptic relationship with DARPA, there could be projects I don't know about. It goes without saying, my security clearance doesn't entitle me to every secret.

"A long way to come for a launch," I point out, and she's quick to remind me that Pandora is in the business of building its own rockets.

"As you no doubt know," and I don't like the familiarity of her words or tone, "we're very much into satellites, lunar missions and beyond the beyond. I've had my eye on the spaceport at Wallops for a while as an excellent East Coast presence for us," she feels some need to share with me.

Smiling, adjusting her fancy glasses just enough for me to notice scratches on her hand. As I envision the furrows and contusions around Vera Young's neck.

−00:25:44:1 . . .

"Was invited to visit as a prospective client," Neva Rong is saying, "a guest at the

469

launch in the event I should decide to get a contract with NASA and put a pad out here . . ."

"Let me confirm," I interrupt her firmly. "Dr. Vera Young was your sister?"

"Sadly, that's correct. But it's just Vera or Mrs. Young," she's quick to insist, disavowing me of any foolish notion that her deceased sister had more than a few measly master's degrees to her name.

"Not a physician, although I did encourage her to go to med school," Neva Rong says, and she's not a physician either but does have her doctorate.

Actually, more than one, she makes sure I know, "In neuroscience and quantum physics . . ."

Passing the 7-Eleven again, lit up in the snow, and I can see the same clerk reading a magazine at the counter. Not a single customer inside or at the gas pumps.

34

"I tried many times to get Vera to write her dissertation, to just get on with it," her sister says without a trace of warmth from my phone's display. "But she was one of these savant-esque researchers who can't quite finish what she starts. I've no doubt you're familiar with the type. Procrastinators. Such an awful word."

−00:23:52:1 . . .

"Was she unhappy at work?" Passing Hardee's, nobody home, the snow swirling around light poles in the parking lot.

Not letting on that Vera Young told me yesterday she wasn't pleased about being relocated to Hampton. She even used the word *boonies.* Now I'm wondering what Neva's real motive was with dispatching her procrastinating sister here. Maybe to help her hack into the Yellow Submarine tunnel, and I think of the blood spatter on the asbestos-covered steam pipe near FOD-1.

Let's see who the DNA comes back to, because I'm betting on Vera Young. I'm betting this is what she was really up to when she supposedly went home with a migraine yesterday. Hacking, playing swift tricks with badges, my sister not the only one who can do stuff like that.

"Frustrated. Always frustrated. That's Vera," her cold-blooded CEO sister goes on. "No matter how many times I'd remind her that education is just an invitation to learn, Captain Chase. Or do most people call you Calli? And I'm glad you went ahead and finished your doctoral program, by the way. I looked you up as soon as I was given your name."

"I'd appreciate it if you'd tell me who did that and how you got this phone number."

"Why? Is it the wrong one?" she asks, and I can't tell if she's being funny. "Excuse the pun," she actually says that next. "And I'm sure you realize that when people are traumatized, they can be inappropriate," she continues her inappropriate comments and seems about as traumatized as a rock.

"Why are you calling?" I don't sound sympathetic, don't bother trying.

"Well," she says, "it would seem Vera took her own life. As you might expect, I need to know what's going to happen next."

"Maybe you could answer a few questions of mine. Was she acting unusually of late? Did she give any indication that she might be thinking suicidal thoughts?"

No way in hell-o I'm telling Neva Rong that it's looking like her sister was murdered, and I sure hope nobody else has filled her in. In the first place, I have no doubt she already knows. And knows all too well. But she doesn't know that I do, and I don't want her to. Nor can I imagine why she would, I decide as her face flashes back and forth on my phone while I switch between her and the NASA feed.

Give her nothing.

"I'll tell you the same thing I told Mason Dixon just a very few minutes ago . . ." she starts to say, and I cut her off a second time.

"Did he give you my number?" Furious with myself all over again for ever letting him have it.

But the director of the Langley Center in addition to Fran and the police chief have been clear since I was hired three years ago that I have to be reasonably competent at dealing with the media. Especially if the journalist in question is the nephew of the governor and has ties to the White House. Last summer, Mason wanted my number for a NASA-related story about drones, and here we are.

What makes no sense to me is why he would know Neva Rong. Why did he think to contact her about an alleged suicide at Fort Monroe? Nothing about her calling is making sense, not in a good way, and every circuit in my body is lit up with warnings.

"Mason and I go back a long way," and it's all Neva has to say to explain so many things.

Such as the two of them being together at Wallops right now when she's making a bid to install a launch pad there. Such as her perhaps knowing about her sister's death before the rest of us did, and is the one who told him. He in turn alerted the local affiliate that showed up at the scene. And if all of the above is true, that would be more than a little incriminating.

"Any indications that might make you think she was depressed, that something wasn't right?" I'm asking Vera's so-called bereft loved one the expected questions as my suspicions swirl faster and faster like a summer twister. "What about depression or life changes that were disruptive? Being relocated here to Virginia, for example. I've heard it suggested she wasn't thrilled to be so far from home."

"Of course, I didn't see this coming." Neva's eyes like tiger eyes, her mouth pressed in a thin line. "I would never have allowed her to be relocated had she complained. And further, had she seemed depressed, moody, anything *off-nominal,* we would have whisked her back to Houston right away."

—00:20:42:1 . . . Passing Wendy's, getting closer . . .

"I'm just wondering what to expect from the medical examiner," Neva's voice as I monitor the NASA feeds.

The rocket shining white on the pad, everybody gathered and watching the clock. Including the CEO of Pandora Space Systems. She probably has the same view I do, looking up at the flat-screens everywhere, dozens of cameras trained on LP-0A. I imagine her in the VIP area at Mission Control, looking through glass, maybe over Rush's shoulder.

I check the International Space Station live feed to see what's going on with the EVA, and I can't stand it that I'm running late. The two astronauts are in what's known as *depress operations,* meaning all systems are a go, and they're suited up, about to open the hatch for the spacewalk. The quantum node on its pallet has been removed from the cargo hold and is outside

secured to the truss, awaiting the installation.

". . . Just wondering how much is really
necessary when it's so obvious what happened . . . ," Neva Rong's voice goes on.

−00:19:52:1 . . .

The film crew Ken mentioned earlier is
Mason Dixon, of course, and I keep wondering if Dick is there. Maybe close enough
for Neva to touch.

"There will be a postmortem examina-
tion," I inform her unhelpfully. "And then
you can make arrangements with a funeral
home . . ."

"That's the thing. She needs to come
home. To Houston. And while this is a
delicate topic, but will she be viewable?
How did she look, and how disfiguring is
the autopsy? Because I've heard horror
stories about people having all their organs,
even their eyes removed. And limbs if need
be. Of things gouged out of them . . ."

−00:18:22.2 . . . Passing Bojangle's,
reminded how freakin' starving I am, and
I've got to alert Fran that I'm coming.

". . . Never been one to watch all those
crime shows, and I'm afraid I really don't
know what to expect. But I understand
some medical examiner's offices have CT
scanners these days . . ."

476

She knows about the sensors. And that explains the bleach.

Carme.

It and the missing container give the appearance of someone attempting to tamper with evidence, and that was the only point. To give the appearance. So we'd take a second look. And a third. And more looks to come, and driving with one hand, typing with the other, I send an urgent text to Fran:

Meet me at the main gate NOW.

". . . Because I should think if one is carefully examined externally and scanned, then why cut the person open?" Neva Rong outrageously goes on, and I'm not going to answer that either.

"I suggest you call the death investigator," and I give her the information for Joan, who won't tell her jack squat.

Then I tell *Dr. Rong* I have to go, and it's now 16 minutes out from launch with the EVA soon to go on. All those Iowa kids must be right there, and I can't imagine her holding court like the evil queen in *Snow White.* Smiling and paying attention to people from the *sticks,* as she probably thinks of rural America, if she's anything

477

like her sister.

  −00:16:03:1 . . .

On Langley Boulevard now, opening the text that just landed.

10-23, Fran letting me know she's waiting for me at the guard gate, and she must have been out in her car and in the area to get there that fast.

I can see her black Tahoe alone in the Badge and Pass Office parking lot, where I don't need any fancy credentials to get in. I park next to her, driver's door to driver's door as usual.

"How did you manage to lose your frickin' badge?" she says as our windows hum down.

"I didn't lose it, and it would seem someone used it several hours ago to access the Durand Gate and may be on this campus," I let her know instantly, but I'm not going to mention my sister.

"Not that same trick again! Are you kidding me?" Shaking her head, the cold wind ruffling her hair. "Well, I hope you don't end up hanging from your closet door," she adds unpleasantly.

"I just know that somebody used it to get through the guard gate, and it wasn't me," I turn up the heat as high as it will go, having no intention of telling her the rest of the story.

That my ID apparently has been used to access the AFB for the past three days. And it's probably my fugitive twin sister doing it.

−00:13:00:1 . . .

"And Neva Rong clearly knows her sister's dead," I add. "She just called me. Neva did . . ."

"Yeah, I figured you didn't mean Vera." Always the smartass, lighting a cigarette.

"Wanting to know what the medical examiner is going to do to the body," I explain. "And I didn't like the way she was asking it or anything about her call. Out of the blue. Thanks to Mason Dixon, who gave her my number, the two of them at Wallops right now. The important point is I think Neva Rong knows about the sensors."

"They already dug them out," Fran holds up her hands, fingers splayed. "I talked to Joan a little while ago, and she said she tried what you said, using a wand like TSA has. And they were able to extract some sort of teeny-tiny square chips. About 20 of them from her fingers, wrists, ankles."

−00:12:31:1 . . .

"Sensors, and we should look at them here," I reply. "And I've got to get to MC. I'm already late."

"Now I've got a question for you," the tip of the cigarette glowing orange. "While Scottie and Butch were dealing with the evidence at HQ a little while ago, something weird was found inside the fridge . . ."

"I know, I know. I tucked the swabs in there from earlier. Despite your belief I shouldn't have bothered . . ."

"Not those." Fran taps an ash in the dark, her frozen breath laced with smoke blowing out in a plume. "A tube of blood labeled *1111-A,* I kid you not."

"What?" My mind goes blank.

"You heard what I said. A blood tube like they take in the doctor's office. In the fridge next to the swabs you put in there. A label on it that says *1111-A.* Maybe the blood that matches the drops you found on the steam pipe, huh?" She's being funny and she's not.

Carme.

"So, you want to tell me where that tube of blood came from? Maybe the dead lady from Fort Monroe?"

Vera Young was dead for hours by the time anyone checked on her. There was plenty of time for someone to stick a needle in her femoral artery and take a blood draw. Then drip several drops on the steam pipe in the Yellow Submarine tunnel, and I think of the alert on my phone at 3:38 in the afternoon while I was giving my briefing.

Carme.

Who's a whiz at hacking into anything and altering parameters of pretty much whatever she wants. And she sure as heck knows how to get my attention.

"If you've got an explanation, I mean, I'm listening . . . ," Fran fills the windy cold silence, smoking as I think.

−00:10:04:1 . . .

"Well?" she pushes.

"I don't know."

"You don't know who the hell drew a tube of her blood at the scene, if that's what the hell we're talking about? Someone did that *before* we got there, for Chrissakes?" Taking a deep drag on the cigarette. "Jeez, Calli," in a quieter tone. "What the frick's going on?"

"I don't know."

"Where's your sister?"

I shrug, don't know. And she doesn't say anything more, smoking in the dark, snow falling everywhere and blowing inside our trucks. Whatever I might know, Fran is quite clear that I'm not going to tell her. That it's not the good old days anymore. It can't be. Another hit on her cigarette, and she puts it out in a Dunkin' Donuts coffee cup.

−00:09:31:1 . . .

"Here you go. Don't lose it." She hands me a generic smartcard so I can access doors.

Tells me to follow her Tahoe through the guard gate, where I sit behind her ruby-red brake lights, watching her talk to the female officer. Celeste. Both of us know her, and she glances several times in my direction. We wave at each other, friendly enough. But she stares hard at me as I drive through, studying my face as my phone rings again. This time Fran.

"You're the one who came through the Durand Gate." Her voice inside my truck.

"Excuse me?"

"Celeste says you came through about midnight. That a military cop named Crockett alerted her that there was something weird going on. Because he'd seen you earlier with General Melville in your police truck. And then you were in and out, most recently around midnight."

"What was I supposedly driving?"

"A white Prius," Fran's pushy voice over speakerphone. "Which is what your dad has. That for sure wasn't you, was it, Calli?"

"No. It for sure wasn't me, Fran. At midnight I was getting showered and dressed."

"Where's your sister?"

"I don't know," and it's true, because I don't.

−00:07:51:0 . . .

We don't pass a single car, the campus deserted. Only those of us who have to be here, and I peel off into the parking lot of Building 2101, the main building on the Langley campus, the second floor lit up. Fran keeps driving, and I promise her we'll get into everything in greater detail later.

But it isn't good enough.

"Calli? Where's your sister?" she says in that tone she uses when she knows I have the answer but am not going to hand it over.

"I don't know," I reply, and technically it's not a lie.

I can't say where she is right now, and when we're talking about Carme, all bets are off. The only thing that's certain is you can expect the unexpected, and for once there's no problem finding a parking spot close to the door.

"What should concern you at the moment is Neva Rong," I reply, getting out of my truck, locking up. "The Pandora CEO who's at Wallops this very minute. And I'm gonna lose you inside the building, Fran."

I might not until I'm on the elevator, but I don't want to stay on the phone with her a second longer, and I come close to hanging up on her, over and out. Because she won't stop asking questions, even though she's darn sure I'm not going to answer them. Feeling threatened by my connection to Carme, and I know that Fran wouldn't put anything past her.

−00:06:22:1 . . .

Using my temporary smartcard, I open the front door, and my boots are loud on polished granite. Not a soul inside. Walking so fast I'm close to trotting, past the cafeteria and exchange, the lights low, outer doors locked, nobody home. Riding up alone to the second floor, looking a bit like a one-woman SWAT team in my field clothes and gear. Walking past the offices for senior management of the research and engineering directorates.

The usual NASA photographs everywhere, and outside Mission Control, a glass showcase filled with models of the Space Shuttle. The new Space Launch System super rocket. The James Webb Space Telescope with its sunshield coated in gold. Our Mission Control Center is modest compared to Johnson Space Center and Cape Canaveral, nobody paying any attention to me when I walk into the tan carpeted open area of workstations cheek to jowl, only about a third of them occupied.

−00:01:11:2 . . .

Computer displays glow with tightly packed acronyms, numbers and codes depending on which system is being monitored, the controllers facing a data wall displaying the rocket on LP-0A, and the EVA in progress outside the Space Station.

Commander Whitson with her high-tech drill Pistol-Grip Tool (PGT) on a swing arm at her waist, her checklist on her wrist, is tethered to the faux LEAR on its pallet and the robotic arm.

−00:00:50:0 . . . T-minus 50 seconds . . .

Moving through the vacuum toward the research platform on the most remote area of the truss, the Station as bright as polished silver, receding slowly. I listen to the countdown displayed big enough to see across the room, the live feed of the rocket quietly ticking away above it. Ken is at his console, busy on the comms, an array of displays monitoring every system and subsystem that he needs to know about.

In jeans and a sweater, he's stubbly and his eyes look tired, a plate of fresh fruit salad and a pastry in easy reach.

−00:00:30:0 . . . T-minus 30 seconds . . .

We shoot each other a quick smile as I walk past, headed to my station, the payload deployment officer on my left, the instrument and communications officer on my right, two rows back from the food table. Everybody riveted to the data wall, and I sit down, putting on my headset to monitor Rush talking to EV1 and EV2, our astronauts outside in their big white spacesuits, their EMUs. As the countdown continues.

−00:00:10:0 . . . T-minus 10 seconds . . .

Typing in my password.

". . . 5, 4, 3, 2 . . ."

When the robotic arm suddenly stops midflight. At 17 meters (56 feet) from the Station.

00:00:00:00 . . .

As the rocket explodes like a bomb on the pad in a towering eruption of rolling fire while the Station's telecommunications go dead. The audio and video instantly knocked out. Leaving us blind, deaf and dumb in outer space and on the ground.

"Holy mother of . . . !" under my breath.

My fingers click-clicking on the keyboard, loading a NORAD special coordinate file for tracking objects in space. I can use the 3-meter parabolic antenna dish on top of our hangar to reconnect with the astronauts as long as that red tab is pulled on the node and the beacon turned on. As long as Commander Whitson remembers, we can complete the quantum network and talk. Sort of

486

like tin can telephone again.

Entering commands to power on the servos so I can reposition the antenna dish's 3-axis motors. Except the circuits don't engage. Nothing happens.

35

The explosion paints an orange afterglow on the black horizon that can be seen from as far away as Washington, DC, according to reports already on social media.

Emergency crews are putting out the fire, the island shrill with sirens, and pulsing with lights based on video feeds in Mission Control from a moment ago. The road leading on and off Wallops has been closed, leaving spectators with no way back to the mainland. Police cars and fire trucks everywhere.

In dramatic contrast to the barren planet I'm driving through at 0713 Greenwich Mean Time. Thirteen minutes past 2:00 a.m., and the Langley campus is so deserted one might think the mothership showed up and left some of us behind.

". . . It broke out the glass in a lot of the buildings, those closer to the pad," Rush is saying over the phone through the speakers inside my truck. "It happened so fast, a lot of people are just standing around in a stupor. We're fine where we are here in Mission Control except I've never felt anything like that. And hope I don't again. I now understand the meaning of *bone rattling.*"

An off-nominal launch in addition to a robotic arm failure as the Space Station's comms go dead, Rush summarizes. Just as he was in the middle of telling Peggy Whitson over Space to Ground 1 that she had a lot of kids from her hometown watching. Such an irony when everything awful happens at once.

"We got any idea how *both* strings of S-band plus *both* strings of Ku-band comms could have been knocked out?" I inquire, driving through blowing snow, the streets empty and white, the buildings dark and in lockdown.

"No clue," Rush replies. "And not just one catastrophic failure but *three* of them almost simultaneously . . ."

"Sounds like that's the point."

"Whose point?"

"Whoever hacked into NASA, because that's sure as shooting what we're talking about," I reply. "Taking out our rocket while targeting the robotic arm and the Space Station's telecommunications during an extremely dangerous EVA involving a classified quantum node installation. Primary, secondary and tertiary attacks happening at the same time. Works like a charm. Just ask terrorists."

"Then you believe it's all connected. All from the same source of ugly."

"You know what I say about coincidences."

"You're not getting an argument from me," he agrees.

"What was Neva Rong doing during all this?" rolling past the massive white metal spheres that generate velocity in the wind tunnels. "You know, the VIP guest sitting under your nose whose NASA contractor sister's badge was supposedly stolen before she was found suspiciously dead yesterday."

"Don't think I knew about that. Hmmm. Well then. To answer your question, she was watching in a special guest room with all the Iowa kids . . . ," Rush's voice, and it's been a while since I heard it.

Langley's up-lit giant spheres shine vaguely through the snowy fog like prehistoric full moons that seem to follow me in my mirrors as I speed to the hangar. I envision the PONG attached to the pine tree near my closet, wondering if it's still there. Wondering where it is this minute. Almost missing it as much as I do Carme. And I must be tired. Running on empty as I speed to the hangar.

"Is Dr. Rong still there?" and I have no doubt of it.

My subroutines are running like high-speed trains beneath my thoughts. The blood spatter cooking on the steam pipe's asbestos cover in the Yellow Submarine tunnel. The mysterious blood tube in our protective services evidence refrigerator. The tampered-with crime scene and stolen badges, including mine. Landing on a lot of things Carme could be blamed for and maybe already is.

But I'm not so sure she's done anything wrong. Quite the opposite, and it's obvious that if she had something criminal to do with the hacking into 1111-A and all of NASA, then she wouldn't leave blood right by the FOD-1. But I'm pretty sure that's exactly what she did. Left blood because she wanted me to find it, and it won't turn out to be hers, that's for sure.

". . . Oh yeah," Rush's voice. "Everybody's waiting on you to save the day, getting those comms back up so we can watch you rescue our astronaut. Hopefully."

"Based on the mess she's in, I think she'll have to rescue herself," I reply, and I probably could say the same about my sister. "Commander Whitson is stuck, and nobody can get to her. This could turn out really, really bad."

"I hope they're not freaking out up there, wondering where everybody went." Blowing out a tired breath. "If we can't get the arm working, Calli, I honestly don't know what they're going to do."

"And I honestly wonder how all these so-called mishaps will affect Pandora Space Systems doing business with Wallops," I reply with just the slightest whiff of sarcasm. "Because I'm not so sure I'd want to install a pad at a spaceport where a rocket just blew up right in front of me. Or if I did, and this is the more likely scenario, then I'd expect to have some serious leverage while negotiating the deal."

Dr. Rong was in Virginia yesterday for sure. Had to be if she was going to make it to Wallops in time for this morning's launch. And I have to ask myself. Would she come here and not try to see her relocated dis-gruntled sister? The unfortunate Vera, who couldn't get her doctorate, and worked for her CEO sibling, and was suicidal.

The poor robotics and sensors scientist in Prada, implanting devices, doing research on her own body. A body that Neva doesn't want autopsied and is much too eager to have flown to Texas. Who might have benefited from Vera never talking again to anyone about her missing badge or anything else?

It's going to be a bear to prove.

". . . Maybe Neva Rong's lucky day. Maybe Mason Dixon's too. Our mishaps are their jackpots and headlines," Rush's soothing voice.

Never frazzled, he doesn't sweat the little stuff or much of anything, making me feel like a jitterbug by comparison. Awkward and antsy around him, never saying exactly what I feel or mean especially when he locks me in with that green-gold stare. Those luminous eyes that seem to have an unlimited power supply, so intense they feel hot like the sun through a magnifier, going back to when Carme and I were seniors in high school and he was starting at Langley.

My sister doesn't play her game of trading places when it's someone she wants all for herself, and it's true what that lawyer said 22 years ago. Most people can't tell the two of us apart, especially if that's our intention. Even Rush has his confused moments when the three of us are together. Most recently when Carme was home last month, and he walked into Mom's kitchen while I was peeling carrots in the sink.

Replaying it like a movie in my head, the two of us alone, my sister out on one of her punishing 8-mile runs along the fitness path at the air force base. I can still feel his breath on my neck and my thoughts shorting out as he wrapped his arms around my waist from behind.

Holding me hard, sliding his hands up alarmingly. "How are we besides beautiful?" nuzzling my ear.

"Rush . . . ?" His name catching in my throat, tucking my elbows in close, cueing him to stop before he finds his mark.

But too late for that, and he says, "Huh," with a perplexed frown.

As I twist myself around, facing him. "Rush? Ummm . . ."

"Yeah. Sorry." Letting go, stepping back apologetically, and I could see it in his eyes.

Passion cooling rapidly from smoldering to unsure to uh-oh. Looking me up and down, trying not to be obvious. Because Carme and I have never been constructed exactly the same, our topographies as different as geography.

"You know I'm Calli, right?" and I've had to say it too often in life.

The word out of the gate is that the off-

494

nominal event is being investigated. Period. End of story at only 15 minutes out since everything hit the fan.

That doesn't mean we don't have some idea, and we do. At T-minus 30 seconds in the countdown, a dish antenna near LP-0A was hacked by some unknown bad actor attempting to take control of the rocket, which is basically a missile minus a warhead.

For sure less dangerous than an atom bomb but you wouldn't want it headed in your direction. A 130-foot Roman candle blasting off with 800,000 pounds of thrust would pack a devastating punch if diverted off course. Away from the water, over land, headed toward a dense urban environment, for example.

I've been saying forever that a hijacked rocket could level the Wallops spaceport. The navy base. The Pentagon. Quantico. The CIA. The White House. Take your pick of the high-value targets in this part of the world. Were it not for our masters of space antenna ninjas in their blockhouses, I don't know what might have happened.

They spied the rogue signal in the nick of time and were quick on the trigger with the kill signal. Or in our usual understated nerdy parlance, *"The safety officers resorted to the flight-termination system to disable the*

495

vehicle." We blew it up our freakin' selves. Millions of dollars in equipment and research projects lost in a massive eruption of fire and brimstone.

But beyond the substantial financial loss and plasmic egg on our face, the damage is minimal in the grand scheme of things. Nobody was hurt. Not yet.

Deep breaths.

Driving fast toward the hangar off Runway 8, at the end of a taxiway we share with the air force base. Along Langley Boulevard in blowing snow, my adrenaline pumping. It's all I can do not to panic.

Focus! Focus! Focus!

"The worst part is getting up there," and Rush isn't talking about outer space, but he may as well be. "I'm sorry I'm not around to help."

"Not a big deal. I've been up there enough times before," I reply, and it's not true.

It is a big deal. Freezing cold, snowing on a deserted campus in the pitch dark, and I'm supposed to climb up on the roof of the NASA hangar. Normally, I'd never do such a thing in these conditions, but we have an astronaut and her top secret payload tethered to a failed robotic arm that quit 56 feet from the Space Station. We don't know what happened to cause the malfunction, and if the international crew in their various modules do, they can't tell us.

That's the reason I need to climb up on the roof, and it's not child's play on the prettiest of days. First, I'll have to enter through a lower door and climb 10 stories of stairs or see-through metal catwalk grating. If you do the math, that's 160 steps, plus catwalks and ramps. Once I reach the ceiling, I'll exit through another door to an outdoor platform, where I'll climb an iron ladder up the side of the building like a human fly. Exposed to the wind and cold some 100 feet above the tarmac, and were it not for the urgency of the situation, I would take a pass.

But there's no choice. Houston has a problem this time. A much bigger one than NASA knows, because everywhere I look, I'm seeing sabotage. The Station loses communication, and I find out our rooftop dish magically got switched from Remote to Local mode. To do that, someone had to physically access the antenna pedestal the same way I'm about to, by climbing up to the roof.

Hauling butt through the snowy parking lot, I notice light spilling on the ramp in front of the huge retractable door on the other side of the fence. I don't know why the bay would be open, certainly not at this godforsaken hour and in this weather. No aircraft are being towed in or out, and I wouldn't expect anybody to be here for any reason, especially during a furlough.

Taking off my ballistic vest, my gun belt, I place them on the floor behind the front seat. Because I can't climb a ladder in all that, but I'm not leaving my gun. The Glock goes in my backpack, and I work my arms into the shoulder straps, fastening the sternum strap. Pulling on my black leather gloves, I lock the truck.

Trotting toward a side door, I hope like mad that my temporary smartcard works. And it does. Stepping inside the prewar tiled hallway, not seeing anyone. Listening, hurrying past NASA showcases and photographs, then Flight Operations, lights on inside but don't see anyone. Almost passing up the ladies' room but the last thing I need on top of everything else is to feel like I've got to pee while climbing up the side of the building in a snowstorm. Just the thought, and I can barely make it, dashing inside, unzipping and untucking as I hurl myself into a stall, cargo pants dropping to the floor, snatching at toilet paper. Flushing and running.

Banging through that door and out another, this one solid metal and leading inside a hangar big enough to shelter a fleet of fixed-wing and rotorcraft of all sizes and descriptions. Well, some of them defy description. Not everything that ends up in here is for public consumption. Some things a lot of people are better off never knowing about. I can't and won't talk about a lot of what I've seen over the years, and I suspect what I'm looking at right now is a good example.

Six black Suburban SUVs, a black Ford F-150 pickup with all their domes and antennas. And the Secret Service agents who go with them, including the bearded man I noticed earlier at the 7-Eleven and the woman who was with him. Military officers I don't recognize are busy at mobile workstations, and Dick Melville is sitting at a table with my father.

Nobody's looking in my direction as I creep up a flight of maintenance stairs, hoping like crazy I'm not spotted. No question they wouldn't take kindly to me sneaking up to the roof. And I can't announce myself in an emergency when there's not a second to spare, and up the metal steps I bound, as quiet as a cat, eyeing the table of signal analyzers.

From two stories up, I can make out

colorful waves on the lighted displays, and good thing I left my phone in the truck. But I have the remote control key that's transmitting a signal even as we speak, stupid me! And I frantically pat myself down, as if it matters now. But it's not in my jacket, and none of my pants pockets. I know I didn't put it in my backpack, meaning it must have fallen out while I was in the bathroom. And just this one time, that's a good thing. No question the Secret Service agents are scanning even as I'm climbing, and I don't need anybody interfering.

Moving fast and stealthily, climbing and climbing. Those below none the wiser, the length of a soccer field away and sufficiently preoccupied near the open bay door. Near a mountain of unmarked wooden crates on pallets flown in here late last week on a C-17, destined for a classified storage facility on the air force base. I don't know what's in them, didn't ask, don't always want to know.

Five stories up and sweating, my heart about to hammer out of my chest as I hurry, looking down through the red-painted mesh metal steps at everything below. The T-38 trainer jets. The gutted Gulfstream packed with electronic and radar equipment. The Chinook helicopter that's been squatting here for months. Watching my dad in his corduroys and button-up denim shirt, light winking off his glasses as he sits at a table, laptops open around him.

He doesn't look happy, and I can tell from his mussed-up gray hair that he's been running his fingers through it the way he does when he's frustrated. Dick hovering nearby, I can't think of any reason for my dad to be here with him unless it's about my sister. Unless what I'm seeing gathered below is the posse out to get her. All these people are in here because of Carme.

What have you done!

Or more likely, what do they *think* she's done? Or might do? What really? The things Dick said and all that's occurred don't quite add up to my sister turning into a monster. Not a consummate one. Until there's proof, I don't accept that she's hurt anyone. Not the missing Noah Bishop. Not the dead Vera Young. Certainly not my parents or me. She's had ample opportunity, has been inside the barn while I was. She could have hurt me. She could hurt everyone. And she hasn't.

The PONG can spy on all of us, and it might. But Carme won't harm us. No matter what she's gotten involved in, she wouldn't hurt her family. She wouldn't hurt

Rush, and even as I think of him, everybody below looks up at me at the same time like a spotter plane finding a whale. That's when I remember his birthday gift. Still wrapped in an expired sectional flight chart, forgotten inside my backpack.

The motion-charging sensors I built into the tactical pen are transmitting signals that the analyzers are picking up in the noise floor. It took but a few minutes for their algorithms to do their continuous subtractions, and catch me in my own trap. Any low-level noise from the pen's GPS and other sensors is showing up as something new in the room. Then everyone zoomed in on the source, and now the chase is on.

I haul open the heavy metal door 10 stories up as I hear a herd of booted feet pounding across the concrete floor below, headed to the stairs.

They think I'm her.

They're looking for Carme and not expecting me to be here. They'll confuse me with my twin like everybody else, only this time I might get shot. Slamming the door behind me, and I'm blasted by snow and frigid wind, my eyes watering badly as I grab a rung of the iron ladder attached to the outside of the hangar 100 feet above the asphalt. Gloved hand over gloved hand, never looking down, climbing as the wind grabs at me, tears streaming down my face.

One rung to go as I calculate how much time I have, maybe 5 minutes before they overtake my head start and are on this same ladder. Hauling my legs over the lip of the snowy roof, and it's slippery as crap up here, flat in the middle but pitched just enough on the sides to make gravity a worse enemy than usual. Rather much like taking a tumble in outer space if you lose your balance, can't stop yourself from sliding downhill to the edge and going over.

The snow is about three inches deep, and I feel around in it for the walkway safety matting that leads directly to the radome, and I'm mindful of the men coming after me. I don't know how many or who, but the longer I duck them, the harder it will be to explain why I'm up here and that I'm not my fugitive sister.

Moving as fast as I can toward what looks even more like an igloo surrounded by snow. I don't see the footprints leading away from the maintenance door until I'm about 20 paces out, fresh tracks without the lightest dusting of snow. Only one set of them. Left as recently as minutes ago.

My feet almost go out from under me, making me feel a lot like that stranded astronaut I'm trying so desperately to help.

Flailing in an environment that couldn't be more unfriendly, slip-sliding on snow in a blustery wind, my eyes so flooded I can scarcely see. And a bad slip could send me tumbling into the ether. Trying for all I'm worth to make it to the radome's access door, to scan my temporary smartcard and get my hands inside the pedestal.

Breathing hard, working out of the backpack's shoulder straps, ditching it because it's throwing off my balance. And I can't pull out my gun. That's the quickest way to end up dead on this winter wasteland at the top of the world, my ears frozen, my nose and eyes running like faucets, and I dig into my coat pockets for the smartcard.

I feel my heart sucked out of my body, patting myself down frantically as it dawns on me. The temporary ID was in a pocket of my cargo pants and must have fallen out when the truck key did in the ladies' room.

"Shit!" This time I say it, the entire word.

Turning around, my boots going out from under me, landing on my ass. Scrambling up and retrieving my backpack, not for the gun but for the damn pen that's caused all this damn trouble. Tearing open the flight-chart gift paper, ripping into the small box, snatching the pen out of its lightly magnetized sheath as I flip up the white polyurethane cover over the fail-safe keypad.

The old-style metal-button numbers are protected under glass that I shatter with one sharp tap of the pen's carbide tip. I punch in the master code, the lock clicks free, and I sling open the access door as I hear voices shouting in the wind. The posse is on the roof, headed toward me. I have maybe two minutes. Inside the radome, and it's dark as a movie theater.

I don't want to make myself an easier target. But I didn't bring a flashlight, didn't think I'd need it. But I can't afford to press the button for the low-noise lighting. It would illuminate the radome enough to be seen from the ground. Feeling along the antenna's pedestal, I knock against something that crashes to the floor. Leaning down, I feel for what it was. A small laptop computer, and when I flip it open and tap a key, the screen lights up, the display streaming with waves and peaks of spectrum analysis going on in real time.

And I realize with horror that my sister picked up the same rogue signal the Secret Service did. From my pen, and not knowing who was coming, she fled. Or if she knew it was me, she feared both of us would get shot if she hung around. So, she bolted but left a calling card that also could be used to track her had she carried it with her. My sister deliberately left the computer. I'm certain of it.

She was just here, had been hiding up here for a while. No doubt switched the dish to Local mode so someone didn't remotely move it, possibly injuring her as she was controlling the PONG.

Focus. Focus. Focus.

Finding the control pendant. Then the rectangular box that I know is yellow and connected to a junction box by a 10-foot multi-wire electrical cable. Recognizing the big switch, red if I could see it right now, and I flip it from Local to Remote mode.

Then I step back outside, shutting the access door behind me, and I put my hands in the air. Because I really would prefer not to end this day being dead. Walking fast, slip-sliding toward the agents, three of them and Dick.

"It's me, Calli!" yelling at them. "My gun and creds are in the backpack! Get me to Mission Control now!"

The arm remains broken, and Peggy Whitson and I are on a tether. A quantum one. Or simply *Q*, as I think of our radio connection.

The astronauts are happy that Mission Control is back. Sort of back. But they don't know what's going on, why the Space Station lost telecommunications and power to the arm. Commander Peggy Whitson and Jack Fischer likely don't know that a Wallops antenna dish was hacked or that the resupply rocket blew up with all their holiday goodies in it.

Even if the crew inside the Station got that Grinch-worthy news, it wouldn't be shared with astronauts on a dangerous spacewalk when paying attention and staying calm are the difference between life and death.

"Captain Chase, do we have comm back?" Commander Whitson sounds in my headset as I sit at my station just like before.

Only now Dick is next to me, and next to him is the bearded guy from the 7-Eleven.

And next to him is the woman with long hair.

"No, I'm transmitting through Q," I radio back to outer space.

Both video and audio are up and running on Q, and I can see what Commander Whitson is looking at through the camera built into her helmet. There's also a camera on the dead robotic arm, the images severe-clear of her stuck in outer space while tethered to a quantum node that she remembered to power up, just as she'd been told.

Sort of a Space Force portable "cop" radio, but a terribly expensive and cumbersome one. Of course, by the time they actually make such a thing, it will be small enough to wear as a watch.

"Can you relay to Houston the plan?" Commander Whitson asks me over our now-activated Q-comm, because she can't ask Rush.

He's at Wallops, and it isn't on Q yet. Only Ames, the Space Station and Langley so far, and there's no one else to sit in this pilot's seat, so to speak, except me right now. The plan we're to relay to Houston is what the astronauts have improvised during a crisis so they can install the node anyway.

Thinking on their feet in microgravity,

they've decided the safest option is for Commander Whitson to do some sleight of hand with tethers. The pair of 3-foot-long ones at her waist made of webbing instead of 3/32-inch-thick braided stainless steel wire. We watch on the live feed as she hooks the two waist tethers together, looping them like a belt around the arm's tip boom.

I hold my breath during the really risky part, when she disconnects her safety tether from the arm. Before connecting this off-nominal rigging to a D ring on her suit as if she's an astro-lineman. Slowly shimmying along a telephone pole, only this one is 35 centimeters (14 inches) in circumference and weighs close to 2 tons. Inchworming her way along in an unprecedented maneuver never taught, trained for or anticipated. Minutes ticking by, and everybody nervous. But it's working like a charm, already dubbed "doing a Whitson," doing whatever it takes to save your bacon when lost in space.

Down she goes while Jack Fischer waits for her by the truss, ready to snag her with a safety tether. Together they'll move hand over hand, walking their precious payload the length of the station to that remote research platform. From there they can just head home on their own. It's only a tether away should they take a spill.

"Can I get you something?" Dick keeps asking me that, and I know he feels bad.

Not sorry but regretful that I had to be patted down. That he pulled off my right glove to check the scar on my finger, making sure it was me. Not to mention all his lies.

"This may take a little while, and you should eat something." Trying to be paternal again, trying to be my friend. "Eat a little of the fruit at least."

Pushing the plate farther away. I couldn't possibly, and it's all I can muster to block out those images. The boot tracks in the snow, one set headed away from the radome to an area of the roof where there's no ladder. No maintenance stairs. Nothing but air.

"Coffee?" Dick persists.

Shaking my head, staring straight ahead at the live feed of the astronauts and their long wires shining like spaghetti-thin laser beams. Moving along the truss with their payload on its pallet.

"Don't punish me," under his breath, in my ear.

"If you weren't going to let me look, then show me the pictures," I sotto voce him right back, and if people didn't know better, they might think we're having a lovers' spat.

As windblown and teary as I must look, shaking inside like that rocket before it blew apart. All because Dick won't offer me the common courtesy of proving my sister is alive. I don't see how she could be. But her body hasn't been found, not on the snowy ground by the hangar where she should have landed. I know that for a fact because Fran keeps checking, sending me texts.

Carme hasn't turned up dead or alive anywhere as far as I know, and everybody's looking. Nobody's offering me data. But I know what I saw. One set of boot prints leading to the edge and stopping. No place to go but down.

Or up.

I suspect Carme was on the roof before the snow started, probably about the time the PONG decided to introduce itself to me while I was getting out of the shower. My sister could have ensconced herself in the windowless egg 10 stories off the ground. Who would think to look for her up there?

No doubt she had a small tactical light and could see just fine while she was there, and the radome also has a low-noise heater that I'm sure she turned on. She could have made herself reasonably comfortable for hours or days, out of the elements, inside her protective shell, virtually above the fray and invisible to it.

"Captain Chase, do you have the PGT settings?" Commander Whitson in my headset.

"Yes," I radio back. "Bravo 2, clockwise 2, expecting 10 turns on each bolt."

"Starting turns on bolt 2, settings bravo 2, clockwise . . . 9.5 turns, green light," she fires back, and Jack Fischer floats closer to help, moving along the handrails.

"I'll stabilize and you go for bolt 4 next . . . ," his voice in my ear, as I feel Dick's shoulder pushing against me.

Setting down his phone in front of me, a photograph on the display of the boot prints at the edge of the roof. I never got that close to look, was in too much of a panicked hurry to get back here. And nobody was of a mindset to let me wander anywhere, not that there was time.

Picking up Dick's cell phone, enlarging the image of the disturbed snow. The boot-shaped impressions with an unusual tread pattern. Terminating a good 6 feet from the rooftop's edge, telling me everything as I remember the jogger in non-reflective black. The powerful gait, running after dark on ice and in bitter weather as if it was nothing. Remembering the creepy feeling I had, as preoccupied as I was driving Dick back to Dodd Hall. Reminded of the barking dog, and the light that blinked on.

It makes more sense now that Dick would act nonchalant when I inquired about who else might be staying there. Because it had been my impression that nobody else was. Just him on such a desolate night only hours before a furlough. He didn't want to tell me that members of a Secret Service cyber-posse were staying there. He didn't want me to know that they were looking for Carme even as I sat in my truck talking to him about her.

I'm pretty sure that's who was out running the very same fitness path she always runs. Maybe it was my sister who scared the dog that was barking nonstop as if confronted with an extraterrestrial or a Darth Vader–ish robot. My sister was out and up to something, and probably hiding in a Langley radome when she wasn't on the farm, and I never knew it.

"Captain Chase," Jack Fischer raises me on the air again, "after lever is over center, do you want the backup data connection next?"

"Yes. It's the smaller cable," I reply, watching him on the data wall sorting through cable labels. "W1111 mated to J-1," I remind the two of them. "After you get that in place, we will do the power-on procedures from here."

"W1111 mated to J-1," Commander Whitson repeats. "It's a tight fit for my hand . . . ," struggling to get the plug-socket connector's lever over center. "I am having problems getting my hand in here . . ."

Not good. Bad if after all this they can't get the blasted thing up and running, but what I say is, "Copy."

". . . Let me try a different position . . . ," her voice comes back, and I can hear her working hard. ". . . Maybe I can do it with my fingertips . . ."

"Copy," reminding me of one of those tasks in space I might not have been able to do had my accident in the break room turned out worse than it did.

And I recognize the big hand gently gripping my shoulder, the gleam of the simple gold band on Dad's wedding finger. Then a plate piled high with bacon and a bagel slathered with cream cheese magically lands next to my keyboard. Looking up at Dad's kind face, one arm holding Easton in his space-dinosaur pajamas, like a mini-me crash dummy, sound asleep.

"Eat," he says, his eyes keen behind his old-style black-framed glasses, his thick gray hair sticking up everywhere.

"Here, hon." Mom's right beside him with a carton of cranberry juice, straw already in it.

"Captain Chase, how much time left?" Jack Fischer asks me from space for all of Mission Control and my family to see.

Including Carme. Hoping she's watching from somewhere. Somehow.

Please be alive.

"We're ready here as soon as the data connection is mated," I reply as I think of sensors and robotics, of flying cars, tourists orbiting Earth, of jet packs, habitats on the moon . . .

"Working on it . . . ," Commander Whitson struggling away.

Most of all, I'm thinking about exoskeletons. Ones being designed for superhuman chores in space, and all sorts of helpful tasks down here. Humans outfitting ourselves to do the work of machines, ironically. Lifting great weights, running faster without fatigue. And flying without a cockpit or a cape.

"Mated!" Commander Whitson announces, and everyone inside the control room begins cheering and applauding the way they do when watching in real time as a rover lands perfectly on Mars or flies by Ultima Thule and beyond Pluto.

Some people are even hugging each other, having no idea that what just got plugged in isn't an atmospheric reader named LEAR. Taking a sip of my juice, chewing on a piece of bagel, looking at Mom smiling proudly at me, not worried about Carme, I can tell. Dad's just nodding his head, and as frazzled as he is, he's not worried either.

If they're okay, then I am, too, and we know exactly what to do, know all about not asking and telling.

"Okay," I radio back to outer space. "Let's get the prime power and data hooked up so we have redundancy."

As a video file lands on my mobile phone, and starts playing on its own. The mirror ball PONG in my bathroom again, filming in the mirror over the sink, taking a selfie as it slowly spins.

ABOUT THE AUTHOR

In 1990, **Patricia Cornwell** sold her first novel, *Postmortem,* while working at the Office of the Chief Medical Examiner in Richmond, Virginia. An auspicious debut, it went on to win the Edgar, Creasey, Anthony, and Macavity Awards as well as the French Prix du Roman d'Aventure prize — the first book ever to claim all these distinctions in a single year. Growing into an international phenomenon, the Scarpetta series won Cornwell the Sherlock Award for best detective created by an American author, the Gold Dagger Award, the RBA Thriller Award, and the Medal of Chevalier of the Order of Arts and Letters for her contributions to literary and artistic development.

Today, Cornwell's novels and iconic characters are known around the world. Beyond the Scarpetta series, Cornwell has written the definitive nonfiction account of Jack the Ripper's identity, cookbooks, a children's book, a biography of Ruth Graham, and two other fictional series based on the characters Win Garano and Andy Brazil. While writing *Quantum,* Cornwell spent two years researching space, technology, and robotics at Captain Calli Chase's home base, NASA's Langley Research Center, and studied cutting-edge law enforcement and security techniques with the Secret Service, the US Air Force, NASA Protective Services, Scotland Yard, and Interpol.

Cornwell was born in Miami. She grew up in Montreat, North Carolina, and now lives and works in Boston and Los Angeles.

LP 3899